Economic Growth, Stagnation and the Working Population in Western Europe

Economic Growth, Stagnation and the Working Population in Western Europe

Leif Ahnström

Belhaven Press
A division of Pinter Publishers
London and New York

© Leif Ahnström, 1990

First published in Great Britain in 1990
by Belhaven Press (a division of Pinter Publishers),
25 Floral Street, London WC2E 9DS

British Library Cataloguing in Publication Data

A CIP catalogue record for this book is available from the
British Library

ISBN 1 85293 125 6

Library of Congress Cataloging-in-Publication Data

Ahnström, Leif, 1934–
    Economic growth, stagnation and the working population in Western
Europe / Leif Ahnström.
        p.   cm.
    ISBN 1-85293-125-6
        1. Europe—Economic conditions—1945–   2. Europe—Industries.
3. Europe—Occupations.   4. Labor supply—Europe.   I. Title.
HC240.A5944   1990
338.94—dc20   90-33775
                                                                                          CIP

Typeset by Florencetype Ltd, Kewstoke, Avon
Printed and bound by Biddles Ltd, Guildford and Kings Lynn

To William William-Olsson

Contents

List of Figures

List of Tables

Foreword

The research which has materialized into this book was initiated at the Stockholm School of Economics in the mid-1970s. I had completed a geographic study of functions of administration and control in twelve West European countries, and wanted to embark on more broadly conceived research on 'regional economic development in Western Europe'. Before I could proceed with the kind of inquiry I had in mind, it seemed necessary to improve my knowledge and understanding of the economic life of the various countries: What was actually happening in the economy? What factors accounted for the rapid change?

Earlier studies of the ways economic activities are treated in population censuses (which I had carried out as a research assistant to Professor W. William-Olsson at the Department of Geography, Stockholm School of Economics) led me to concentrate on the changing structure of the working population: the evolution of industries, occupations and socioeconomic groups. The research, which also touched upon the post-war economic growth of Western Europe, covered the period 1950 to 1970, and was reported in a series of (not widely circulated) working papers.

When I moved to Norway in the late 1970s, these reports had become outdated because of the phenomenon of 'stagflation', which at that time was puzzling. Under the influence of a general change in interest from issues of growth to issues of stagnation (and the 'crisis of capitalism'), I felt obliged to revise and update my earlier findings. As new population census reports appeared in the 1980s, it was also possible to extend the study of the restructuring of the working population until about 1980. This second round of research, first at the Norwegian School of Economics and Business Administration in Bergen, and later at the University of Oslo, gave rise to new working papers and reports, but no comprehensive account.

When I contacted Pinter Publishers in 1987 to inquire if they were interested in publishing a monograph on economic growth, stagnation and the working population in Western Europe, I received a very positive response, but also met with concern that my study did not look any further than the beginning of the 1980s. Although detailed data on the working population would not appear until well into the 1990s, I decided to consider also some 'tendencies and bearings of the 1980s'. Hopefully, this brings the book more in touch with current issues — although I now realize that as a writer preoccupied with current change, you can never really keep up.

Writing as a geographer, and addressing other geographers, I have occasionally asked myself: Is this geography? My answer is that it should be considered an attempt at 'macro-geography', or *geographic social analysis* (parallel to the notions of 'macro-history' and 'historical social analysis'). Although the study covers several countries, it is not comparative in the sense of discussing what distinguishes one country from another. The aim has rather been to discover what the Western European nation-states in question have in common. The book, therefore, demonstrates what has been called the 'tyranny of the model': the pressing of concrete reality into a conceptual mould.

Although I have not worked in close contact with research workers in the same field as my own, I have, of course, adopted many views and ideas developed by other students of economic change. Some of these writers are referred to in the book, others are not. The main reason for their omission is that their thinking, as time passed, has become incorporated into my own.

The research covering the 1950s and 1960s was generously funded by the Swedish Social Science Research Council. In more recent years I have benefited from the financial support of the Norwegian Council for Social Science Research (RSF). In the last few hectic weeks, Lynn Parker has corrected my occasionally strange English, for which I am grateful.

Leif Ahnström
November 1989
Department of Geography
University of Oslo

1 Introduction

Purpose and Scope of the Study

The purpose of this study has been to provide a considered account of post-war changes in the economy of Western Europe: to assess and explain the growth and decline of the various industries, occupations and employment status groups into which the economically active population of a country is customarily divided; and to monitor and discuss the simultaneous changes in the size and composition of the gross domestic product. Thirteen countries are included: Great Britain, Ireland, the Federal Republic of Germany, France, Italy, the Netherlands, Belgium, Austria, Switzerland, Sweden, Norway, Denmark and Finland. The time-span of the reported research is approximately the 35-year period between 1950 and 1985. The reason for covering both changes in the activity structure of the working population and the issue of economic growth (and stagnation) is the conviction that the causes of the post-war economic growth are also the main factors behind the evolving industrial, occupational and employment status structure of the economically active population. By identifying certain practices and motives of private and non-private agents which account for the expanding volume of supplied goods and services (and which seemed to some extent deficient in the second half of the 1970s and early 1980s), it is also possible to explain the concomitant restructuring of the working population. Hence economic growth and stagnation will be related to the same social forces and processes as the growth and decline of the various industries, occupations and employment status groups.[1]

Causal Analysis by means of Retroduction

The method used in the explanatory parts of the study is similar to the *realist approach* developed by Andrew Sayer.[2] Explanation, or causal

1

analysis, requires a specification of what has 'generated' or 'led to' the studied phenomena. More precisely, the phenomena should be related to 'underlying structures', or sets of 'non-contingent' interrelationships between crucial agents. The structures are arrived at by means of abstraction, an isolation of (or focusing on) particular aspects of the study object. Explaining a phenomenon means the postulation, or identification, of certain 'liabilities' or 'ways of action' which connect it in a logical way to some conceived social structure. In the language of Sayer, this means a *retroduction* from the observed phenomenon to certain practices of some agents, their goals and interests and non-contingent relations to other agents. The realist approach, or causal analysis by means of retroduction, is illustrated in Fig. 1:1. Using the terminology of the philosophy of Charles Pierce, it can be said that retroduction makes the phenomenon to be explained 'a matter of course', the logical outcome of a set of postulated (and partly verified) circumstances.[3] The figure conveys a very simplified presentation of the retroduction procedure. The conditions evoking certain practices of one particular agent may be the result of practices adopted by some other agent(s). Practices are confined by *technology*, the state of the art of 'the possible';[4] goals and interests reflect *ideology*, the ways reality is conceived and posited by agents in purposeful practice.[5]

In trying to explain changes which result from reactions to changing conditions within *populations* of agents (such as business firms and public institutions), it is proper to speak of *processes of change*. A process is a recurrent practice that gives rise to the phenomenon to be explained, the *explicandum*, as it is initiated and subsequently propagated within an agent population. The processes are consistent with certain goals and interests of the agents: they are propensities of behaviour, which can be derived from (or which are consistent with) *theorems*, generalizations concerning the goals and interests of the agents. The goals and interests motivate the initiation and adoption of certain practices and hence are the *driving forces* behind the effective processes and the ensuing social change. As processes evolve due to the adoption of certain practices by one type of agent, the situations of other agents often change, inducing certain reactions; agents create conditions for each other; change induces further change.

The conditions, or situations, of the agents do not only bring about certain processes, they may in some cases inhibit them. Therefore, a studied phenomenon (such as 'economic stagnation') may be due to conditions impairing the opportunities of some agents to realize their goals and interests (in certain known and earlier-trodden ways). The phenomena are non-intentional and result from impotence of agents in specific situations.

The processes of change are in principle finite: they start as the practices are initiated, and evolve as they are successively adopted; they

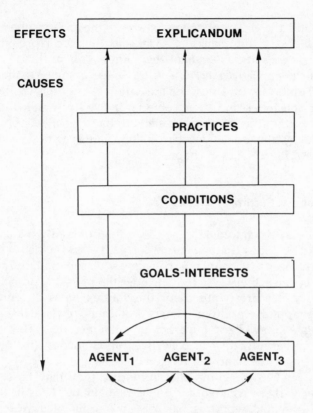

Figure 1.1 The realist approach: causal analysis by means of retroduction

terminate as they gain general acceptance among a population of agents (or when they no longer offer any advantage to the agents in question). In such situations, which are compatible with an equilibrium of the social system, new or modified practices are presumably introduced which keep the system in motion.

The phenomena which are to be explained in this study are, on the one hand, the growth or decline of certain industries, occupations and employment status groups, and on the other hand, the accompanying changes in the rate of growth and composition of the gross domestic product. Explaining these interrelated phenomena means relating them to the same non-contingent interrelationship between some 'economic agents', as well as identifying or postulating some recurrent practices which are consistent with the supposed goals, interests and structural positions of these agents (which may be business firms, public institutions, governments, trade unions or political interest groups).

In the following parts of this chapter a few words will be used on the conceptual and theoretical foundation of the study: the concept of the *economy* and the different *sectors* of work, the major spheres of paid work, which are the *commodity sector* and the sector providing *public services*, the *goals* and *interests* of the main agents of these sectors and their *structural interrelationships*. After some comments on the geographical units of analysis (which are nation-states), this chapter defines the basic categories and direct objects of the study, i.e. the working population and the gross domestic product. Finally it presents the concept of dominance and subordination, an analytical device which will be used in subsequent chapters.

The Economy: Sectors of Work

The 'economy' is conceived of as the system of paid work and unpaid household activities that substitute for paid work, which relate to the wants and needs of people as consumers of commodities and public services. As an activity system it includes the physical and non-material resources which are required for the various types of work: natural resources, appliances and machinery, buildings, physical infrastructure, technology, knowledge of market potentialities, etc. The needs and wants may be individual or collective, 'spontaneous' (in the sense of materializing as demand for marketed goods and services) or imposed by some public (or semi-public) authority; they may be satisfied by means of market exchange, by public regulation, or (as in the case of unpaid household work) as part of some order of pure reciprocity.[6] Work, in turn, comprises those activities of a productive, distributive, regulatory or reproductive character which are either carried out by economically active persons, or which are carried out as substitutes for paid work by unpaid household members.[7] Always using the word 'economy' in the singular serves to remind us that the only relevant work system of today is the global world economy. Although there is today only one relevant system of work, the global world economy[8], the word economy will be used in the plural. It should be remembered, however, that the economy of a particular country is only a *segment* of the global system of work, a national *'economeri'* to use a term suggested by William Olsson.[9] It is regulated by the authorities of a state, and hence, to some extent, subject for politically determined use of economic resources. The economy of a country is the work activities of a national sphere of political priorities.

In the following chapters three sectors of work will be distinguished: the private sector of production (which is also called the 'commodity sector'), the public sector of production (or the sector of public service provision) and the household sector of various substitute activities (i.e. work that can be transferred to or from the private or public sector). The relations between the three sectors are depicted in Fig. 1:2. The

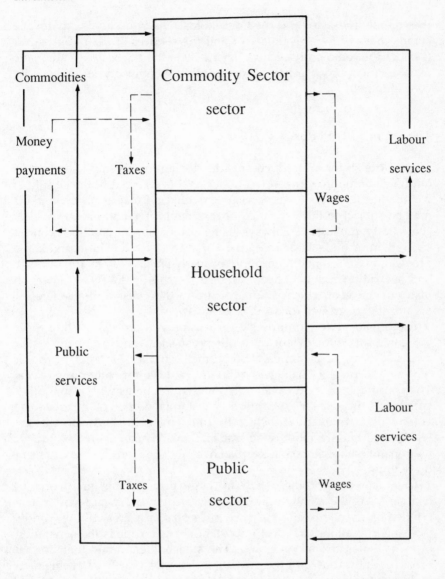

Figure 1.2 The three sectors of the economy: commodity (private), household, and public

households provide labour services for the commodity sector and the public sector; the economically active members of the households receive payment for their work (in the figure these are called 'wages'). The private sector of production supplies the households (and the public sector) with commodities; the public sector provides services for the commodity sector and the households. The households pay for the commodities of the private sector and the services of the public sector (as does the commodity sector). Payments to the public sector are made as taxes (in a broad sense, also including compulsory social security contributions).

The Commodity Sector

The private sector of production is the domain of large and small firms (and own-account workers), economic agents engaged in the supply of commodities, i.e. goods or services provided for markets. The markets may be subject to little or much government intervention. The goal of commodity providers is always some profitability: that the revenues derived from the sale of the goods or services cover the costs of the provisioning. Profitability, or more properly *profits*, may be the ultimate and overriding goal of a firm, but also (as will be developed later) an instrumental goal which is subordinate to the quest of its leaders for organizational growth (or survival).

The private sector comprises a great variety of firms, but all of them are guided to some extent by profit prospects. The core of the sector consists today of a comparatively small number of large firms, or *corporations*, run by 'managers' who are, at least formally, employees. The corporations are typically oligopolists. Together with a few other enterprises they are able to capture a substantial portion of the total sales volume of the industries in which they are engaged. Their markets may be national but are more often transnational. They generally know of their major competitors and keep an eye on the actions and reactions of these firms.

The theoretical prototype of the large firms is the 'megacorp' of Eichner.[10] As the name implies, a megacorp is a very large enterprise typified by the companies included in *Fortune*'s directory of the world's largest corporations. Its most important characteristic is the separation of management from ownership. The stockholders retain their formal property rights, but with the growth of the firms they have proliferated to become passive *rentiers* whose major concern is the size of the dividends and (or) the current price of the shares. The actual decision-making power has been turned over to professional and technically trained managers; the firms rely on these executives for the success of their operations. Since managers wield the effective discretionary power, it is this class of men which determines the behavioural patterns of the organizations, and the decision rules. The firms seem to be permanent institutions. Though they may suffer temporary reverses, their position within the overall economy assures against their outright demise in all but the most unusual of circumstances. This sense of permanence pervades the actions of the executives and they are able to make decisions based on long-term considerations that would be unthinkable to those in charge of firms with less certain life expectations. The tendency to take far-sighted views is reinforced by the fact that the executives have only an indirect personal stake in whatever net income the firms may earn. The executives prefer more rather than less net income; but a high net income is desirable not so much because of the dividends it makes possible, but more because of the financial strength it offers. Dividends are claims on the firm's revenue similar to wages, salaries and interest, and therefore form part of costs. The status and sense of accomplishment of the managers reflect the standing of their companies in the larger business community. In working to enhance that position, the executives are simultaneously adding to their own prestige. Several factors mitigate any divergence of interest between the managers and their organizations. The officials are carefully screened as they rise through the organizational hierarchy; only those deemed to have the necessary loyalty are permitted to advance to a higher position. Group norms emphasizing loyalty to the company are reinforced.

It can be assumed that the largest Western European firms share a basic characteristic with the megacorp: the preoccupation of their leaders, or *technostructures* (as they have been termed by Galbraith), is with the size and the growth of the firm. As has been developed by various writers, the overriding goal of large oligopolistic firms is to expand sales, absolutely or in terms of market shares.[11] A growing sales volume, which sooner or later entails expansion in terms of employees and physical production facilities, creates opportunities for the advancement of ambitious junior managers and technicians; able employees do not leave for a career in a competitor firm, but can be kept within the organization; expanded sales make use of resources which are otherwise idle, or underused, because of the indivisibility of physical and human capital, the fact that production and sales facilities can often only be acquired in lumps. If an increase in the sales volume 'soaks up' unused capacity it reduces the 'opportunity costs' of the firm (i.e. the costs represented by the revenue lost by not using the facility). If growth implies mergers and acquisition of other firms, it may further reduce the costs and inconveniences of the market: economic activities are not regulated through the capricious forces of the market but by means of more reliable corporate planning.[12] From a more general point of view, it can be maintained that growth in sales, or more properly, *real sales revenues*, belongs to the logic of capital accumulation under managerial capitalism: by expanding sales, larger parts of the costs of labour and other inputs can be regained and recycled, thus providing the means for further accumulation (i.e. corporate growth).

As oligopolists, the large firms cannot use price cuts to increase their sales volume and market share. But, as pointed out by Eichner, this does not prevent corporations from achieving growth. The industries to which they belong are likely to expand as general economic growth (i.e. an expansion of the gross domestic product) leads to growing demand for their products. The growth of the economy is, in fact, the primary source of opportunities for expansion, and by simply maintaining its share of the total industry market(s) any corporation will be assured a minimum rate of growth. In addition, the firms are able to increase their sales volume and market share by means of non-price competition.[13]

Growth as the overriding goal of the corporation, as pointed out by Eichner, prescribes a maximization of the realized *gross profits*, i.e. the amount of revenue over and above the current expenses. An increase in this sum will mean an increase in the amount of discretionary income that management commands for reinvestment, a lessening of the budgetary constraints on expansion.[14] Increasing gross profit, while keeping down *net* profits (which are arrived at after deductions for obsolescence of the production facilities), may then be regarded as an instrumental goal of the firm, the means to accomplish the goal of growth, or 'accumulation'.

Maximization of gross profits demands not only that management tries to increase the (real) sales revenues of the firm, but that measures should also be taken to reduce (real) costs. Cost reductions can be attained through rationalization which increases the efficiency of the operations: labour and other inputs are used in such ways that they are compatible with the largest possible growth potential of the firm, the largest gross profits. The general objective of efficiency[15] thus becomes embedded into the prescripts of any corporate technostructure, which are:

1. to increase the sales proceeds (in real terms);
2. to reduce the incurred costs (in real terms); and
3. to use as large a part as possible of the gross profits for investment in new production and sales capacity.[16]

The private sector is in many countries marked by *dualism*, a clear discontinuity in the size distribution of the firms.[17] The sector comprises, on one hand, a small number of large firms accounting for a substantial share of the private sector output and employment, and on the other hand, a great number of much smaller commodity providers. While the large and growth-oriented firms have considerable (but far from unlimited) power to enhance the demand for their products, determine the prices and quantities of their output, and regulate the generation of internal funds for investments, the smaller firms generally work under more competitive conditions. Excluding agriculture and a few other industries of minor quantitative importance, they are typically so dependent on the market that it virtually determines their prices, output and investment opportunities. Their leaders, who are generally the owners of the firms, are basically motivated by a desire to remain in business or to earn a net profit and personal income, rather than to promote the growth of the firm. From a theoretical point of view, they represent neo-classical proprietorship,[18] the empirical foundation of the Marshallian theory of the firm.

There are several reasons for dualism. Basically, dualism reflects the financial and market strength of the large firms *vis-à-vis* the small firms. The large firms may be more financially able to exploit major innovations. New or substantially modified products can be launched when those of the existing product line approach maturity and hence declining profitability. (The large firms may be assumed to prefer operating on the intermediary sections of the imaginary life curves of the products, shunning not only maturity but also the introductory stages, as pioneering seldom pays: the segments of introduction and maturity are thus deliberately left to small-scale producers.) The large corporations can introduce new and more efficient production methods when their once vanguard methods have been brought into general use and therefore no longer offer any competitive advantage. The timely and profitable use of available technology may be due to the ability of large firms to finance the required research and development activities, but also to their capacity to acquire smaller firms which are the possessors of desired technologies, markets or physical assets. The greater ability of the large firms to exploit innovations can be considered both a cause and an effect of their financial and market strength: it gives them an adaptive capacity, not necessarily in terms of ingenuity but rather in terms of the means to put new ideas into profitable use. This greater capacity for adaptation reinforces their strength.

Another reason for dualism is the economies of scale which stem from the ability of the large firms to reserve for themselves the *minimum and certain* demand for the kinds of products they provide, leaving the *non-predictable* parts (which offer no or only small economies of scale) to their small-firm competitors. This is, according to Piore, the main technological foundation of dualism in advanced industrial countries. Drawing on Adam Smith's conception of the division of labour, Piore divides the demand for products into two segments: a minimum and predictable segment, which will be realized under whatever conditions, and a possible but non-predictable segment. While the large firms, which operate on declining average cost curves because of economies of scale, are catering for the predictable and largely stable (or consistently growing) part of the demand, the small firms are left to satisfy the unpredictable and fluctuating part.[19]

A third reason for the discontinuity in the size distribution of firms is the preference of large firms for growing by means of the acquisition of small firms which seem to offer them complementary resources of some kind. Many leaders and owners of small and successful firms are inclined to sell their enterprises if no relative is able to take over; their firms therefore never attain the size of the largest firms. Selling the going concern to another firm is also a common practice of owners of larger but less successful enterprises; the value of the viable parts of the companies can thereby be realized.

Another circumstance of great importance for the observed dualism is the ability of large firms to mobilize outright or hidden support if they get into a precarious situation. The corporations often play vital roles in the economy of their countries and any government is likely to provide means for a financial restructuring, or to initiate mergers with other large firms, thereby supposedly increasing the viability and international competitiveness of the industry. It should be remembered, however, that the discussed dualism does not preclude mobility within the size hierarchy of firms. There are always some ascending and descending enterprises, successful and unsuccessful performers, firms which are affected positively or adversely by structural changes in the economy.

Because of the dualism discussed above, the commodity sector has been conceived of as comprising two sub-sectors, an *oligopolistic* or *corporate* sub-sector, and a *competitive* or *small-firm* sub-sector. The functional relationships between these sub-sectors is marked by dominance and subordination: a change in the volume of production (or sales) of the oligopolistic sub-sector may be expected to give rise to a change in the volume of production (or sales) of the competitive sub-sector, while the opposite does not hold, or does not hold to the same extent. The sub-sectors are interdependent, but the interdependence is asymmetrical. The subordination of the small commodity providers may be due to their roles as subcontractors to the large firms, as suppliers of their inputs, or as the providers of goods or services which are complementary to the commodities supplied by the larger firms. (The small firms may be, for instance, the retailers of products produced by large corporations, and are hence dependent on the ability of these large firms to promote the demand for the products.) That there exists a relationship of domination and subordination between the two sub-sectors means that the growth-oriented strategies of the large corporations provides a key to an understanding of the development of the private sector as a whole (or at least, to a substantial part of it). The ascribed quest for growth of the corporate technostructures may be assumed to work as the major force of growth of the commodity sector as a whole. If the large firms are, on the whole, successful in their attempts at organizational growth, they create opportunities for an expansion of the competitive sub-sector as well (provided that they do not grow only by encroaching upon the traditional domains of small firms).

The large and small firms of the two sub-sectors are the main agents of the commodity sector. But the commodity sector also comprises other economic agents who do not fit into either the oligopolistic or the competitive sub-sector as described above. It contains small suppliers of goods or services who do not work under strictly competitive conditions, or who are not dominated by large firms. There are farmers competing with each other; but they are so dependent on agricultural policy that their prices, net incomes and investment opportunities are determined by the state rather than the market. There are medical practitioners providing services which are exempted from the forces of the market (with production costs covered mainly by taxes or social security contributions), and self-employed professionals and artists occupying oligopolistic market positions due to highly valued and rare qualifications. Such agents of the commodity sector can also be brought into an analysis.

The Public Sector

The public sector of production is the area of government institutions providing services on a non-profit basis. The service provision is always to some extent financed by means of taxes or other compulsory contributions by the population, the supposed beneficiaries of public services.

The institutions of the public sector provide non-marketed services for individual or collective consumption. Some are responsible for the sovereignty and internal cohesion of the state, the authority of its leaders, law and order or relations with other nations. Some are entrusted with regulatory functions in areas which are not the prerogative of the state, but are nevertheless areas where public agencies should, for one or more reasons, exert some influence or control. Some provide for services which would not be carried out at all unless entrusted to the public sector, or which could be consumed by only a minor part of the population if priced according to the principles of the market, or which are the responsibilities of any state that cares for its inhabitants. Examples of the latter categories of public services are research and provision of physical infrastructure, education, medical services and social welfare. Some of the bodies of the public sector secure the financial base for public activities by collecting taxes and administering the fiscal system. What all these activities have in common, and what distinguishes them from services supplied by the private sector, is that they stem from political decisions. Financed (at least to some extent) by means of taxes and compulsory social security payments, their provision is dependent on allowances made by central and local decision-making bodies. This is a circumstance which bears on the amounts and kinds of services which are made available.

According to O'Connor and many other Marxist writers, the functions of the public sector essentially serve the interests of capital; or, more specifically, the leaders of the corporations of the oligopolistic sub-sector, either by enhancing the profits of the firms, or by contributing to the legitimization of the 'capitalist state'.[20] The theoretical stance of this study is that public services are designed primarily to secure political parties electoral support, and that public service provision is (in itself) an interest of the public servants. The chief motivating force behind public sector growth is the interest in this growth of the leading public service providers and their allied members in the political decision-making community (which comprises both political parties and organized interest groups). This view is not inconsistent with the idea that the functions of the public sector benefit large corporations (and particularly such firms), or that they serve the interests and welfare of large segments of the population. By their successful attempts at expanding the services of their sector, the leading public service providers further not only their own interests, but also the interests of other social groups who can provide the necessary electoral support and/or an economic base for the required government spending. Of crucial importance is the reliance of the sector on funds raised by taxation. The services must be sold 'politically' in the sense that major factions of the political community consider them consistent with the wishes of 'their people', and are therefore apt to concede the necessary financial means. But although these political decision-makers raise the necessary funds in a technical sense, the public sector is virtually dependent on the private sector of production for its growth and sheer existence. The limits to its expansion are determined by the capacity and willingness of the taxpayers to allow for the appropriation of an economic surplus, that is, a compulsory withdrawal of some share of the incomes of the private sector members for allotment to public consumption intended to serve the community as a whole.[21]

The postulated interests in public sector growth of the leading public service providers and their political allies constitute an important motivating force behind economic growth (and a motivational factor behind the expansion of certain industries and occupations). They are highly conditional though, as they cannot be realized unless there is a politically commandable surplus: the surplus appropriation capacity of the political decision-makers works as an efficient constraint to the realization of the goals and interests of any public technostructure.

The alleged motives and structural constraints of public sector growth are consistent with the conception of the state developed by Offe and Ronge, who discard the idea common among Marxist students that there is a particular instrumental relationship between the ruling capitalist class and the state apparatus. The state (viewed as a social agent) does not patronize certain interests, and it is not allied with certain classes.[22] What it protects and sanctions is a set of rules and social relationships which are presupposed by the rule of the capitalist class. The state does not defend the interests of this class, but the common interests of the members of the capitalist class society. An important characteristic of the capitalist state is, according to the authors, that political power is prohibited by its own political criteria from organizing production: property in labour power and in the means of production is private. But political power depends indirectly, through the mechanisms of taxation (and the reliance of the state on the capital market) on private accumulation. Occupants of power positions are in fact powerless unless the volume of capital accumulation allows them to derive, through taxation or public borrowing, the material resources which are necessary to promote a political end.

Since the state depends on an accumulation process which is beyond its control, persons holding state power are basically interested in promoting conditions which are conducive to accumulation. This is an institutional self-interest of the state in capitalist societies, conditioned by the fact that the state is denied the command of the flow of economic resources, which is indispensable for the use of state power. The state must guarantee and safeguard a 'healthy' accumulation process upon which it can thrive. In democratic political regimes, Offe and Ronge emphasize, any political group or party can win control over public institutions only to the extent that it wins sufficient electorate support. There is thus a dual determination of political power in the capitalist state: access to political power is determined through the rules of democratic and representative government; the use of political power is controlled by the requirements of the accumulation process.[23]

Structural Relationships between the Commodity Sector and the Public Sector

The structural relationships between the public and private sectors will be emphasized in the following chapters. The public sector, it should be remembered, provides services which benefit the firms of the private sector by lowering their costs of production, and by furthering the demand for private sector goods and services. Public activities such as higher education, research and the supply and maintenance of physical infrastructure promote the productivity of the firms. In the words of O'Connor, parts of the necessary human and physical capital are 'socialized', i.e. financed by means of taxation.[24] (In accordance with the earlier reasoning, it can be maintained that the costs of the capital provision are borne, in the final instance, by those who derive their income from work in the private sector of production.) Services are made available to the firms free of charge, or at prices which do not cover production costs. Other services, such as public health, social security and general education, which are considered attributes of the welfare state, lower labour costs, either by tempering the wage demands of the work force or by raising labour productivity. The activities of the public sector support the demand for commodities supplied by the private sector, either directly through acquisition of goods and services for public consumption and investment, or indirectly by securing employment and income for a considerable and growing share of the working population, or by organizing transfers of income to low-income segments of the inhabitants. Public sector growth thus implies growing demand for the commodities of the private sector, which is a basic condition for public sector growth and capital accumulation of firms.

As the public sector enhances the growth potential of either some firms or the private sector as a whole, its agents are able to create, under certain conditions, the basic requirement for the realization of their goals and interests, i.e. an expanded institutional capacity for the provision of their particular services. An important condition for the agents of the public sector to create the economic requirements for further public sector growth is that the expansion of the sector does not give rise to wage inflation for which the firms cannot compensate themselves by raising prices or by rationalizing the use of their input of labour; another condition is that public sector growth does not lead to increased public borrowing which induces firms to make purely financial investments instead of mobilizing the disposable labour by investment in new and enlarged production capacity. Such disturbances in the desired working of the accumulation process are likely to impede further public sector growth.

Agents of the Economy

In subsequent chapters, the development of the GDP and the working population will be related to the supposed goals and interests of the agents of the private and public sectors, discussed earlier, and the techno-structures of the large firms and their public counterparts (i.e. the leading providers of public services and their allied members of the political decision-making community). But sometimes explanation also requires that other agents are brought into the analysis, parties who are not producers, but nevertheless have a considerable (and in some instances determining) impact on the economy. Three types of such 'exogenous' agents should be brought to the fore:

1. governments, which through their policies affect to a large extent the conditions of not only the private and public sector agents, but also the households (as consumers, taxpayers and suppliers of paid work);
2. associations of farmers and other small-scale producers which are

able to act as the defenders of the interests of some types of commodity providers;

3. trade unions, which, because of their bargaining strength or connections with political decision-makers, are able to affect the labour costs of both the private and public sector.

Geographical Units of Analysis: Nation-States

The geographical units of this study are the thirteen nation-states of Western Europe, national economies and (paraphrasing Taylor) 'spheres of ideology'.[25] As such, they are all headed by a government and central decision-making bodies which serve as the focal point of expectations and main target for organized pressure, and which (responding to these expectations and pressures) make for politically determined redistribution of incomes and employment opportunities. As emphasized by Giddens, nation-states are the main 'power-containers' of the contemporary world.[26] The power derives not only from the traditional and highly developed resources of authority of the state surveillance system, but also from the ability of policy-makers to exert a considerable influence on the actual use of economic resources (through taxation, public expenditure and provision of employment for a growing share of the working population). The allocation and reallocation of incomes through the activities of the public sector make nation-states the most suitable units for an identification of processes which have shaped the economy of the West European countries in the post-war period.

The Working Population: Industry, Occupation and Employment Status

The working (or economically active) population, which is of main interest in this study includes all those persons who work for pay in cash or in kind, or who compete with such suppliers of services on a labour market by either running a small business of their own or by assisting a family member in a family firm. The latter kind of economically active persons, who are usually called *unpaid family members*, are nowadays found mainly in agriculture and some service industries (notably retail trade and hotels and restaurants). The working population usually comprises those who are temporarily out of work, but not persons who perform unpaid household work, retired persons and full-time students. The core of the economically active population consists of those offering their labour services on a labour market.

The members of the working population are customarily classified with reference to their industry, occupation and employment status.

The *industry* of a person refers to the kind of goods or services the person provides, or takes part in the provision of. Examples of industries are agriculture, forestry and fishing (forming the so-called 'primary sector'), manufacturing (which is part of the 'secondary' or 'industrial' sector) and wholesale and retail trade, transport, banking, insurance and real estate, public administration, defence, and education (which are industries of the 'tertiary' or 'service' sector of employment).

Occupation refers to the kind of work the economically active person carries out when providing, or taking part in the provision of, certain goods or services. Examples of occupations are farmers, forestry workers and fishermen, machine minders and operators, salesmen and shop assistants, motor vehicle drivers, administrators, managers and office clerks, military officers, professional soldiers and teachers.

Farmers, forestry workers and fishermen are found almost exclusively in the industries of agriculture, forestry and fishing; machine minders are rarely encountered outside manufacturing. But some occupations, such as managers, clerks and motor vehicle drivers are found in many industries. For example, they may work in manufacturing, wholesale or retail trade, banking, insurance or public administration. The economically active persons of an industry may thus represent many different occupations. In manufacturing there are not only machine operators and other production process workers, but also engineers and other technicians, accountants, truck and crane drivers, security guards and janitors. In defence we find officers and other kinds of military personnel, but also draughtsmen, office messengers, sociologists and medical surgeons. In education there are teachers, but also administrators, telephone switchboard operators and catering personnel.

The third aspect of differentiation, *employment status*, makes a distinction between employers and own account workers, who employ themselves, and unpaid family workers and employees, who are dependent on a family member or an employer. The self-employed are typically found in agriculture, repairing, land transport, retailing and other private service pursuits, they work with the assistance of few or no other persons and represent the socioeconomic category of small-scale entrepreneurs and petty traders.

Data on the economically active population by industry, occupation and employment status are provided by the population censuses. Although most countries use their own standard of classification, the international comparability of industrial and occupational statistics is generally satisfactory for attempts to uncover major differences between countries in the quantitative importance or development of certain kinds of paid work. This holds at least when data for the 'minimum' items of the national classification systems are available, and thus may be recombined to form comparable activity clusters for cross-national study. What restricts comparisons between countries and census years are changes in the criteria used to decide whether persons should be considered members of the working population or not. It is usual to base such judgements on a minimum number of hours worked during a specified time period. Intercensal changes in such minimum requirements of work may obstruct assessments of the evolution of industries and occupations. International differences in the mode of operationally defining the working population also impair the possibility of comparing nations with respect to the relative frequency of certain industries and occupations.

The Gross Domestic Product

The gross domestic product, which is the basis for any assessment of the economic growth of a country, is the estimated value of all goods and services supplied in a year by the working population. The GDP is estimated in current or fixed prices. It represents the *net* money value of all goods and services, the accumulated *value added* of each stage of the production or service provision. It includes the value of exports with deductions for imports. The GDP may be analysed with reference to the use of the provided goods and services, or by reference to their origin (e.g. various industries or institutional sectors of paid work). In the former case it is customary to make a distinction between consumption (which may be private or public) and various types of fixed capital formation (e.g. provision of physical production facilities such as machinery, factory buildings and transport equipment). Data on the size and composition of the GDP are given on an annual basis in national accounts statistics. Expressed in fixed prices, such data are commonly used to judge a country's 'growth performance', its rate of current or compounded economic growth.

Dominance and Subordination: Development Blocks

An inherent characteristic of both the working population and the complex of activities that constitute the GDP is the relationship of dominance and subordination that may be uncovered in an analysis relating the quantitative development of certain parts of the aggregate to others: changes in the size of certain segments of the working population or the GDP give rise to changes in the size of other segments, while the reverse is not the case (or is not the case to the same extent). The former are the dominant parts, the latter the subordinate. The dominant and subordinate segments, or units, may be production sectors, industries, branches of an industry, or even large firms; or they may be types of expenditure distinguished in an analysis of the GDP from the point of view of use or type of demand (such as private and public consumption and various forms of capital formation). The dominance–subordination may be due to relationships of supply and demand (if these words are used in a wider sense as also covering relations of supply and demand regulated by political decisions). The dominating (and change-inducing) units are the 'demanders' of the goods or services of the subordinate units.[27]

A dominating unit and its subordinate units may form a 'development block' or *filière*, a complex of activities which grows or declines in terms of employment or output because of the growth or decline of the dominating unit.[28] The notions of dominance and subordination will be used in the analysis of both the working population and the GDP.

Contents and Plan of Presentation

Although this book contains a lot of statistical information concerning the working population and the gross domestic product, the subject is essentially the economic and political *processes* which have transformed the thirteen West European economies from the early 1950s until the second half of the 1980s, the motivated but changing practices of the agents of the private and public sectors. As the aim is principally causal analysis, changes described by means of statistics will be related to supposed goals, interests and agent interrelationships. Chapters 2–6 deal with patterns and causes of changes in the 1950s, 1960s and 1970s. The subjects are economic growth and stagnation, and the changing industrial, occupational and employment status structure of the working population. Chapter 6 attempts a systematic presentation of processes at work in the thirty-year period, 1950–80. Chapter 7 highlights factors transforming the West European economies in the 1980s. Basic tenets are deliberately repeated (with some variations) to form the common thread of the book.

Notes

1. As an attempt to cover both these kinds of change, this study can be placed in the tradition of research established by Fisher, Clark and Kuznets. See A.B.G. Fisher, *The Clash of Progress and Security* (London: Macmillan, 1935), C. Clark, *The Conditions of Economic Progress* (London: Macmillan, 1940) and S. Kuznets, *Modern Economic Growth: Rate, Structure, and Spread* (New Haven & London: Yale University Press, 1966).

   But as will be shown below, perspectives on work developed more recently will also be incorporated. See, for instance, J. Gershuny, *Social Innovation and the Division of Labour* (Oxford: Oxford University Press, 1983), J.I. Gershuny & I. Miles, *The New Service Economy: The Transformation of*

   Employment in Industrial Societies (London: Frances Pinter, 1983) and R.E.
   Pahl, *Divisions of Labour* (Oxford: Basil Blackwell, 1984).
2. A. Sayer, *Method in Social Science: A Realist Approach* (London: Hutchinson, 1984).
3. W.B. Gallie, *Pierce and Pragmatism* (Harmondsworth: Penguin, 1952) p. 98.
4. J. Ellul, *The Technological Society* (New York: Vintage Books, 1964).
5. A. Gouldner, *The Dialectic of Ideology and Technology* (London & Basingstoke: Macmillan, 1976).
6. For these three modes of economic circulation (or economic integration), see K. Polanyi, *Trade and Market in the Early Empires: Economies in History and Theory*, ed. C.M. Arensberg & H.W. Pearson (New York & London: Collier-Macmillan, 1957) p. 251 ff.
7. This definition of the ambiguous notion of work, which gives primacy to the labour market, has been considered most consistent with the purpose of this study. It includes domestic self-provisioning and the so-called 'informal work' of households, but only to the extent that it is probable that such unpaid activities can be either substituted by, or be the substitutes for, work done by members of the economically active population. For a discussion of various ways of looking at work, see Pahl, op. cit. and Gershuny, op. cit.
8. The concept 'world economy', has been developed notably by Wallerstein and Braudel. According to the latter, it is historically a segment of the globe which has provided for most of its own material needs, thus engaging in very little trade with the outer world. See F. Braudel, *Civilization and Capitalism 15th-18th Century* Vol. III, *The Perspective of the World* (London: Collins, 1984) p. 27.
9. W. William-Olsson, *Europe West of the Soviet Union* (forthcoming).
10. A.S. Eichner, *The Megacorp and Oligopoly: Micro-Foundations of Macro-Dynamics* (Cambridge: Cambridge University Press, 1976) p. 19.
11. W. Baumol, *Business Behaviour, Value and Growth* (New York: Macmillan, 1949); E.T. Penrose, *The Theory of the Growth of the Firm* (Oxford: Basil Blackwell, 1959); R. Marris, *The Economic Theory of 'Managerial' Capitalism* (London: Macmillan, 1964); and J.K. Galbraith, *The New Industrial State* (Boston: Houghton Mifflin, 1967).

   'Economists who have spent time observing operations of business enterprises come away impressed with the extent of management's occupation with growth. Expansion is the theme which (with some variations) is dinned into the ears of stock-holders, is constantly reported in the financial pages and in the journals devoted to business affairs. Indeed, in talking to business executives one may easily come to believe that growth of the firm is the main preoccupation of top management. A stationary optimum would doubtless be abhorrent to the captains of industry, whose main concern is not at what size their enterprises should finally settle down . . . but rather how rapidly to grow.'

   W.J. Baumol, 'On the Theory of the Expansion of the Firm', *American Economic Review*, Vol. 52 (December 1962), 1078.
12. The costs of using the market for economic transactions were emphasized by R.H. Coase in 'The Nature of the Firm', *Economica*, Vol. 4 (1937).
13. Eichner, op. cit., p. 28.
14. Ibid, p. 23.

15. See, for instance, C.W. Churchman, *The Systems Approach* (New York: Dell, 1968) p. 17: 'Any manager who is alert looks around his system and discerns where unreasonable wastes are occurring; if he's a good manager, he does his best to eliminate those wastes in order to reduce total costs of operation. . . . As Taylor and his "scientific managers" saw it, there is an efficient way to do a job, and it's up to the manager and his staff to find it.'

16. By 'ploughing back' parts of the gross profit, rather than using it for the payment of dividends, the corporations become to a large extent their own suppliers of the needed venture capital. Dependence on external funds is relaxed and the autonomy of top management is increased. A requirement for a high degree of financial self-reliance is, of course, that the firms are not affected deeply by general economic downturns or other adversity. In such situations there are great risks that major owners and other outsiders with a stake in the corporation will try to interfere in the strategic dispositions of top management; cf. Galbraith, op. cit., p. 167.

17. The following paragraphs on dualism draw heavily on C.F. Sabel, *Work and Politics: The Division of Labour in Industry* (Cambridge: Cambridge University Press, 1982). See also R.T. Averitt, *The Dual Economy: The Dynamics of American Industry Structure* (New York: Norton, 1968) and S.J. Prais, *The Evolution of Giant Firms in Britain* (Cambridge: Cambridge University Press, 1976).

18. Eichner, op. cit., p. 21.

19. M.J. Piore & S. Berger, *Dualism and Discontinuity in Industrial Societies* (Cambridge: Cambridge University Press, 1980).

20. J. O'Connor, *The Fiscal Crisis of the State* (New York: St Martin's Press, 1973).

21. The idea of an *economic surplus*, which could support an 'unproductive' part of the economy, was vital to classical political economy (including that of Marx). As noted by Smith, for instance: 'The sovereign, with all his officers both of justice and war who serve under him, are unproductive labourers. They are servants of the public, and are maintained by part of the annual produce of other people', i.e. kept by means of a share of the produce of the productive labour or a withdrawn surplus. See A. Smith, *The Wealth of Nations*, Book 2, Ch. 3, 'Of the Accumulation of Capital, or of Productive and Unproductive Labour', London, 1776 (Harmondsworth: Penguin, 1979).

    The notion of an 'economic surplus' has reappeared in non-Marxist studies of contemporary economic issues. Drawing a parallel to the view of the French physiocratic economist François Quesnay, who in the eighteenth century held that agricultural rents provided the surplus which supported the Court of Versailles, the French aristocracy, the armed forces and the church, Bacon and Eltis have mainly attributed the slow growth of the British economy in the 1970s to the allegedly exorbitant growth of a surplus-consuming and unproductive sector of the economy. Their argument is that there is a part of the economy which produces a surplus that makes it possible for the remainder of the economy to function. If the surplus-producing part grows rapidly, the economy grows rapidly; if the former declines, the economy crumbles. The surplus-producing sector is conceived of as the part of the economy which supplies marketed goods and services, i.e. commodities which are sold at home or overseas. The surplus-consuming activities provide non-marketed goods and services. See R.W. Bacon & W. Eltis, *Britain's Economic Problems: Too Few Producers* (London & New York: Macmillan, 1978). The economic surplus of the private sector is in this study conceived of as the amount of the sector's income over and above the total expenditure of the members of the sector on *commodities* supplied domestically or imported from abroad (net of exports). The members of the sector derive their income from wages or profits (or access to profit, as in the case of unpaid family members). It is believed that surplus-consuming activities, such as the services of the public sector, can be productive and conducive to economic growth in the sense that they indirectly enhance output per unit of input in the private sector. An essential facet of the economic surplus is, however, that it is appropriated by some authority: withdrawn from direct use of the income earners.

22. C. Offe & V. Ronge, 'Theses of the Theory of the State', in C. Offe, *Contradictions of the Welfare State*, ed. J. Keane (London: Hutchinson, 1981).

23. Ibid., p. 119 ff. Parallelling corporatist views of the state, Offe maintains that political power selectively favours groups whose acquiescence and support are crucial to the untroubled continuity of the existing order: oligopoly capital and organized labour. The state defrays part of the costs of production of capital (e.g. by supplying cheap energy through pricing policies of nationalized industries) and offers a range of benefits for organized labour (e.g. by tacitly supporting high demands and enhanced wage differentials). The representatives of these strategic groups increasingly step in to resolve threats to political stability through informal, extra-parliamentary negotiations. See D. Held, 'Theories of the State', in *The State in Capitalist Europe: A Casebook*, ed. S. Bornstein (London: Allen & Unwin, 1984) p. 17.

24. O'Connor, op. cit. p. 8.

25. P. Taylor, *Political Geography: World Economy, Nation-State and Locality* (London & New York: Longman, 1985) p. 29.

26. A. Giddens, *Violence and the Nation-State: Volume Two of Contemporary Critique of Historical Materialism* (Cambridge: Polity Press, 1985) p. 13 ff.

27. F. Perroux, *L'Economie du XX:e Siècle* (Paris: Presses Universitaires de France, 1961) p. 85.

28. This is, in essence, the growth pole of Perroux, see 'La Firm Motrice dans une Région et la Région Motrice', *Cahiers de l'Institut de Science Economique Appliquée*, Suppl. No. 111 (March 1961). The word 'development block' derives from E. Dahmén, *Entrepreneurial Activity and the Development of Swedish Industry, 1919–1939* (Homewood, Ill.: Irwin, 1970).

2 Economic Growth and Stagnation, 1950–80

Abated Growth Rates

During most of the post-war period, the countries of Western Europe could report exceptionally high rates of economic growth, i.e. increases in their gross domestic products at fixed prices. In the 20-year period 1953–73, which is conventionally defined as a period of pronounced economic growth, the annual rate of growth of the GDP exceeded 3 per cent in almost all countries; for Germany, France, Italy, the Netherlands, Austria and Finland annual rates of growth were in the order of 5.0–5.5 per cent (Table 2:1). The high rates of economic growth were accompanied in most countries by moderate inflation and low rates of unemployment. The period 1973–82 brought more feeble economic growth; annual rates lower than 2 per cent were far from exceptional and only a few countries (Ireland and Norway) reported rates exceeding 3 per cent a year. Other characteristics of the post-1973 period were mounting rates of inflation and unemployment. The turn from high to low rates of growth is usually described as a change from *growth* to *stagnation*.[1]

This chapter consists of four parts. Part 1 deals with processes and forces which gave rise to the substantial economic growth prior to 1973; Part 2 deals with circumstances accounting for the abated growth rates in the second half of the 1970s and the early 1980s—the 'stagnation'. Variations in the rates of growth of the GDP will be related to four factors:

1. The degree to which socially necessary activities, such as the care of children, elderly and other dependants, are carried out as *unpaid household work*, or as *remunerated work* in the private or public sector of production.
2. The actual *volume of paid work*, or *employment* (conceived of as number of man-hours).

Table 2.1   Gross domestic product: annual rate of change (%)

	1953–73	1973–82
United Kingdom	3.0	0.8
Ireland	3.3	3.4
Germany	5.5	1.7
France	5.3	2.4
Italy	5.3	2.1
Netherlands	4.9	1.5
Belgium	4.3	1.9
Austria	5.7	2.4
Switzerland	4.6	0.3
Sweden	3.9	1.4
Norway	3.9	3.7
Denmark	4.3	1.6
Finland	5.0	2.7

Sources: A. Boltho, 'Growth', in *The European Economy: Growth and Crisis*, ed. A. Boltho (Oxford: OUP, 1982) and OECD, *National Accounts*, Vol. 1, *1953–1982* (Paris: OECD, 1984).

3. The *productivity of labour* (defined as the average real value added per hour of paid work).
4. *The scope and accurateness of registration*, i.e. the extent to which goods and services provided for by means of paid work are actually reckoned in national account statistics.

The volume of paid work, or employment, is regarded as a function of two factors: the aggregate demand for goods and services, and labour productivity. The evolution of domestic demand, which is registered as private and public consumption and fixed capital formation in the private and public sector, is highlighted in Parts 1 and 2. External demand is considered in Part 3, which deals with foreign trade. In connection with foreign trade, capital formation in other parts of the world is also taken into account. While the analysis of the first three parts focuses on conditions of demand, Part 4 considers the change from high to low rates of growth from the point of view of supply. The low rates of economic growth in the post-1973 period are related to a supposed (and more or less evidenced) *profit squeeze* of the commodity sector. It is maintained that a depression of aggregate gross profits constrained the expansion of the activities of both the private and public sector. This chapter provides a statistical demonstration of the evolution of certain macroeconomic categories as defined in the national accounts. Seven countries have been chosen for particular evidence: the United Kingdom, Germany, France, Italy, the Netherlands, Belgium and Sweden.

Causes of Economic Growth 1950–73

When looking for causes of economic growth, one should keep in mind
that a change in the size of the GDP may partly be due to institutional
relocation of some kinds of work, a transfer of the activities to (or from)
the part of the economy where work is remunerated and registered (more
or less accurately) in the national accounts. If unpaid household work is
brought into the realm of the private or public sector of production it is
reckoned as a contribution to the GDP; if it is withdrawn from these sectors
its relocation is conducive to a contraction of the GDP. In the same vein,
the size of the GDP is affected by changes in the extent to which paid work
is actually recorded. Economic growth reflects an increase in the volume
of remunerated work accounted for in the national accounts statistics.

A major factor of economic growth in the pre-1973 period was
transfers of unpaid household work to the registered parts of the
economy. The care of children, the elderly and the disabled increasingly
became the responsibility of the public sector, activities of institutions
where the formerly unpaid (and female-dominated) work was carried
out by (mainly female) public employees. The 'formalization' of the
work, to use a term proposed by Gershuny,[2] added to public consumption expenditure, and it induced investment in the public sector which
was recorded as government gross fixed capital formation. Other
household work, such as the preservation and preparation of foodstuffs,
was taken over by firms in the food industry (or the catering business) as
households increasingly relied on pre-processed food (or got some of
their meals in a workplace canteen). Such relocation of work added to
the rise of recorded private consumption expenditure and, through
investment inducements, to capital formation expenditure.

As has been emphasized by Gershuny, transfer of work was also
taking place from the paid and formal parts of the economy to the
unpaid household sector.[3] The most conspicuous example is personal
transport work which became, to a large extent, a do-it-yourself activity
carried out by means of privately owned automobiles. Such a transfer
implied declining demand for paid transport work (entering the GDP)
but the net effect of the institutional shift was certainly growth of the
GDP, as the unpaid transport activities implied expanded use of goods
and services provided by both the private and public sector of production.
If one considers the growth of the volume of unpaid transport work
carried out by means of private cars, one should keep in mind, however,
that it was more an effect of the increased availability of private cars—
and increased need for movement of people—than a relocation of
already existing work. In fact, it can be regarded as the most important
facet of the emerging mass consumption of industrial goods, which (as
will be elaborated below) derived its dynamics from the growth motives
of the firms of the private sector.

Contributing also to the growth of the GDP, but not necessarily the volume of actual work, was the increased commercialization of agriculture. The national accounts include imputed values for the part of agricultural output which is used by the producers for their own consumption. But the consumption of self-provided goods is presumably underestimated. As agriculturists became more dependent on the market (and on government subsidies related to the sale of their produce) their work probably entered into the accounts more fully. A second major factor accounting for the rapid rise of the GDP was the increased economic productivity of industries in the private sector, i.e. the growth of their real value added per hour worked.[4] Paid work was used by employers in ways conducive to increased output (in physical or value terms). The growth in productivity resulted from the efforts of the producers to rationalize operations, i.e. to use the disposable labour resources in ways enhancing real value added per hour. Rationalization of the production process and changes in the product range of the firm were the standard reactions of employers to the increased hourly compensation of the employed labour force.[5] The rising nominal wages, which induced the productivity-enhancing practices of the firms, reflected the relatively strong position of organized labour *vis-à-vis* the employers. The demand for operative labour was high. In most countries immigration of labour from other parts of the world was moderate (the major exception being Germany), or kept within limits which secured favourable wage-bargains for many categories of operatives. As the wage increases were generally not offset by increases in the general level of prices, real incomes rose.[6] The inflated wage bill required private sector producers to organize, equip and substitute labour in ways which seemed at any time consistent with the lowest labour costs per unit of output. Economizing in the use of paid labour was a condition for the survival and growth of any private sector producer. As emphasized by several writers, it was both the stick and carrot which induced firms to adapt to changes in their environments. Producers who did not adopt labour-saving practices were forced out of business, thereby contributing to the rise of the productivity in their industry. Firms which played the game successfully grew at the expense of their less efficient competitors and increased their relative weight in total output.[7] By investing in labour-saving equipment, firms could compensate themselves for wage increases at the same time as they took part in the satisfaction of the growing aggregate commodity demand which characterized the period.

As pointed out by Maddison, the rise in the general level of prices lowered the real costs of borrowing and made it more expensive for firms to keep assets in the form of cash. In order to cater for some flexibility with respect to future changes in the pattern of demand and production techniques, investment in projects which seemed to have a short pay-off period was preferred.[8] Firms could therefore keep pace with technological development in their industry and acquire the most up-to-date production equipment. The efficiency of the production facilities in general approached the limits defined by the most efficient producers.[9]

A third major factor of economic growth in the pre-1973 period was the low unemployment rates, which resulted from the sustained growth of output of industrial commodities and increased provision of public services. A large proportion of those willing to work for an employer were offered employment and could participate in the formal and registered economy. The crucial factor behind the low rates of unemployment—and the presumably expanding volume of paid work in the pre-1973 period—was the substantial fixed capital formation: the expansion and ongoing modernization of the physical production facilities of the firms, the growing demand for physical capital in the public sector, and the considerable residential construction.

A main characteristic of the Western European countries in the pre-1973 period, and the major inducement to physical capital formation, was the growing effective demand for consumer goods, notably durables such as primary and secondary homes, cars and other personal transport equipment, 'white' household appliances and consumer electronic goods. High and growing household expenditure on durables, which became items for large-scale and standardized production, were part of the logic of rising real incomes and low rates of unemployment. Production and distribution of these kinds of industrial commodities engaged, directly or indirectly, an increasing share of the working population. The economies of scale and rationalization attained in their provision partially benefited the customers as the price of durables fell compared to many other commodities, in particular to personal services supplied by the private sector. As argued by Gershuny, their cheapening (in terms of real and comparative prices) enhanced, in combination with the rising costs of private services, a move towards a mechanized and capital-intensive self-service economy. Personal service work supplied by firms was transferred to the households, where the work could be carried out with the use of machinery supplied by other (and typically large) firms. The pattern was one of substitution, Gershuny maintains.[10] But, as already noted, the substitution was associated with an increase in the volume of household work, which implied the use of consumer durables. The symbol of the emerging mass consumption society was the privately owned car, which in a decade or two became the main means of personal transport. For many households it became a necessity, whether conceived of as an implement of work or for recreation. The automobilization of the population implied a rapid growth in the stock of passenger cars. In the period 1950–82 the number of registered vehicles in most countries grew more than tenfold (according to *U.N's Statistical Year Book*). In Germany it increased from 620,000 to 24 million;

in Italy from 350,000 to 19.5 million. A (temporary) break in the growth trend was experienced only in the years of rapidly rising oil prices of the 1970s and early 1980s. The growing demand for consumer goods (durable and non-durable) induced firms to expand their production capacity, to acquire more machinery, space for operative and non-operative work, transport equipment and industrial inputs. In many firms it also induced expanding employment. Hence the demand for producer goods increased, as well as the demand for production facilities and inputs for the producers of producer goods and services. In the ensuing high and growing aggregate demand for industrial commodities—and the consequently low rates of unemployment—each of the countries experienced the emergence and growth of large *development blocks*, clusters of economic activities which were dependent for their growth on the growing household expenditure on durables. The most conspicuous of these blocks (or *filières* as they have also been called) was that of the privately owned automobile. This is not limited to the production, sales, repair and servicing of cars, and the provision of fuel, lubricants and spare parts. It can also be conceived of as comprising the production of the inputs of passenger-car manufacturers (such as steel, plastics, instrument and electrical components), the required petroleum-refining capacity and the transport equipment and services needed to ship the input and output of the refineries, the construction and maintenance of roads, some part of the insurance business, the surveillance apparatus of the state, facilities for surgery and rehabilitation of victims of car accidents, breakers' yards, scrap dealers, etc. All these activities expanded, in terms of output and employment, as a result of the growing household ownership and use of cars.

As already emphasized, many firms were also forced to rationalize their production. Rationalization, which in general terms meant a more efficient use of operative labour, required substantial expenditure on new production facilities, and added therefore to the growing demand for producer goods. Because of its implicit high demand for factory buildings, machinery and other equipment, the extended rationalization did not lead to contracting private sector employment. The saving of labour required the engagement of a substantial amount of labour in the production of labour-saving equipment. Substantial investment in machinery and other production facilities was also made in the primary industries. The rationalization of these industries was associated with a contraction of their employment, but it also added to the demand for labour in other parts of the economy, particularly in industries supplying agricultural machinery and inputs.

A further characteristic of the pre-1973 period was growing government expenditure on public consumption and investment. Priority areas for the expanded public sector in most Western European countries were health, social welfare and education—services which could be claimed to promote the productivity of the labour force at the same time as they symbolized the emerging welfare state. Simultaneously, the geopolitical situation of the countries called for growing defence expenditure, a tribute to the 'warfare state'. The consumption of public services added to the demand for goods and services supplied by the private sector; it offered employment opportunities for a growing part of the working population, people who were both buyers of private consumption goods and beneficiaries of public services. It also entailed a growing demand for public producer goods, notably commodities supplied by the industrial sector: buildings to house public institutions, a transport infrastructure for the movement of goods and persons, appliances for medical services, military installations and equipment for defence etc.

The expanded private and public consumption of households secured a rate of capital formation which was consistent with high rates of economic growth. But when one considers the substantial build-up of physical capital which boosted the GDP and kept a large portion of the working population in employment, one should keep in mind that it was part and parcel of the continuous reorganization of the economy. When firms in the industrial sector tried to attain economies of scale by concentrating their operations on larger plants, the associated distributive functions were necessarily extended over large geographical areas (or extended to new categories of customers). The rationalization of commodity production thus implied growth of intermediary industries, for example wholesale and retail trade and transport, storage and communication (or the kinds of functions these industries represent). The expanding intermediary work required new and proper kinds of physical capital and, through the demand for physical structures, transport equipment and other facilities, it added to the aggregate physical capital formation expenditure of the countries. Increased demand for physical capital also resulted from the industrial shift in work which was part of the modernization of agriculture and other primary industries. As will be developed in subsequent chapters, rationalization of agricultural work implied movement of distributive work, construction, repair activities and provision of energy to other industries (where the work could be done more efficiently in terms of the required labour inputs). A third example of such reorganization of the economy, which engendered substantial demand for new production facilities, was the shift from coal (as the main source of energy) to oil, or a mix of imported and domestically produced oil and natural gas, supplemented by nuclear power. Such changes in the energy economy, which all Western European countries went through, generated considerable construction work and investment in transport facilities—as did the accompanying locational shifts in the work and residence of the population, the urbanization, suburbanization, and spread of urban population to areas beyond the residential zones of large cities. The urbanization and suburbanization of the population (which meant an increase in the percentage of the total population living in urban settlements) reflected the declining employment opportunities in agriculture and the creation of jobs in urban industries. The (more recent) tendency of urban workers to settle in the countryside, and at considerable distances from large city centres, allegedly signalled a new preference for living in less congested areas, in surroundings which offered some rural amenities. This preference could be realized by more people as they became owners of cars and could use an extended network of public roads in commuting daily to a place of work in an urban area.[11] But the move of the urban population to formerly rural areas was surely also a result of changes in the locational patterns of industries which are traditionally considered urban. The most important example is manufacturing, which invaded many rural and less central parts of the countries. In any case, the overall agglomeration of the population, and the almost simultaneous deconcentration of some part of the urban (and traditionally agglomerated) population, entailed substantial fixed capital formation: investment in dwellings to house the growing urban population; physical structures for the provision of private and public services; transport facilities to bridge the growing distance between the home and place of work; and roads and other forms of infrastructure which allowed for a high degree of functional integration of the geographically dispersed urban industries.[12]

The high rates of economic growth in the pre-1973 period thus resulted from transfers of work from the households to the sectors of paid (and registered) work, from increased labour productivity, and from low (or falling) rates of unemployment. The high degree of participation of the labour force in the provision of goods and services, and the presumably growing employment (in terms of man-hours) were corollaries of the specific demand conditions of the sub-period, particularly the substantial physical capital formation in the private and public sector of production.

The high and growing demand for both commodities and public services in Britain, Germany, France, Italy, the Netherlands, Belgium and Sweden is evidenced by means of national accounts statistics in Tables 2:2–2:9. The slowest growth of private final consumption expenditure in the 1953–73 period was registered for Britain and Sweden, the highest (well above 5 per cent) for Germany, Italy and France. That the growth of private consumption of households was not a reflection of merely an increase in the number of consumers is made clear by Table 2:3, which shows population growth in the seven countries. Although the rate of population growth was comparatively high in Germany, France, Italy and (particularly) the Netherlands, it did not match by far the growth rates of aggregate private consumption expenditure. Extraordinary high rates of growth were recorded for household expenditure on the purchase and use of personal transport equipment, i.e. essentially privately owned cars (Table 2:4). This type of expenditure is highly susceptible to aggregate demand policy (not to mention the price of oil). The fairly low rate of growth recorded for Sweden reflects a decline in the early 1970s. The growth of expenditure on residential construction is shown in Table 2:5. Residential construction (which, although considered as capital formation, indicates the consumption standard of the population) showed very strong growth in most countries in the 1950s and early 1960s, France and Italy being notable examples. The later decline of residential construction started in some countries in the second half of the 1960s, and therefore affected the rates for the selected period. The growing provision of public services is reflected in the growth of government final consumption expenditure (Table 2:6). The slowest growth of public consumption between 1953 and 1973 was registered for Britain, the highest for Germany, Belgium and Sweden. The steady expansion and modernization of the production facilities of the private sector is reflected in Table 2:7, which shows the rate of growth of gross fixed capital formation expenditure on machinery and other equipment. Rates between 7 and 10 per cent a year were recorded for France, Germany, the Netherlands and Italy. Growth rates of capital formation in the public sector are presented in Table 2:8. Rates exceeding 7 per cent a year are shown for Britain, France, Germany and Belgium. As demonstrated in Table 2:9, the rates of growth of aggregate gross fixed capital formation in the period 1953–73 were, for all seven countries, in the range of 5–8 per cent a year.

Table 2.2   Private final consumption expenditure: annual rate of change (%)

	1953–73	1973–82
United Kingdom	3.0	0.9
Germany	5.6*	1.8
France	5.2*	3.3
Italy	5.5*	2.1
Netherlands	5.1*	2.1
Belgium	3.8*	2.2
Sweden	3.2	1.2

* 1954–73

Source: OECD, *National Accounts*, Vol. 1, *1953–1982* (Paris: OECD, 1984).

Table 2.3 Population growth: annual rate of change (%)

	1953–73	1973–82
United Kingdom	0.5	0.0
Germany	1.0	−0.6
France	1.0	0.4
Italy	1.3	0.4
Netherlands	2.2	0.7
Belgium	0.8	0.1
Sweden	0.6	0.2

Source: OECD, *National Accounts*, Vol. 1, *1953–1982* (Paris: OECD, 1984) and various editions of the countries' statistical year books.

Table 2.4 Private final consumption expenditure, personal transport equipment: annual rate of change (%)

	1960–73	1973–82
United Kingdom	7.7	−2.2
Germany	9.3	1.6
France	9.1*	1.6
Italy	10.0**	4.4
Belgium	8.5	1.8
Sweden	2.1***	0.2

* 1962–73   ** 1964–73   *** 1963–73

Sources: OECD, *National Accounts of OECD Countries 1950–1968* and *1952–1970* (Paris: OECD, 1970 and 1982), *National Accounts of OECD Countries*, Vol. 2, *1962–1979* (Paris: OECD, 1981), *National Accounts*, Vol. 2, *1970–1982, 1971–1983, 1972–1984* and *1973–1985* (Paris: OECD, 1984, 1985, 1986 and 1987).

Causes of Stagnation in the Post-1973 Period

The 1950s and 1960s were characterized by rapidly increasing productivity of labour, but, as the productivity growth was matched by rapidly growing provision of goods and services, unemployment was low measured in both absolute and relative numbers. In the post-1973 period stagnating commodity provision and rapidly growing productivity combined to produce substantial unemployment. In absolute numbers,

Table 2.5   Gross fixed capital formation,
residential construction: annual rate of change (%)

	1953–73	1973–82
United Kingdom	2.5	−4.8
Germany	4.4	−2.0
France	9.1	−1.5
Italy	6.0	−0.9
Netherlands	5.7	−2.7
Belgium	3.3	−4.3
Sweden	4.6	−2.0

Sources: OECD, *National Accounts of OECD Countries 1950–1968* and *1952–1970* (Paris: OECD, 1970 and 1982), *National Accounts of OECD Countries*, Vol. 2, *1962–1979* (Paris: OECD, 1981), *National Accounts*, Vol. 2, *1970–1982, 1971–1983, 1972–1984* and *1973–1985* (Paris: OECD, 1984, 1985, 1986 and 1987).

Table 2.6   Government final consumption
expenditure: annual rate of change (%)

	1953–73	1973–82
United Kingdom	1.4	1.5
Germany	4.8*	2.3
France	3.4*	2.8
Italy	3.9*	2.4
Netherlands	2.4*	2.5
Belgium	4.8*	2.6
Sweden	4.4	3.0

* 1954–73

Source: OECD, *National Accounts*, Vol. 1, *1953–1982* (Paris: OECD, 1984).

registered unemployment grew in Britain from about 600,000 persons in 1973 to more than 2.9 million in 1982; in Italy 2.38 million persons were reported as unemployed in 1982 compared to over one million in 1973; in the Netherlands the number of unemployed was 4.7 times as large in 1982 as in 1973; in Belgium the number of unemployed increased fivefold between 1973 and 1982.[13] Among the few countries with no or only a small increase in the unemployment rate was Sweden.[14] It can be assumed that rising unemployment was accompanied, in most countries,

Table 2.7 Gross fixed capital formation,
machinery and other equipment: annual rate of
change (%)

	1953–73	1973–82
United Kingdom	5.3	1.3
Germany	8.2	0.9
France	9.7	2.8
Italy	6.6	0.6
Netherlands	7.8	−0.3
Belgium	5.4*	0.7**
Sweden	4.9	0.7

* 1957–73   ** 1973–81

Sources: OECD, *National Accounts of OECD Countries
1950–1968* and *1952–1970* (Paris: OECD, 1970 and 1982),
National Accounts of OECD Countries, Vol. 2, *1962–1979*
(Paris: OECD, 1981), *National Accounts*, Vol. 2, *1970–
1982, 1971–1983, 1972–1984* and *1973–1985* (Paris:
OECD, 1984, 1985, 1986 and 1987).

Table 2.8 Gross fixed capital formation,
government: annual rate of change (%)

	1953–73	1973–82
United Kingdom	9.9	−6.8
Germany	7.7*	−1.2
France	8.0**	1.2***
Italy	4.0	0.6
Netherlands	2.7	−2.3
Belgium	7.2	−0.3
Sweden	5.8	−0.4

* 1959–73   ** 1956–73   *** 1973–81

Sources: OECD, *National Accounts of OECD Countries
1950–1968* and *1952–1970* (Paris: OECD, 1970 and 1982),
National Accounts of OECD Countries, Vol. 2, *1962–1979*
(Paris: OECD, 1981), *National Accounts*, Vol. 2, *1970–
1982, 1971–1983, 1972–1984* and *1973–1985* (Paris:
OECD, 1984, 1985, 1986 and 1987).

by a contraction of the total number of hours worked, i.e. a declining
volume of actual employment.[15]

A main cause of the contraction in the volume of registered work was
that physical capital formation stagnated or declined. Another main

Table 2.9 Gross fixed capital formation: annual
rate of change (%)

	1953–73	1973–82
United Kingdom	5.1	−1.2
Germany	5.6*	−0.2
France	7.7*	0.8
Italy	5.6*	0.2
Netherlands	5.8*	−1.8
Belgium	4.8*	−0.5
Sweden	4.9	−0.9

* 1954–73

Source: OECD, *National Accounts*, Vol. 1, *1953–1982*
(Paris: OECD, 1984).

cause was increased labour productivity. As for physical capital formation, the changing character of labour-saving measures seems to be
crucial (the move of commodity producers from pure mechanization to
automation). A further factor in the contracting volume of employment
was probably the increased self-provisioning of households and growth
of clandestine work, a factor which affects the GDP but not necessarily
the volume of actual work.

In the 1970s, private consumption expenditure evidently increased
less rapidly than in the 1950s and 1960s. For some types of commodities
it seems that the demand approached saturation. The privately owned
car was just such a commodity. (With hindsight it may be more
appropriate to maintain that the slackened growth rates in the number
of passenger cars indicate a cyclical pattern of investment in consumer
durables.) Further decreases in the real prices of products did not lead to
a substantial growth in the real sales volume of the producers. The
aggregate demand for consumer goods was further hampered by
growing unemployment and rising energy prices (which followed the
upturn of the import prices of oil in 1973). As for durables (the demand
for which had played such a crucial role in the earlier decades), sales
reflected, to a much larger extent than earlier, replacement of obsolete
equipment, or a wish of customers to acquire better (or more sophisticated) product variants. The major exception was certain kinds of
household electronic goods. Consequently, and in sharp contrast to the
1950s and 1960s, the demand for consumer durables induced only
modest additions to the aggregate production capacity of the private
sector. Investment was made for the purpose of rationalization, or
replacement of obsolete equipment. A further circumstance that had a
dampening effect on capital formation in the consumer goods industries,

and particularly industries producing durables, was that the household demand for manufactured goods was increasingly satisfied by producers in other parts of the world. In the 1970s Japan emerged as the leading exporter of household electronics and automobiles. Japanese firms penetrated not only the home markets of the Western European producers, but also infiltrated their overseas markets. The large development blocks, which had created the growth requirements for the public sector in the pre-1973 period, thus lost much of their momentum (or, rather, their momentum in Western Europe).

The tempered output growth of the private sector and the rising unemployment were also caused by the ongoing rationalization of commodity provision and (which was probably more crucial) the changing character of capital formation and technical modernization. In the 1950s and 1960s rationalization generally implied mechanization, accompanied by changes in the organization of operative work. Mechanization saved labour but generated substantial expenditure on physical production facilities, machinery for more widespread and intensive use, as well as factory buildings to house the new and more efficient machinery. Mechanization saved labour, but at the same time enhanced the demand for labour, particularly as firms were eager to use the most up-to-date models of labour-saving devices available. In the 1970s rationalization increasingly assumed the form of *automation*, i.e. the use of self-steering mechanical equipment which could be operated with very little human attendance. The purpose of rationalization efforts by firms was the same as earlier, but not the effects on aggregate output and employment. Automation, as compared to sheer mechanization, meant that a certain reduction in the amount of labour required to produce a given amount of commodities could be attained by means of the use of amounts of physical capital which represented a smaller addition to aggregate gross capital formation and total employment. Because of technical progress, the costs of the labour-saving equipment were lowered, in terms both of money and of man-hours. As automated operations required less labour than non-automated operations, the saving of labour power caused by the more widespread use of automated machinery by far exceeded the amount of labour spent in the production of the labour-saving equipment. The substitution of automation for pure mechanization thus had the effect of reducing both physical capital formation and employment. In addition, certain indirect effects on the total spending power of households may be ascribed to the automation process if redundant workers did not find alternative employment.

The public sector growth rate was also slower in the 1970s than in the earlier decades, and far from sufficient to compensate for the stagnating commodity provision. The moderate growth of public consumption expenditure and the declining gross capital formation expenditure of the public sector symptomized the reluctance, or inability, of economic policy-makers to restore economic growth and full employment through increased government spending, directly by expanding public services, or indirectly by stimulating the demand for private sector goods and services. The major constraint to expansionist policies was the abated growth of the private sector—the very cause of the stagnation to be remedied. Substantially increased government expenditure was not allowed, as the main objective of governments was generally to curb inflation. Faced with a real (or perhaps only believed) trade-off between inflation and unemployment, most governments seemed to tolerate high rates of unemployment (or were forced to do so). Because of the deteriorated terms of trade between the Western European countries and the oil-exporting countries, economic policies were highly influenced by balance of payments considerations. A pronounced goal in many countries was to promote the international competitiveness of the exporting industries. Increased public spending was ruled out as a remedy for maladjustments in the economy, as it would stimulate imports and raise the labour costs of the exporters (by strengthening the position of organized labour in bargaining for wages). The deteriorated balance of payments situation called for restrictive policy measures.

Considering the industrial restructuring of the economy, an important growth factor in the pre-1973 period, it seems reasonable to suggest that it generated less demand for physical production facilities. While the reorganization of the system of commodity provision was in the earlier decades largely geared to attempts by firms to secure economies of scale by means of a capital-requiring expansion of both the production and sales facilities (which was consistent with mass consumption), the restructuring of the economy in the 1970s was dictated more by attempts at cutting costs by adoption of production methods requiring less labour and energy. Automation of mechanized operations has already been mentioned. Another example is computerization of office work, the application of new technology to the compilation, storage, processing and communication of information. Although the new methods of information work required much new physical equipment, the implied demand for physical capital was modest compared to the needs of the earlier decades. Rationalization furthered to a much larger extent than before the accumulation of knowledge, to a lesser degree the accumulation of physical capital in the form of buildings, machinery, transport equipment and infrastructure. Also contributing to the tempering of the fixed capital formation expenditure was the delay, or definite cancelling, of some nuclear energy programmes in the late 1970s. Suspended and cancelled investments were due to a combination of growing political opposition, and mounting construction and maintenance costs, as well as revised energy demand prospects. Furthermore, urbanization, conceived of as an overall agglomeration of the population, slowed down in the 1970s; it thus contributed less to the aggregate physical capital formation expenditure than in the 1950s and 1960s. As some writers have remarked, urbanization, in the sense of growth in the share of the population living in urban places, is a finite process. The share can approach but never exceed 100 per cent.[16] As the actual percentage limit to the agglomeration of the population is much lower, many Western European countries entered a stage where geographical redistribution of the population meant relocation and spread of the urban (and generally agglomerated) population. The physical capital requirements of such relocations may have been considerable, but were presumably less than the demands for physical capital generated by the massive movement of people from agricultural areas, which almost all Western European countries experienced before 1973.

In discussing factors accounting for the low economic growth rates in the post-1973 period, this chapter has hitherto focused on the mismatch between output and labour productivity, on circumstances which brought a decline in the volume of paid work. Also contributing to the depressed growth rates of the 1970s were probably net transfers of work from the private sector of production to the households and the growth of clandestine work (which does not contribute to the GDP).

Evidence and reasons for the increasing amount of 'do-it-yourself' in households in advanced industrial countries have been presented by several writers.[17] According to Pahl, certain forms of self-provisioning increased considerably among British households in the 1970s: 'A substantial amount of production once again took place in the home by household members, which earlier in the century might have been done by employing another individual or firm'.[18] Major causes of such transfers were, according to the same writer, the government-encouraged spread of owner-occupied dwellings, the declining disposable income of middle-class homeowners, and shorter working days. By the late 1970s, do-it-yourself had become the fastest growing sector of the building industry. The growth of this particular area of self-provisioning was attributable to the appearance of new tools and cheap, readily available materials; another factor was accelerating inflation, which induced many homeowners to improve what appeared to be their strongest hedge against inflation. As a further factor, Pahl mentions the mounting costs of formally contracted labour.[19]

In the 1970s it was also observed that growing numbers of people had begun to participate in economic activities which were not covered by the surveillance apparatus of the state. Seeking to evade taxes and avoid compliance with government regulations, many otherwise law-abiding citizens, it has been maintained, began to engage in what was called underground, black, hidden or clandestine work. In the words of Mattera: 'What all these terms refer to are transactions that . . . do not conform with the rules set down by the state in its role as overseer of the economy'.[20] It is impossible to make a definite judgement on whether such statements reflect increased attention to the phenomenon, or an actual growth of clandestine work.[21] Reasons for thinking that in the post-1973 period there was both a growth of the self-provisioning of households and a growth of remunerated but unreported work (compared to the paid and reported work activities of the population) are the rising costs of some kinds of service provision and the increased tax burden on households.

The costs of service provision (as any kind of work paid for by customers or clients) rise whenever the economic productivity and/or the efficiency of the firms (or public service providers) do not keep pace with the increases in the compensation of the engaged labour force, when the wage increases of the providers of the goods or services outstrip the capacity of producers to raise the value added per any unit of time by rationalizing the work or by changing the character of the provided services in such ways that they become less labour requiring. Rising costs generally induce firms to raise their prices (provided that the demand is not highly elastic); public service providers, which do not depend on pricing, are compelled to ask for larger financial allowances (which generally means increased taxation).

In the case of private service provision, rising costs probably worked as an impetus to increased self-provisioning in the entire post-war period. The strength of the impetus has been a function of the ability of private service workers to raise their hourly wages and the extent to which customers have experienced the rising costs in the form of increased prices. A circumstance that has made rising prices of services more crucial over time is increased taxation. Paid service work became not only more expensive compared to household machinery; it became more expensive in terms of the number of hours that the average household member has to work in order to pay for contracted service work after deduction of income tax.[22] The increased taxation of households reflects the growing volume of public sector work, the difficulties in raising the efficiency of some public sector work (without degrading the quality of the services) and the fact that the financial means which were appropriated for the running of the public sector were extracted on the basis of a contracting, or only slowly growing, amount of paid work (due to the stagnation of the economy). The evolution of direct taxes as a percentage of the aggregate incomes of the households is shown in Table 2:10. The pattern for the thirty-year period as a whole is an overall rise, headed by Sweden; in the late 1970s more than a third of aggregate household income was used for direct taxes in the late 1970s (as compared to less than 20 per cent in the 1950s). In addition to direct taxes, households had to bear a substantial share of indirect taxation such as VAT. In the 1970s, indirect taxes made up between 10 and 20 per cent of the private sector contribution to the GDP, as shown in Table 2:11.

Table 2.10 Direct taxes and contributions to social security (% of aggregate household incomes)

	1950	*1973*	*1982*
United Kingdom	13.6	19.3	20.2
Germany	16.5	26.9	27.0
France	15.6	19.8	23.7
Italy	–	16.1	22.6
Netherlands	17.1	29.5	29.6
Belgium	12.7*	22.7	27.3
Sweden	13.0	30.0	34.3

* 1953

Sources: OECD, *National Accounts of OECD Countries 1950–1968* (Paris: OECD, 1970) and *National Accounts*, Vol 2, *1970–1982* (Paris: OECD, 1984)

Table 2.11 Indirect taxes as percentage of private sector value added (contribution of 'industries' to GDP)

	1970	*1975*	*1982*
United Kingdom	20.6	16.8	22.4
Germany	15.5	15.2	15.0
France	18.4	17.0	17.8*
Italy	12.5	9.7	11.7
Netherlands	–	14.3**	13.6
Belgium	15.3	13.9	15.5
Sweden	17.6	19.1	22.3

* 1981   ** 1977

Source: OECD, *National Accounts*, Vol 2, *1970–1982* (Paris: OECD, 1984)

The rising relative costs of some private service work, and the fact that a growing share of the rising real incomes of households was used for payments of direct and indirect taxes (i.e. for compulsory consumption of government services) suggest that in the 1970s there was a growing tendency among some kinds of service providers (and their customers) to understate, or not to report, their transactions. Taxes raised the prices of formally contracted repair and maintenance work and made it virtually inaccessible to people who could not rely on self-provisioning to a considerable extent. If the demand for such work is highly sensitive to its price, tax evasion is probably a temptation on both parts of the transaction. Popular accounts witness the extended practice of double

pricing among self-employed craftsmen and repairers: the customer
may choose between (an official) price with a receipt and a(n unofficial)
price without a receipt.[23] If the work is done as part of the side-
employment of a person who usually works for an employer, tax
evasion is presumably implicit in the agreed-upon conditions, as it is
supposedly in cases of sheer bartering of work.

Thus many factors combined to curtail commodity demand, and
demand for labour. Statistical evidence of abated commodity demand is
given in Tables 2:2 to 2:9. A decline in the rate of growth of private final
consumption expenditure between 1973 and 1982 compared to the pre-
1973 period is shown for all seven countries included in Table 2:2. France
is the only country where private consumption expenditure grew by
more than 3 per cent a year. That there was a contraction of household
expenditure on personal transport equipment (and commodities
associated with the use of cars) is demonstrated in Table 2:4. In fact, this
type of expenditure proved very sensitive to the rise in oil prices, and
among the seven countries only Italy did not show a temporary decline
in the latter half of the 1970s. The contraction of residential construction
in the post-1973 period is reflected in Table 2:5. (As already noted, the
decline in residential construction had already started in the late 1960s.)
The contraction was most pronounced in Britain. The much weaker
inducements on firms to expand their production capacity is reflected in
Table 2:7, which shows the growth rates of fixed capital formation
expenditure on machinery and other equipment. While, as shown in
Table 2:6, the growth rates of gross fixed formation in the public sector
were depressed in all seven countries (and turned negative in all but
two), the changing growth opportunities of the public sector seem to
have had only a moderate effect on government final consumption
expenditure, although, as shown in Table 2:6, public consumption
expenditure did not grow as fast between 1973 and 1982 as between 1953
and 1973. Aggregate fixed capital formation expenditure declined in five
of the seven countries between 1973 and 1982 (Table 2:9).

The Role of Foreign Trade

The rapid economic growth of Western European countries was
accompanied by an even faster growth in their foreign trade: a growing
part of the demand for their goods and services was derived from
abroad and was hence accounted for as exports; an increasing share of
their demand for commodities was met by imports. The post-war period
witnessed, above all, a strong growth in the *intra*-Western European
trade, eased and stimulated as it was by economic integration policies:
the creation of the European Economic Community and the European
Free Trade Association.[24] The growth in exports of seven countries is

illustrated in Table 2:12. The growth rates, which are in the range of 5–12 per cent a year in the pre-1973 period and 2–6 per cent between 1973 and 1982, reflect such trade liberalization policies, but also reduced transport costs, and an increased awareness of, and ability to comprehend, sales potential abroad. Growing foreign trade was also a corollary of the emergence of international oligopolist markets. The national oligopolies which traditionally characterized some industries were supplanted by international oligopolies; the producers of the various countries became involved in a mutual penetration of their national markets which triggered waves of mergers and acquisitions. The growing organizational and technical scale of production required larger, and increasingly transnational, markets. As a result of these concentration processes, transactions which were formerly taking place within nations passed the boundaries of the integrating national markets as international trade.

Table 2.12 Exports of goods and services: annual rate of change (%)

	1953–73	1973–82
United Kingdom	4.7	2.5
Germany	10.0	4.6
France	9.0	5.0
Italy	12.3	5.9
Netherlands	9.1	2.1
Belgium	8.4	3.3
Sweden	7.3	2.1

Source: OECD, *National Accounts,* Vol. 1, *1953–1982* (Paris: OECD, 1984).

Tables 2:13 and 2:14 show the changes in the geographical distribution of Western European trade which accompanied its strong volume growth. While in the mid-1950s some 55 per cent of the agglomerated EEC-EFTA export value was derived from intra-Western European trade, exports to other Western European countries accounted for more than two-thirds of the total export value in 1970 and 1980. The share of exports to the United States increased between 1955 and 1970, as did the (much smaller) share of exports destined for Japan. Between 1970 and 1980 exports to both the US and Japan declined in relative terms. Developing countries, which had received about 25 per cent of the EEC-EFTA exports in 1955, but only 14 per cent in 1970, had increased their share to 17 per cent by 1980. As for imports (Table 2:14), intra-Western

European trade declined in relative terms between 1970 and 1980. The decline was mainly due to the inflated value of oil imports from the OPEC countries. Between 1970 and 1980 the percentage share of these countries increased from 15 to 20 per cent. Imports from the United States declined from 13 per cent in 1955 to 7 per cent in 1980. In the same period, imports from Japan gained absolute and relative weight.

Table 2.13   EEC-EFTA merchandise exports, by region of destination (% of total export value: f.o.b.)

	1955	1970	1980
EEC-EFTA	55.3	66.8	67.8
United States	6.7	8.0	5.5
Japan	0.4	1.2	1.0
Developing countries	25.7	13.6	17.4
OPEC	–	3.2	7.6
Non-OPEC	–	10.4	9.9
Socialist countries of Eastern Europe	3.2	4.2	4.4
Total export value ($m)	35,300	137,500	809,500

Source: UNCTAD, *Handbook of International Trade and Development Statistics 1983*

Table 2.14   EEC-EFTA merchandise imports, by region of origin (% of total import value: f.o.b.)

	1955	1970	1980
EEC-EFTA	49.8	64.2	62.0
United States	13.0	9.8	7.1
Japan	0.5	2.0	2.4
Developing countries	26.6	15.1	20.6
OPEC	–	6.0	13.1
Non-OPEC	–	9.1	7.5
Socialist countries of Eastern Europe	3.6	4.4	5.0
Total import value ($m)	39,200	143,100	885,300

Source: UNCTAD, *Handbook of International Trade and Development Statistics 1983*

With the exception of Germany, which could register a positive balance of trade in almost the entire thirty-year period, the value of merchandise imports of Western European countries tended to exceed their exports. The import surpluses were as a rule paid for by factor incomes from abroad or neutralized by capital inflows. It was only in the post-1973 period that balance of payments deficits forced governments to adopt policies which, in fact, forestalled capital accumulation processes. One reason for the trade deficits in the 1970s was the reliance of Western Europe upon imported fossil fuels; another reason was the growing imports of Japanese manufactured goods. The former factor lost some of its weight as oil consumption stagnated and some countries began to exploit their domestic oil and natural gas resources (and when the European producers raised their export prices).

Although most Western European countries reported deficits in their merchandise trade, and it thus did not add in an accounting sense to their gross domestic product, it can be argued that their increased involvement in, and dependence on, foreign trade was a main factor behind their economic growth. It helps explain the increased technical and organizational scale of production: by supplying larger markets, firms could attain economies of scale in both production and distribution. It implied increased international competition, compelling producers to rationalize their use of labour and other resources. It induced substantial physical capital formation: the build-up of production capacity to meet demand in other parts of the world. Of paramount importance was the ability of the Western European countries to increase their exports to the United States. While most countries entered the post-war period heavily dependent on imports from the United States, many lessened their trade deficit with this country in the 1950s and 1960s. The growing US demand for Western European exports was no doubt the major external cause of Western European economic growth. In the 1970s, when the value of the dollar depreciated in relation to the currencies of Western Europe, imports from the United States tended to grow faster than Western European exports. The US replacement of imports from Western Europe added to its economic stagnation in the post-1973 period. When most Western European countries ran into balance of payments problems because of deteriorated terms of trade with the oil-exporting countries, increased foreign trade worked as a structural constraint to the traditional economic growth policies of the countries. As already stressed, balance of payments considerations restricted the possibilities of governments expanding domestic demand.

An external growth factor in the 1970s was the demand for European capital goods in the industrializing countries of the Third World. In the 1950s and 1960s many Third World countries entered a process of social transformation which implied rapid industrial growth and modernization of their agriculture (not to mention the creation of a technologically advanced military apparatus). Economic restructuring processes were often promoted by policies emphasizing the creation of a manufacturing industry (expected to look for its customers at home or abroad). As the industrializing countries could not produce all the required capital equipment (and the kinds of manufactured goods demanded by their relatively small but rapidly growing middle class of managers, technicians and public bureaucrats), they relied on imports from the industrial countries. Their import of physical capital was to a large extent financed by borrowing in the industrial world (in fact, a recycling of OPEC current-account surpluses). When the Western European countries supplied the machinery and other production facilities, and to some extent also the financial means for importing these commodities, they alleviated their own economic problems. At the same time, they contributed to the development of manufacturing industries which tried to gain access to their domestic (and traditional overseas) markets by offering cheap manufactured products.[25] Such attempts at market infiltration followed from the fact that the only way for borrowing countries to service their debts was by earning foreign exchange from exports. The recessions and sharply rising unemployment in the 1970s prompted an upsurge of protectionism in many industrial countries.[26] But despite the marked increase in barriers against imports from the Third World in the 1970s, many developing countries were able to increase their share in the developed countries' imports of some commodities. Their market penetration reflected in many cases a diversification in their exports.

As shown in Table 2:15, the share of the developing countries in the total EEC/EFTA export value of machinery and transport equipment (a major and growing component of their expanding export) increased from 0.4 per cent in 1955 to 23.5 per cent in 1980. The intra-Western European trade, which captured more than 80 per cent of the total export value of machinery and transport equipment in the mid-1950s, accounted for only 55 per cent in 1980; Table 2:15 thus illustrates the restructuring of exports to Third World countries that took place in the post-war period as a result of their industrialization. As demonstrated in Table 2:16, the share of the developing countries in the total import value of textiles and clothing of the EEC-EFTA countries increased from 13.8 per cent in 1970 to 18.9 per cent in 1980. While Western Europe was a net importer of machinery and transport equipment in the mid-1950s, it was a net exporter in 1970 and 1980.[27] Between 1955 and 1980 Japan increased its share in the total EEC-EFTA import value of machinery and transport equipment from 0.4 to 6.0 per cent. The percentage share of machinery and transport equipment imports from the United States increased between the mid-1950s and 1970; between 1970 and 1980 the share declined.

Looking for factors contributing to economic growth in the foreign trade of these countries, one should also observe the effects of their

Table 2.15 EEC-EFTA exports of machinery and transport equipment, by region of destination (% of total export value: f.o.b.)

	1955	1970	1980
Developed countries	98.3	77.6	72.2
EEC-EFTA	81.8	55.8	55.4
Developing countries	0.4	17.6	23.5
of which OPEC	–	4.2	10.1
Socialist countries			
Eastern Europe	1.2	4.4	3.7
Asia	–	0.3	0.6
Total export value ($m)	4,000	46,300	252,000

Sources: UNCTAD, *Handbook of International Trade and Development Statistics 1976* and *1984*.

Table 2.16 EEC-EFTA imports of textiles and clothing, by region of origin (% of total import value: f.o.b.)

	1970	1980
Developed countries	82.5	76.2
EEC-EFTA	71.3	64.8
Developing countries	13.8	18.9
Socialist countries		
Eastern Europe	2.7	3.3
Asia	1.0	1.6
Total import value ($m)	11,100	57,100

Sources: UNCTAD, *Handbook of International Trade and Development Statistics 1976* and *1984*.

terms of trade with other parts of the world. In the pre-1973 period, it was possible for Western Europe to import petroleum, minerals and other primary commodities at falling real prices (see Table 2:22). A certain amount of export revenue could buy an increasing amount and value of such commodities. The more favourable terms of trade represented a saving in economic resources: labour and physical capital could be used for other purposes; the transfer of production to other parts of the world contributed to the recorded productivity growth of the private sector and some of its industries (such as agriculture). When the prices of oil and many other primary commodities went up in the 1970s, the import of these commodities became more expensive in terms of the work and physical capital that was embodied in the reciprocal exports. But as most countries paid for the more expensive imports by balance of payments deficits (or by drawing on their foreign currency reserves) the deteriorating terms of trade did not work as a negative factor of economic growth (if their effects on economic policy is not taken into account). As the rising prices of oil stimulated indigenous production of petroleum and natural gas in some countries (notably Britain and Norway) they rather had the effect of mobilizing work and capital. The deteriorated terms of trade thus affected GDP and employment in a positive way (although at the expense of higher energy prices ultimately paid by households).

Reactions of Manufacturing Industry and the Public Sector

The shift from high to low rates of economic growth, which almost all Western European countries experienced in the 1970s, has been related to contracting commodity demand, particularly demand for the purpose of physical capital formation. It has been maintained that the reduction of fixed capital formation expenditure of the private and public sector was the single most important factor behind the abated growth rates. In this section, physical capital formation will be considered with respect to manufacturing industry and the providers of the public sector, or, more precisely, the oligopolistic firms of the manufacturing industry and the public spending bodies of the state. It will be argued that many commodity providers suffered from a profit squeeze in the post-1973 period, which restricted not only the room for further private sector expansion, but the growth opportunities of the public sector as well. The stagnating commodity provision (and the presumably declining volume of paid work) which resulted from curtailed capital formation brought governments to a situation where it was no longer possible to enhance commodity demand and mitigate unemployment by means of increased public spending. Conventional economic policy measures could not be used by the governments to restore the growth of their economies.

Concentrating on manufacturing industry is justified by the fact that its development (in terms of output, productivity and employment) has a considerable impact on both the evolution of the private sector as a whole and the growth of the public sector (granted some time for adjustment). The influence that manufacturing has on the development of the private sector as a whole derives partly from the fact that it generally makes up a substantial (although in the 1970s, declining) portion of aggregate commodity provision, and partly from its domination of the industries of wholesale and retail trade, transport, and other intermediary activities. A change in the volume of manufacturing output gives rise to a change in the output value of the latter industries, and presumably also their employment—provided that the productivity of the industries does not change in the same direction and to the same extent. The reverse is not true (or not true to the same extent). As the performance of the manufacturing industry conditions the evolution of much of the private sector (in countries where the agricultural sector is small), it may be argued that it also determines the long-term growth opportunities of the public sector (which cannot thrive unless the commodity sector is expanded).[28]

In manufacturing large oligopolistic firms play an important role in the performance of the industry as a whole (in terms of output, productivity and employment), partly because of the great weight of these firms in the total value added and labour input of the industry, and partly because of the dominance that many large firms exert over smaller manufacturers which operate under competitive conditions as their subcontractors, or as producers of supplementary goods. The crucial role of large firms offers an opportunity to relate manufacturing development (and the development of industries which are dominated by the manufacturing industry) to the behaviour of large corporations in general. The growth of the manufacturing industry, and, in effect, a substantial part of the private sector, may be regarded as the logical outcome of growth goals, and practices to enhance organizational goals in such large firms. Economic stagnation, on the other hand, reflects an inability of large firms to realize their growth objectives for either one or a combination of reasons. Foundation for these assumptions is given by the theory of the growth of the firm, which maintains (as elaborated in Chapter 1) that corporate technostructures are motivated by a wish to promote the viability and growth of their own organizations; that they will exploit every opportunity to increase the gross profits of their firms by expanding sales in real terms while simultaneously keeping down operation costs. To the extent that they are successful in their efforts to expand sales, they contribute to the expansion of the private sector output value; to the extent that they succeed in economizing on the use of labour and other inputs, their behaviour is consistent with a rise in private sector productivity. The assumed goals (and group interests) of the corporate technostructures is the chief social motivating force behind the growth of the commodity sector; the ways in which the technostructures attempt to realize corporate growth objectives are the agent practices conducive to economic growth. In the same vein, it can be argued that stagnating commodity provision reflects an inability of corporate technostructures to realize their growth aspirations, i.e. if it implies contracting commodity demand and curtailed gross profits. (As will be developed later, this does not mean that stagnating commodity demand impairs the ability of the corporations to grow in a subsequent period of more favourable demand conditions.)

Applying the theory of the growth of the firm to the specific conditions of the pre- and post-1973 period, it is proper to emphasize the reactions of the firms to the rising compensation of their employees. It can be assumed that the larger and growth-oriented firms in particular tried to counteract the negative effects on their gross profits (and hence their potential for growth and survival) of any increase in the prices of their labour inputs through one, or a combination of, the following types of measure:

— rationalization of production processes (which seemed to secure economies in the use of both human and non-human inputs, such as energy and raw materials);
— changes in the product composition of their sales and production lines (which seemed to allow for a larger positive contribution to the aggregate gross profits of the firm);
— increases in the prices of their products (which could mitigate, at least temporarily, their deteriorating terms of trade with the providers of labour services).

These measures represent, in fact, processes which had a great impact on the Western European economies in both the pre- and post-1973 years, and therefore each sub-period will be considered with regard to the specific conditions facing the agents.

The attempted causal analysis also reflects the concept of public sector growth developed in Chapter 1; that is, it is in the interest of leading public service providers to expand their own institutions; the limits to actual public sector expansion are defined by the willingness and ability of the spending bodies of the state to grant the necessary financial means, and the limits to the growth of the sector are determined by the performance of the commodity sector.

It can be assumed, therefore, that the development of manufacturing industry, which is dominated by large oligopolistic firms, is crucial to an understanding of the development of the non-agricultural commodity sector,[29] and, in fact, the long-term growth opportunities of the intermediary industries and public sector as well. The strategic, and essentially growth-oriented, dispositions of the leaders of the large manufacturing corporations, in the thirty-year period under consideration, affected the growth perspectives of almost the entire economy. Variations in the output, productivity and employment of manufacturing industry resulted predominantly from the practices of the large oligopolistic firms in industry, their reactions to the growth of their sales potential, the prices of their material inputs and the compensation of their contractual labour force. These reactions, which are embodied in their investment behaviour, had a direct impact on manufacturing output, productivity and employment; they had indirect effects on the output, productivity and employment of the intermediary industries, as well as the growth opportunities of the public sector. At the risk of being repetitious, this part of the chapter will first sketch the situation of manufacturing industry and the public sector in the pre-1973 period, then turn to the conditions of the post-1973 period.

The pre-1973 period

The rapidly growing private and public consumption, and the substantial physical capital formation which characterized the 1950s, 1960s and (in most countries) early 1970s, implied considerable expansion of manufacturing output: there was a growing demand for homes and household durables (the most important of which was the privately owned car) as well as for machinery, producer transport equipment and physical structures to be used in the provision of commodities and public services. The growing production of manufactured items was both an effect of, and a condition for, successful efforts by firms to expand their sales. To some extent it reflected the sales promotion measures of the firms, and to some extent it resulted from the growth and technical modernization of other industries (such as construction and agriculture), or the growth of the politically determined demand for public services. The expanding manufacturing output induced growth in other private sector industries, notably intermediary industries, and building and contracting. The growth of these industries reflected their ancillary relationship to physical commodity production, but also changes in the scale and spatial organization of physical commodity production, and the concentration of manufacturing operations in larger technical units (or systems of technical units) of firms catering for larger markets. The increased scale of manufacturing operations required increased work for the distribution of products. The output of the private sector as a whole expanded and, to some extent, private sector employment as well.

The consequent high demand for labour in manufacturing and some other private sector industries helped unions in their attempts to raise wages. As a result of concerted action on the part of labour organizations, the hourly remuneration of the hired labour force rose substantially in nominal terms, both in manufacturing and other private industries which relied on contracted labour. As prices were not raised as much as hourly rates of pay, there was also an increase in the real wages of commodity sector employees.

The producers of the private sector reacted to the rising nominal wages in various ways. As a rule, they attempted to raise the efficiency of their labour force by means of mechanization and other forms of rationalization. Some firms also diversified their product lines to include commodities which allowed for larger profit margins, products (or product variants) which had been developed within the firms or elsewhere. In retailing and other service industries, firms introduced (and extended) self-service to compensate themselves for wage increases. Faced with the necessity of paying higher wages, many producers also raised the prices of their products (and added thereby to the moderate inflation). An important effect of the counteractive measures of producers was the growth in the real value added per man-hour, that is, the growth in the economic productivity of the private sector.

The mobilization, and generally more productive use, of labour in the private sector created the economic requirements for the substantial growth of the public sector. The public technostructures could realize their organizational goals and group interests to the extent that the funding bodies of the state considered the aspirations of the service producers compatible with political priorities. The expanding services of the public sector contributed, in turn, to the productive power and mobilization of the disposable labour force. Through its various activities, the sector added to the growth of the GDP and total employment.

Documentation of the crucial development of the manufacturing industry in the pre-1973 period is given in Tables 2:17 to 2:21 (which are based on data supplied by the US Department of Labor, Bureau of Labor Statistics). The expansion of the volume of manufacturing output in Britain, Germany, France, Italy, the Netherlands, Belgium and Sweden is demonstrated in Table 2:17, while Table 2:18 shows the rise of nominal hourly compensation of manufacturing employees in the seven countries. ('Compensation of employees' includes payments of wages and salaries as well as all supplements and social security contributions covered by the employer.) Excluding Britain, output grew by 5–8 per cent a year between 1953 and 1973; while hourly compensation rose by 9–11 per cent a year. Table 2:19 shows the rate of growth of manufacturing productivity (i.e. output per man-hour). Of the seven countries, Britain shows the slowest productivity growth. As the productivity of the industry increased substantially, unit labour costs (hourly compensation at nominal values divided into output per hour) increased less rapidly than hourly compensation (Table 2:20). As manufacturing output tended to rise more rapidly than output per hour, there was in some countries a rise in the total number of hours worked in manufacturing (Table 2:21). In Italy and France (where manufacturing output expanded rapidly) total hours increased by almost 1 per cent a year between 1953 and 1973. In Britain and Sweden total hours declined by 0.4 per cent a year, due to increased labour productivity and moderate output growth.

In the pre-1973 period, aggregate nominal compensation of manufacturing employees increased more rapidly than the manufacturing value added in current prices, according to available statistics. The 'gross profitability' of the industry as a whole thus tended to decrease. This is demonstrated for the six countries in Figure 2:1. (An exception

Table 2.17 Manufacturing output: annual rate of change (%)

	1953–73	1973–82
United Kingdom	3.3	−2.1
Germany	6.9	0.7
France	6.9	1.5
Italy	7.7	2.5
Netherlands	6.4	1.0
Belgium	6.6*	1.5
Sweden	5.0	0.0

* 1960–73

Source: US Department of Labor, Bureau of Labor Statistics.

Table 2.18 Hourly compensation in manufacturing: annual rate of change (%)

	1953–73	1973–82
United Kingdom	8.1	17.8
Germany	10.0	8.4
France	9.3	16.2
Italy	10.7	20.5
Netherlands	11.1	9.4
Belgium	11.0*	12.1
Sweden	9.0	12.6

* 1960–73

Source: US Department of Labor, Bureau of Labor Statistics.

among these countries is France.) But as total output expanded steadily, the aggregate amount of gross profits in the manufacturing industry increased. Figure 2:2 is an attempt to estimate the development of the mass of gross profits in real terms for Britain, Germany, France, Italy, Belgium and Sweden. The gross profits of the industry as a whole have been estimated by multiplying the total manufacturing value added in fixed prices by the reciprocal of the percentage share of total employee compensation in the industry value added.[30] As the value added of the industry is total sales value less purchased goods and services, the estimated gross profits may be regarded at least as a *proxy* of what is left in the industry for investment, the current growth

Table 2.19 Manufacturing output per man-hour:
annual rate of change (%)

	1953–73	1973–82
United Kingdom	3.7	1.9
Germany	6.4	3.3
France	5.9	4.2
Italy	6.7	4.0
Netherlands	6.4	4.3
Belgium	6.9*	6.1
Sweden	5.5	2.3

* 1960–73

Source: US Department of Labor, Bureau of Labor
Statistics.

Table 2.20 Unit labour costs in manufacturing:
annual rate of change (%)

	1953–73	1973–82
United Kingdom	4.3	15.5
Germany	3.3	5.0
France	3.2	11.5
Italy	3.8	15.9
Netherlands	4.4	4.9
Belgium	3.8*	5.6
Sweden	3.3	10.0

* 1960–73

Source: US Department of Labor, Bureau of Labor
Statistics.

potential of manufacturing firms in general. Among the six countries,
Germany, France and Italy show the most swiftly growing gross profits
for the manufacturing industry as a whole in the 1950s and 1960s.

Contributing to the considerable expansion potential of the industry
in the pre-1973 period was the actual decline in the real prices of energy
and many raw materials. The decline in real prices of material inputs
mitigated the effects on total production costs of rising employee
compensation. As shown in Table 2:22, the nominal prices of many
primary commodities entering world trade rose only slightly in the
twenty-year period 1950–70. The decline in the real price of imported
petroleum lowered transport costs and therefore worked as an impetus

Table 2.21 Total hours in manufacturing: annual rate of change (%)

	1953–73	1973–82
United Kingdom	−0.4	−3.9
Germany	0.5	−2.5
France	0.9	−2.6
Italy	0.9	−1.4
Netherlands	0.0	−3.1
Belgium	−0.3*	−4.4
Sweden	−0.4	−2.2

* 1960–73

Source: US Department of Labor, Bureau of Labor Statistics.

to large-scale production. It also furthered labour-saving mechanization through its effect on energy prices in general (including electricity).

Crucial to the growth of the manufacturing industry, and in fact the entire economy, was the 'recycling' of labour expenditure of firms: increases in real wages of manufacturing employees were used largely for expenditure on manufactures, in the form of either private consumption or public consumption. (As already noted, the growing provision of public services implied the use of large amounts of manufactured goods). By paying higher wages, firms fuelled the demand for manufactured goods. The high and growing demand for manufactures had a positive effect on manufacturing employment. It ensured that the saving of labour power through rationalization was counteracted by increases in manufacturing output. (As will be developed in Chapter 7, this was an important facet of the so-called Fordism which characterized Western European countries in the post-war period.)

The post-1973 period

The 1974–5 recession produced a break in the post-war trend of manufacturing growth in almost all Western European countries (exceptions being Norway and Ireland). Although the actual decline of industry output was temporary and most countries could report expanding manufacturing output in the late 1970s, growth performace was modest compared to the pre-1973 period. This is shown for seven countries in Table 2:17. The stagnating manufacturing production which resulted from the contraction of the physical capital formation expenditure of both the private and public sectors of production symptomized

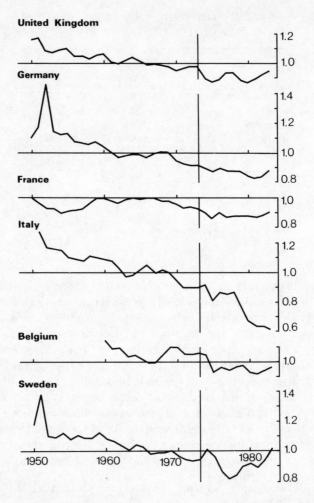

Figure 2.1 Indices of 'gross profitability' in manufacturing (value added divided by employee compensation)

important changes in the national economies, some of which have already been touched upon. The demand for some types of household durables did not grow as fast as in earlier decades, and therefore induced less capital formation; the associated development blocks approached completion (or were partly relocated to other parts of the world). Residential construction, which in the post-war period had become more and more dependent on manufactured inputs, declined. The demand for some kinds of consumer goods was increasingly supplied through imports from other parts of the world. Many firms, it has been argued, established plants in Third World countries which

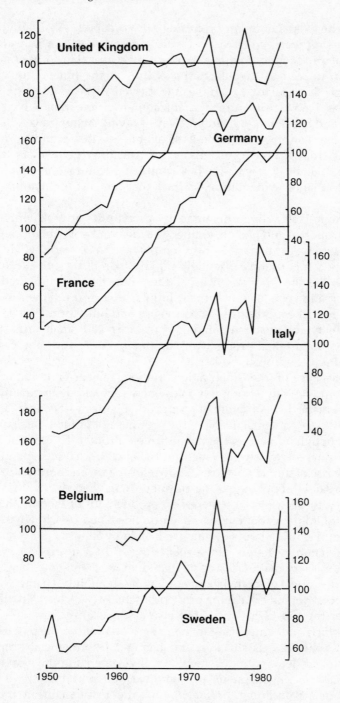

Figure 2.2 Indices of 'aggregate gross profits' in manufacturing

offered cheap labour and/or promising sales prospects.[31] Although such engagements were probably as a rule associated with a considerable export of production equipment, it seems reasonable to assume that they also depressed manufacturing output in the home countries as disposable financial funds for investments were diverted geographically. There was a move from pure mechanization to automation, which was a cheaper and less labour-consuming way of saving labour power. Because of rising unemployment, some segments of the population were excluded from a high consumption of consumer goods, particularly durables. All these factors, which implied a contraction of physical capital formation expenditure, curbed the demand for manufactured products.

Although stagnating manufacturing output and labour-saving rationalization combined to temper the demand for labour, nominal compensation of manufacturing employees rose rapidly. In fact, employee compensation rose more rapidly than in the pre-1973 period (Table 2:18). The industry was at the same time encumbered with sharply rising costs of non-human inputs, due to (as shown in Table 2:22) increased export prices of petroleum and other primary commodities. The typical reactions among both large and small firms to the prospects of curtailed profits were, on one hand, to raise the prices of the products, and on the other hand, to intensify their rationalization efforts. Because of intensified rationalization, the surrendering of firms which could not adjust properly to the new cost and demand situation, and systematic diversification of production by the most adaptable firms of the industry, manufacturing output per man-hour increased substantially, although it followed the downturn of output in 1975. Productivity growth (rates of which are given in Table 2:19) accounts for the less dramatic rise of unit labour costs (shown for the seven countries in Table 2:20). As sales did not induce the output growth which would have been necessary to outweigh the increased productivity of labour, the total number of hours worked in manufacturing declined. As shown in Table 2:21, manufacturing hours declined in Britain by almost 4 per cent a year and in Belgium by 4.4 per cent a year between 1973 and 1982.

As the sales of manufactures stagnated, at the same time there was a rise in the price of both labour and non-labour inputs; many firms experienced not only declining gross profitability (which was part of the reality of the pre-1973 period) but also a squeeze in disposable gross profits which, if not menacing to their survival, reduced the potential for further expansion. There was, on average, less financial scope for (and also less demand inducements to) investments in physical capital and long-term engagements of operative and non-operative labour. Indications of declining profitability in the manufacturing industry in Britain, Germany, France, Italy, Belgium and Sweden are given in Figure 2:1. The aggregated compensation of manufacturing employees,

Table 2.22   World export price indices of primary commodities and non-ferrous base metals

	1950	1960	1970	1975	1980
Food	43	40	47	100	159
Agricultural—non food	65	56	54	100	167
Minerals	15	17	19	100	271
Iron ore	36	62	59	100	121
Fuels	15	16	17	100	281
Crude petroleum	15	16	15	100	295
Minerals, excluding crude					
petroleum	–	–	38	100	134
Non-ferrous base metals	41	51	86	100	186

Source: UN, *Statistical Year Book 1979/80* (New York: United Nations, 1981)

as expressed in nominal values, increased more rapidly than the aggregate value added at current prices.

Indications of squeezed amounts of gross profits, and hence a reduced potential for expansion, are given in Figure 2:2. In contrast to the 1950s and 1960s, when manufacturing output grew rapidly, declining profitability carried highly volatile gross profits for the manufacturing industry as a whole. The rise in economic productivity of the industry was not sufficient to offset the negative effects on the aggregate gross profits of contracting output and rising hourly compensation. As demonstrated in Figure 2:2, aggregate gross profits declined in the years of the two recessions (1974–75 and 1981–82). In Britain the rising compensation and actual decline of manufacturing output brought a trend of contracting gross profits in the years 1973–83. Because of abated growth in the effective demand for manufactured goods, and perhaps also because of the geographical leakage of demand which resulted from changes in international trade patterns of manufactured goods, Western European manufacturers could recapture a much smaller share (compared to the 1950s and 1960s) of their labour costs through increased sales. They were therefore more inclined to raise prices. The growing propensity to retaliate by means of price increases was reflected in accelerating inflation, which motivated unions to press for substantial increases in nominal wages; and it meant that firms were, in general, more ready to accept the wage demands of their employees. Prices and wages spiralled.

The decrease in manufacturing output growth tempered the expansion of the intermediary industries; it also worked as a constraint to public sector growth, as it aggravated the difficulties of the state in covering the rising relative costs of expanded service provision which, if one accepts the reasoning of writers such as Baumol and Oates,[32] resulted from the restricted scope of rationalization in some public sector work, and the ability of public employees to raise their salaries. The predicament of many governments in the post-1973 period was that these rising costs were to be covered in a situation where disposable economic surplus was no longer expanding. Governments experienced an actual or approaching fiscal crisis of the state, which engaged them in extensive public borrowing. The current disbursements of governments tended to outgrow current receipts. Expanded public service provision and public sector investment intended to enhance private output and mitigate unemployment would have required increased taxation and/or a sheer increase in the supply of money. Both options were not feasible. Taxes caught a substantial, and in some countries rising, share of aggregate household incomes; increased liabilities to the state were not expected to promote the support of the electorate. Increased supply of money (or 'money printing') was not compatible with government objectives of combating inflation and reducing the current-account deficits which their countries had run into because of deteriorated terms of trade with oil-exporting countries. The public sector approached (for the time being) the limits to its further expansion and it could not be used to restore economic growth and full employment. The gap between current disbursements and current receipts implied increased public borrowing (a circumstance which contributed to a rise in rates of interest).

The fiscal crisis of the state precluded not only a further expansion of the public sector, but also affected (as will be developed in Chapter 7) the investment behaviour of (at least the largest) firms. Because of the high and rising interest rates of the late 1970s and 1980s, which were necessary for economic policy reasons and in order to attract lenders, it was more profitable for many firms to make financial investment than to engage in productive and employment-creating investment.[33] As interest rates were kept deliberately high by governments, it can be maintained that policy-makers were caught in a self-made trap from which they could not escape by themselves. No wonder the leaders of some countries lent their ears to advocates of a supply-oriented economic policy. An economy freed from excessive fiscal burdens and unnecessary public constraints was expected to induce a new round of innovations and growth-enhancing capital formation. Deregulation would make the entrepreneur emerge as the *Deus ex machina* of the play.

Notes

1. The post-1973 period comprised two major economic recessions. Following the 1973 jump in oil prices, growth rates fell sharply for two years but rose rapidly in 1976. In subsequent years, however, growth was in most countries

well below the rates of the 1960s. The second recession of 1980–2 was shallower than the first, but lasted longer, presumably since countries as a rule tightened monetary controls to bring down inflation. As a result, unemployment, which had stayed high after the first recession, attained even higher levels in the beginning of the 1980s. The World Bank, *World Development Report 1983* (New York: Oxford University Press, 1983).

2. J.I. Gershuny, 'The Informal Economy: Its Role in Post-Industrial Society', *Futures*, Vol. 11 (February 1979).

3. J. Gershuny, 'Post-Industrial Society: The Myth of the Service Economy', *Futures*, Vol. 9 (April 1977) and *After Industrial Society? The Emerging Self-Service Economy* (London and Basingtoke: Macmillan, 1978).

4. As in the writings of Fourastié, a distinction is made here between productivity in the economic and the physical sense of the word. *Economic productivity* refers to the value of output per unit of input (e.g. labour) which in intertemporal comparisons is deflated by means of some price index. *Physical productivity*, or *efficiency*, refers to the amount of output per unit of input. Cf. J. Fourastié, *La Productivité* (Paris: Presses Universitaires de France, 1971).

5. Both kinds of measure, which are interchangeable as well as technically and organizationally related to each other, are in fact *rationalizations* from the point of view of the firm; they both enhance profitability and gross profits.

6. According to calculations made by the US Department of Labor, real hourly compensation in manufacturing industry which was presumably the 'wage-leading' industry in the post-war period, rose between 1953 and 1973 by 300% in Germany, by 260% in Italy and the Netherlands, by about 150% in Sweden and France, and by 100% in Britain. In the period 1973–82 real hourly compensation rose by more than 40% in France, by about 33% in Britain and Germany, and by well above 20% in the Netherlands and Sweden (statistics supplied by US Department of Labor, Bureau of Labor Statistics).

7. Among the most influential students of productivity and technological change in the pre-1973 period was Salter, who focused on 'the new best-practice techniques', i.e. the techniques which at each date employ the most recent technical advances and which are economically appropriate to factor prices. In conformance to the views of Salter, it is here maintained that gross investment is the vehicle of new techniques and that such investment determines how rapidly new techniques are brought into general use and are effective in raising productivity. Cf. E.A.G. Salter, *Productivity and Technical Change* (Cambridge: Cambridge University Press, 1960) pp. 26, 65.

8. A. Maddison, *Economic Growth in the West* (New York: Twentieth Century Fund, 1964) p. 49. That the length of the pay-off period was the most widely used criterion for choosing among investment alternatives is vindicated in many studies.

9. As for manufacturing, which aside from agriculture, provides the most pronounced demonstration of constant technological adaptation, the resulting productivity growth is evidenced in the final part of this chapter. The increased economic productivity of the agricultural sector is highlighted in Chapter 3, which deals with changes in the industrial composition of the working population.

10. Gershuny, 'Post-Industrial Society' op. cit.
11. Although this facet of the so-called counter-urbanization process, or *turn-around trend*, became a topic for much research in the second half of the 1970s, it is highly plausible that geographic deconcentration of work and residence was a facet of economic change in Western Europe from almost the beginning of the 1950s. L. Ahnström, 'The Turn-Around Trend and the Economically Active Population of Seven Capital Regions in Western Europe', *Norsk Geografisk Tidskrift*, Vol. 40, No. 2 (1986).
12. Bringing locational shifts into the analysis means paralleling the thesis of Brinly Thomas concerning the effect of migration on economic growth, mainly through residential construction. See B. Thomas, *Migration and Urban Development: A Reappraisal of British and American Long Cycles* (London: Methuen, 1972).
13. Eurostat, *Employment and Unemployment 1984* (Luxembourg: Statistical Office of the European Communities, 1984).
14. The apparent non-existence of mass unemployment in Sweden was probably due to extensive vocational training schemes and public initiatives aimed at reducing unemployment. Those covered by such measures are generally not registered as unemployed.
15. The assumption is based on observation of weekly hours worked per employee. Weekly hours declined in all nine European Community countries between 1973 and 1981. At the same time, the total number of registered workers (including part-time workers) increased slightly. However, the increase was much slower than the decline in weekly hours (Eurostat, *Employment and Unemployment 1984*). For manufacturing industry, the actual reduction in the number of hours worked is demonstrated in the final part of this chapter.
16. T. Falk, *Changes in the Distribution of the Population – the 1960s in Focus* (Stockholm: EFI, 1976).
17. Cf. J. Gershuny, *Social Innovation and the Division of Labour* (Oxford: Oxford University Press, 1983); A. Toffler, *The Third Wave* (London: Pan Books, 1983); and *Beyond Employment*, ed. E. Mingione & N. Redclift (Oxford: Basil Blackwell, 1985).
18. R.E. Pahl, *Divisions of Labour* (Oxford: Basil Blackwell, 1984) p. 101.
19. As noted by Pahl, the sale of do-it-yourself equipment and materials appears in the national account statistics; 'what is not formally assessed in the national accounts is the unpaid labour of household members, except in so far as that is reflected in the increased capital value of the domestic property on which their labour is invested'. Pahl, op. cit., p. 104. The capital value of domestic property is recorded as construction and maintenance of residential buildings.
20. Ph. Mattera, *Off the Books: The Rise of the Underground Economy* (London and Sidney: Pluto Press, 1985) p. 1. The transactions were underground as being unregulated, untaxed and unmeasured, i.e. not entering the GDP. As for the amount of contractually remunerated but hidden work, various British and US estimates point in the direction of 10% of the GDP (ibid., p. 53). In Italy, where the existence of a large and growing *economia sommersa* has been a major factor of life since the early 1970s, economists have fixed a figure of about 30% of official national output. In 1979, the central Italian statistical

agency (ISTAT) revised the country's national accounts for the previous two decades, adjusting everything upward about 8% to reflect unmeasured economic activity. 'The process is known to have scandalized officials of the International Monetary Fund which had extended substantial loans to the Italian government and could not countenance such a cavalier manipulation of sacred statistics. But in Italy it is widely agreed that ISTAT had not done enough to bring the official figures in line with reality' (ibid., p. 85).

21. Some writers, such as Pahl, would say that *it was increasingly observed* in the 1970s that a large amount of paid work evades the watchful eyes of the state: the growth of clandestine work is rather a product of increased media and research coverage (op. cit., pp. 91–8). Another position is held by Mattera, who maintains that it reflects fundamental changes in the economy of the industrial world. He ascribes some of these changes to the 'crisis of the State and the labour union movement' and the ways many people earn their living today. Work has become irregular to the extent that the traditional categories of economic activity no longer seem adequate: 'With people piecing together incomes from a variety of regular and unofficial jobs, government benefits and other sources, it is much harder to describe anyone as simply "employed", "unemployed", or "not in the labour force" ' (op. cit., p. 2). It should be noted that Mattera bases his statements on observations of some of the most crisis-stricken industrial countries. His description scarcely holds for all countries covered by this study. For attempts at measuring the importance of the clandestine economy in the countries of Western Europe, see B.S. Frey & H. Weck-Hanneman, 'The Hidden Economy as an "Unobserved" Variable', *European Economic Review* Vol. 26 (1984).

22. The Swedish economist Nils Lundgren provides an imagined example: if a craftsman wants to receive 50 Sw. crowns for a piece of overtly contracted work, net of taxes and other compulsory payments, the customer has to carry out some paid and taxed work that his employer is willing to pay 1,400 crowns for. 'Ekonom om Svenska Familjen: Höjd Standard – Mindre Fritid', *Dagens Nyheter*, 10 March 1986. The possible effects of direct and indirect taxes are based on the assumption that the marginal income tax of the craftsman and the customer is 70%. If the marginal tax of both parties is only 50%, an income of 1,400 crowns for the customer will pay for 200 crowns of taxed craftsman work.

23. The double pricing may work as price discrimination, the charging of different prices to various kinds of customers. It allows service providers to exploit the potential of their markets more fully: if they report all their transactions they reach only customers who are able and willing to pay the openly stated prices of the services; if they do not report all their transactions they are also able to sell their services to customers with a lesser capability and willingness to pay. If unreported work is taken in slack periods, double pricing allows for larger sales revenues for the service provider.

Taxes further contributed to the changing terms of trade for many customers in relation to their service providers: In the early 1950s, a Swedish government employee could buy 1–2 hours of contracted plumbing work by spending the net hourly income of one hour of his own work; 25 years later, his net income per hour was sufficient to contract a plumber for only ten minutes. L. Anell, *Recession, the Western Economies and the Changing World Order* (London: Frances Pinter; New York: St Martin's Press, 1981), p. 113.

24. For a general account of these trade liberalization policies, see, for instance, D. Swann, *The Economics of the Common Market* (Harmondsworth: Penguin, 1984).

25. This has been emphasized by Anell, op. cit., among others.

26. *World Development Report 1983*, p. 13. Among many measures to protect ailing industries, governments erected a formidable set of controls against textile exports of developing countries. The Multifibre Arrangement, which covered as much as 15% of developing-country manufactured exports, was, according to the World Bank, the most extreme example of trade restriction since governments started to undo the protectionism of the 1930s (*World Development Report 1983*, p. 3).

27. UNCTAD, *Handbook of International Trade and Development, Supplement 1976* and *1984*.

28. The sudden contraction of manufacturing output in the 1970s seems to have had an immediate depressive effect on the intermediary industries in Germany, France, Italy and Belgium (and a contractive effect with some delay in Sweden, where the government was most inclined to offset the effect of the international recession by means of counter-cyclical policy measures). (For statistical evidence, see OECD, *National Accounts*, Vol. 2, *1970–1982*, Paris: OECD, 1984)

29. The reason for omitting agriculture in this consideration of major relationships of domination and subordination is that its development in the postwar period seemed to be conditioned mainly by agricultural policy. Although the capability of any government to subsidize agriculture is restricted by the macroeconomic performance of the country, agricultural development is treated here as one of several factors determining the growth of manufacturing and intermediary industries (e.g. through the intensity of its technical modernization and demand for manufactured equipment and inputs).

30. The aggregate gross profits of an industry equals the total industry value added (or output) less total labour costs. As output is value added per hour multiplied by total hours, while total labour costs are hourly compensation multiplied by total hours, aggregate gross profits may be expressed as:

Total hours x value added/total hours − hourly compensation x total hours,

or

Value added/total hours − hourly compensation x total hours,

or

Average (economic) labour productivity − hourly compensation x total hours.

Aggregate gross profits, as estimated above, include government subsidies and are to some extent subject to taxation. Hence they serve only as a crude measure of the capacity of firms to engage in physical capital formation. It needs emphasizing that 'human capital formation' of firms represents salaries and other current expenditure for access to required knowledge and adaptive capacity. In fact, such expenditure reduces the amount of gross profit. Firms may very well engage in human capital formation although their gross profits decline (and the decline may be due to human capital formation expenditure).

For the notion of human (or cultural) capital (which had already appeared in the nineteenth-century writings of Friedrich Lizt), see for instance, A.W. Gouldner, *The Future of Intellectuals and the Rise of the New Class* (London & Basingstoke: Macmillan, 1979), p. 21 ff.

31. See, for instance, *The New Division of Labour, Technology and Underdevelopment: Consequences for the Third World*, ed. D. Ernst (Frankfurt: Campus, 1980).

32. W.J. Baumol, 'The Macro-economics of Unbalanced Growth', *American Economic Review*, Vol. 37 (June 1967) and W.J. Baumol & W.H. Oates, *The Theory of Environmental Policy* (Cambridge: Cambridge University Press, 1975), Ch. 17.

33. Does the alleged propensity of some large commodity providers to turn to pure financial investment in the late 1970s and early 1980s invalidate the theory of growth of the firm? Apparently, but not necessarily. On one hand, it seems that the leaders of the firms were more occupied with the pecuniary aspects of their dispositions than the organizational growth of corporations. On the other hand, by lending some part of their cash to the state at interest rates which exceeded the expected rates of inflation, firms could postpone the actual use of their growth potential, i.e. use it in a future situation when demand conditions were more favourable, or when some product development programmes were more ready for implementation. That corporate technostructures are growth-oriented does not mean that they do not adjust to current conditions in ways which are compatible with pure profitability considerations.

3 Industries, 1950–80

Industry Grouping

In studies of the industrial composition of the working population, a distinction is customarily made between primary, secondary and tertiary industries.[1] The primary industries, which form the agricultural sector, are agriculture, forestry and fishing; the secondary industries, or the industrial sector, are mining, manufacturing, construction and energy and water supply. The tertiary industries, or the service sector, is the residual: what is left of the economically active population when those engaged in the primary and secondary industries have been subtracted. In the following account of the growth and decline of various industries in thirteen Western European countries between 1950 and 1980, the traditional distinction between the agricultural and industrial sector will be observed. The heterogeneous service sector is broken down into four sub-categories: intermediary industries, public services, public-private services and private services. In total six industrial groups are thus distinguished:

1. *The agricultural sector*, i.e. agriculture, forestry and fishing; this group mainly represents agricultural commodity production.

2. *The industrial sector*, i.e. mining and quarrying, manufacturing and repairing, construction and energy, and water supply; these industries comprise industrial commodity production and repairing (of, for instance, motor vehicles and consumer durables).

3. *Intermediary industries*, i.e. retail and wholesale trade, transport, storage and communication, banking, insurance and real estate, and business services; these industries mainly represent physical commodity distribution and activities which are ancillary to the production and distribution of commodities (money-handling and finance, risk-sharing and counselling).

4. *Public services*, i.e. public administration and defence, education and research, and medical and welfare services. The services are

provided for mainly by the state; if supplied by the private sector, they are as a rule exempted from the forces of the market; a substantial part of the costs of their provision is covered by means of taxation and social security contributions.

5. *Public–private services*, i.e. business, professional and labour associations, religious organizations, and recreational and cultural services. These industries are mainly non-marketed and surplus-financed, but they are not necessarily provided by the state. This group even includes some commodity provision (e.g. marketed products of self-employed artists).

6. *Private services*, i.e. restaurants and hotels, domestic services, and sanitary and other personal and household services. This group mainly comprises personal services supplied by firms and individual members of the working population (e.g. domestic servants); sanitation provided by the public sector is also included.

The analysis will be made mainly in terms of these six groups. The statistical data are derived from the population censuses of the countries in (or around) 1950, 1960, 1970 and 1980. Although efforts have been made to regroup detailed (3- or 4-digit level) data available in published or unpublished census tables, one cannot pretend that this chapter presents more than a rough description of the development of the industrial groups and the particular industries. This account will mainly serve as the point of departure for (and a corrective to) the search for processes and agent motives which have reshaped the working population in the thirty-year period. Figures concerning industries in particular countries serve the purpose of illustrating trends and tendencies; they are not intended for cross-national comparisons.

Growth and Decline of Industries

The number of economically active persons in agriculture, forestry and fishing declined, as demonstrated in Figure 3:1, throughout the whole thirty-year period; in France, the Netherlands, Belgium and Denmark the decline was apparently less rapid in the 1970s than in the 1950s and 1960s. In these three decades, employment in the agricultural sector was reduced by more than two-thirds in Germany, Italy, Austria, Norway and Finland; in Germany it contracted from 5.2 million to 1.4 million, in Italy from 8.2 million to 2.2 million, in Austria from 1.1 million to less than 300,000. The decline was less pronounced in Switzerland and Britain, two countries which had highly divergent agricultural policies (in the former country a far-reaching protection of domestic producers, in the latter country a traditional reliance on imports).

The industrial sector, which could report at least a modest employment increase in most countries prior to 1970 (the exceptions being

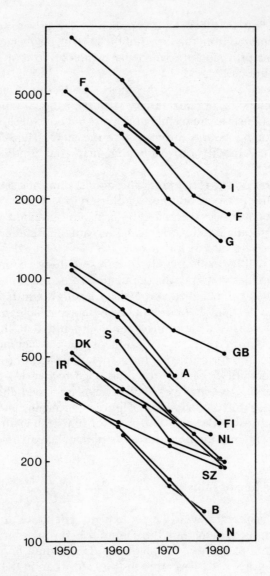

Key to Figures 3.1 to 3.11

Key to Figures 3.1 to 3.11

A	Austria	B	Belgium
DK	Denmark	F	France
FI	Finland	G	Germany (Federal Republic)
GB	Great Britain	I	Italy
IR	Ireland	N	Norway
NL	Netherlands	S	Sweden
SZ	Switzerland		

Figure 3.1   The agricultural sector (000s persons)

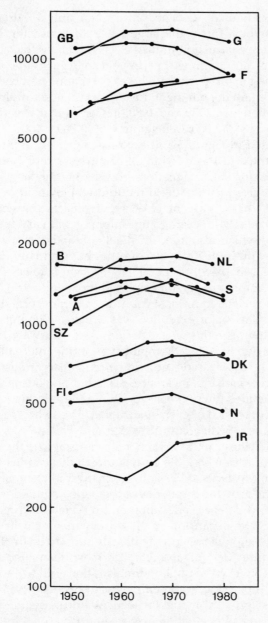

Figure 3.2 The industrial sector (000s persons)

Britain, Belgium, Austria, Switzerland and Sweden), declined in almost all countries between 1970 and 1980. As shown in Figure 3:2, the only countries where the number of persons engaged in the sector grew in the 1970s were France and Ireland. The turn from moderate growth to a more or less pronounced decline reflects not only a curtailment of manufacturing, which forms the largest part of the sector, but also a contraction of the construction industry. The latter contracted between 1970 and 1980 in all countries but Ireland and Austria. Mining and quarrying declined in all countries where coal mining had been of some importance. In Britain the mining industry was reduced by almost half a million persons between 1950 and 1980; in Germany it was reduced by 660,000; in France by 360,000; in Belgium by 160,000.

As demonstrated in Figure 3:3, the post-war growth of intermediary industries continued in the 1970s in all countries except Germany and Norway. In the former, stagnation of the intermediary industries (considered as a group) was due to reduced employment in retail and wholesale trade; in the case of Norway, it reflects the employment decline in the country's ocean-going shipping industry.[2] Retail and wholesale trade, which expanded in the 1950s and 1960s, was also a growing industry in the 1970s in all countries but Germany, most likely because of increased part-time employment (which always affects to some extent the number of persons reported for an industry). Sustained growth was also registered in most countries for transport, storage and communication. The major exception was Britain, where employment declined throughout the thirty-year period. As in Norway, the decline was presumably due to reduced employment in the international shipping industry. The most rapidly growing intermediary industries in the period studied were banking, insurance, real estate and business services. In these three decades the number working in these industries in most countries doubled, trebled or even quadrupled. The swiftest growth was recorded for France, Switzerland, Sweden and Finland. As shown in Figures 3:4 and 3:5, the growth was generally more rapid in the 1960s than in the 1970s. Countries where the growth rate of these industries seems to have abated in the 1970s are Britain, Germany and Denmark.

Also among the growing industries of the period studied were public administration and defence, education and research, and medical and welfare services. The expansion of these industries (which, if they do not form part of the public sector, are heavily subsidized by the state) is illustrated in Figures 3:6, 3:7 and 3:8. The most diversified pattern of development is conveyed in public administration and defence. For this industry Britain reports declining employment between 1951 and 1966, and only modest growth in the subsequent fifteen years. The feeble performance reflects the reduction in the country's armed forces. While the rapid growth of education and research seems to have been curbed in some countries in the 1970s, no such tendencies are noticeable for medical and welfare services. In the three decades the number of persons working in medical and welfare industries grew, according to the population censuses, by 300 per cent in France, the Netherlands and Finland. In Sweden the number increased fivefold.

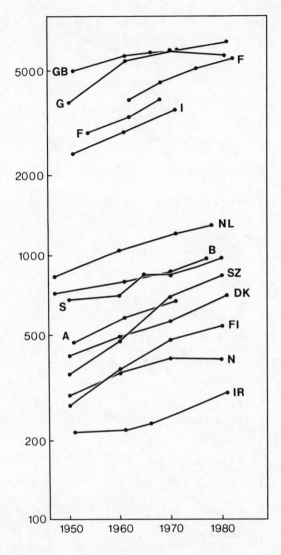

Figure 3.3 Intermediary industries (000s persons)

Business, professional and labour associations also formed a growing industry. Countries where the industry expanded rapidly in the thirty-year period were Germany and Sweden (an increase by 300 and 200 per cent respectively). Religious organizations grew in some countries while contracting in others. Recreational and cultural services show a decline in many countries in the 1950s, but growth in the 1960s and 1970s (Figure 3:9). In Switzerland, Sweden and Norway, employment in recreational and cultural services increased by about 100 per cent in the

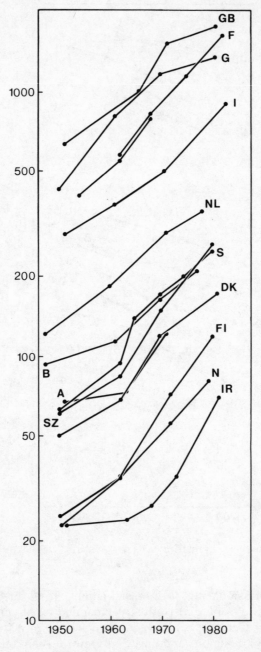

Figure 3.4 Banking, insurance and real estate; business services (000s persons)

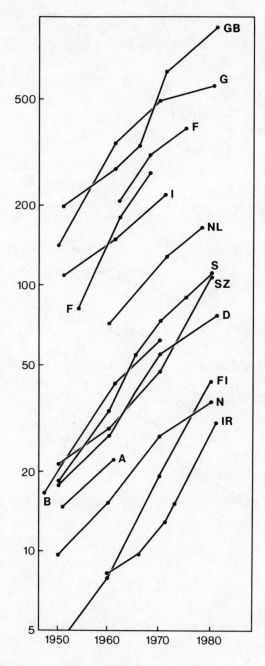

Figure 3.5 Business services (000s persons)

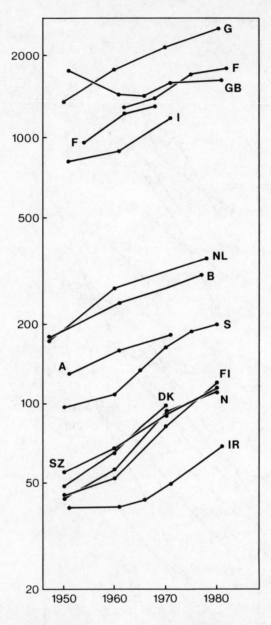

Figure 3.6   Public administration and defence (000s persons)

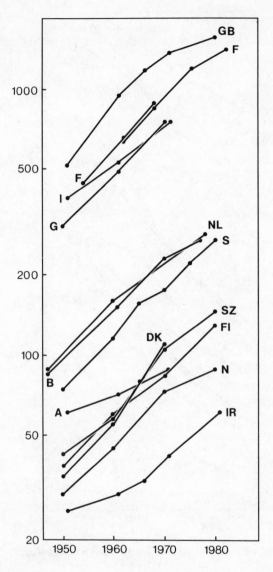

Figure 3.7 Education and research (000s persons)

three decades; in Finland it grew by almost 400 per cent. The pattern of change in restaurants and hotels is far from clear, as shown in Figure 3:10. Growth periods are followed by periods of decline. Domestic services (Figure 3:11) show rapid, and in most countries, accelerating decline. The number of domestic servants was, in some of the countries, reduced by more than 90 per cent (Germany, the Netherlands, Sweden and Norway). Sanitary and other personal and household services

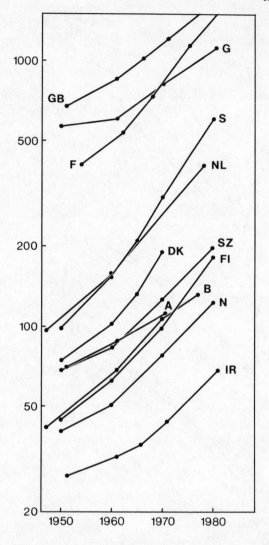

Figure 3.8   Health services and welfare institutions (000s persons)

(which include sanitary services provided by the public sector) engaged more persons in the end of the thirty-year period than in the beginning. In Sweden and Finland the growth of the industry was in the range of 150–300 per cent.

Causes of Growth and Decline of Industries

In the following attempt at explaining the growth or decline of the industries, activities which represent commodity provision (i.e. the

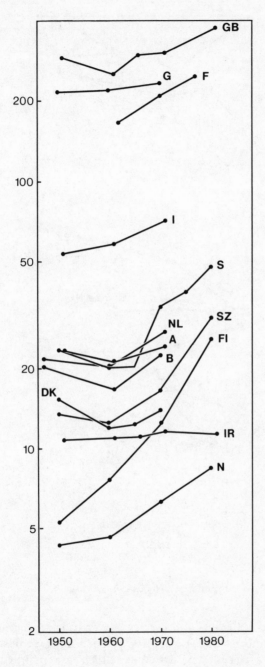

Figure 3.9 Recreational and cultural services (000s persons)

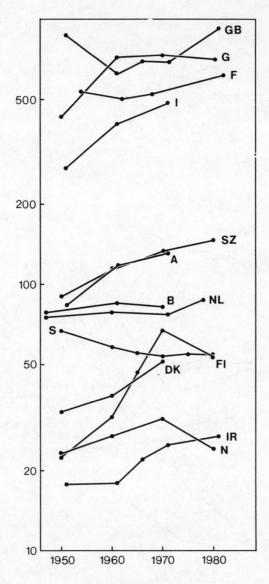

Figure 3.10   Restaurants and hotels (000s persons)

supply of marketed goods and services) have called for a more 'formal' approach than industries representing public service provision or other non-marketed services (i.e. activities which are mainly or entirely financed by means of an appropriation of some economic surplus). As for industries representing commodity provision, which are mainly agricultural, industrial or intermediary industries, attempts are made at assessing employment effects on the industry (or industrial group) of,

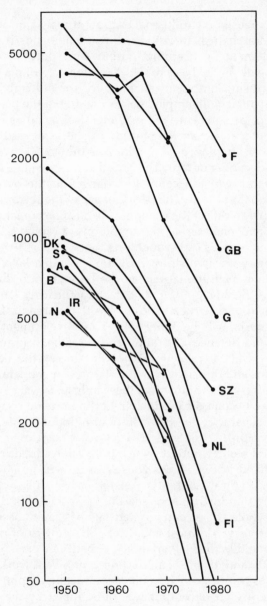

Figure 3.11   Domestic services (000s persons)

on one hand changes in the industrial output (or real value added), and on the other hand changes in output (or real value added) per person employed. Statements concerning output and output per person employed are made on the basis of OECD national accounts and labour force statistics. Rising output of an industry (or industrial group) is considered compatible with employment growth, but the positive effect on the number of persons engaged may be offset by an accompanying change in output per person employed. In the same vein, a rise in output per person employed may reinforce the contractive effect on employment of declining output. The causal analysis will be pursued by a search for factors which account for changes in the output and/or output per person employed. The performance of the sector or industry is assumed mainly to reflect the economic dispositions of large business firms, or, in more general terms, the conditions of capital accumulation in an economy dominated by corporations.

When dealing with industries providing non-marketed services, political and other institutional factors are brought into the analysis. More precisely, the ability of public technostructures and political decision-makers to pursue their specific objectives, organizational goals and group interests will be hinted at. The development of public administration and defence, education and research, and medical and welfare services will be related to the capacity of the economy to generate a surplus and the capacity of the state to appropriate it. The key permissive factor behind the growth of these industries will be considered to be the increased economic productivity of the private sector (i.e. the growth of the real value added per man-hour in industries representing commodity provision).

The agricultural sector's output, which is its value added contribution to the GDP at fixed prices, shows consistent growth in almost all the countries studied. (An exception is Sweden, where the decline of the substantial forestry industry depressed the value added of the primary industries as a whole.) The compounded rate of growth of output was about 2 per cent a year in most countries. The growth of output was extraordinarily rapid in the Netherlands (i.e. between 4 and 5 per cent a year in the 1950s and 1960s). The declining numbers working in the agricultural sector was thus not a result of contracting output, but due to the fact that the growth of output was outstripped by the growth of output per person employed. The rate of increase of output per person employed was, in the 1950s and 1960s, sufficient to produce a decline in agricultural employment by 4–5 per cent a year. In the 1970s output per person employed increased less rapidly, and the employment decline of the sector was therefore not as fast as in the earlier decades. Although a lengthening of the average working day may have contributed in some countries to the recorded loss of numbers employed, it can be assumed that it mainly reflects rising productivity.

In agriculture, which is in all countries the most important of the primary industries, the increased economic productivity resulted from a combination of three factors:

1.   Growing efficiency of farm operations: the physical quantities of output per man-hour, hectare of arable land, or other units of productive resources, increased as a result of changes in the methods and organization of agricultural work (the use of more, and increasingly efficient, machinery, the input of larger amounts of commercial fertilizers and enriched fodder, the application of pesticides and herbicides, the adoption by farmers of more rewarding plants and animal breeds, a less time-consuming layout of operative work, etc.).

2.   Transfers of certain kinds of work to other industries where they could be carried out more efficiently and/or more profitably: maintenance and repair of appliances, machines and farm buildings were transferred to the industrial sector; distributive functions related to the provision of inputs and sale of outputs were taken over by the wholesale trade or transport industry.

3.   Shifts in the composition of agricultural output: labour and other resources were used for the production of commodities, which allowed for a high value added per man-hour when provided for on a large scale and by means of substantial amounts of physical capital; the changing product composition of the real value added of the agricultural industry implied, for instance, that the labour-intensive production of beef and milk gave way to the production of wheat, pork and poultry, commodities which invited farmers commanding the required capital to adopt 'industrial' and highly labour-saving modes of production.

The most important of these factors was probably the increased efficiency of agricultural work, the gains in the physical productivity of the industry which resulted from extended and more intensified mechanization, increased reliance on science and biotechnology in agricultural production and concentration of production on the most 'productive' farms: units which were large enough to offer economies of scale, which were specially endowed by nature, or which could benefit from economies of localization. Mechanization implied increased reliance on petroleum products and electricity. The substitution of these carriers of energy for traditional animal traction power contributed to the functional dismantling of traditional farm work, and certainly also to the rise in the industry's economic productivity, as it was no longer necessary to use labour and other productive resources in keeping horses.

Increased productivity was also secured in other parts of the agricultural sector. In forestry productivity increased through mechanization, more efficient transport equipment and improved infrastructure; in fishing it increased through the use of more appropriate capital equipment (vessels, gears, installations for on-board storage and preparation of the catches).

In manufacturing, which was the backbone of the expanding economy in the 1950s and 1960s, the growth rate of output per person employed increased in some countries by more than 5 per cent a year; but as the real value added at fixed prices grew even more rapidly, the number of persons employed increased. Notable output expansion, which caused considerable employment growth, is recorded for Germany and Italy in the 1950s, when manufacturers in these countries captured substantial market shares abroad for automobiles, machinery and household appliances. In the 1970s, the real value added of manufacturing industry showed a more modest increase. As the growth of output per person employed was, as a rule, more swift than output growth (and in some countries more rapid than in the previous decades), manufacturing employment contracted. As the average number of hours worked by those in employment was shortened in the period, it can be inferred that the economic productivity of the industry rose substantially.[3] The productivity growth reflected:

1. The systematic efforts of the firms to increase the efficiency of physical operations by means of mechanization, automation and other kinds of rationalization of operations.
2. Changes in the composition of the manufacturing output, i.e. an increasing relative weight of products allowing for a high real value per paid hour of work, e.g. machinery and complex work appliances, pharmaceutical products and surgical facilities, sophisticated military equipment and weapons systems, and, not the least, consumer durables.
3. The disappearance of firms which could not survive in an environment characterized by increased competition and rising labour costs.

The repair industry, which here is included in the industrial sector, expanded in terms of its real value added contribution to the GDP, mainly as a direct effect of the growth of the numbers of cars in each country. Although repair-work was rationalized, the efficiency gains were probably not sufficient to offset the growth in the volume of repair activities; the number engaged in repairing increased, presumably also in the 1970s when manufacturing employment contracted.

Construction could report growing output and employment in the 1950s and, in most countries, also in the 1960s. The output growth of the industry was more rapid than the growth in output per person employed. In the 1970s, the reverse was generally the case, so employment declined. In mining and quarrying, declining output was registered for Britain in the 1950s and 1960s and for Germany, France and Belgium in the 1960s and 1970s. In the 1970s, the output of the industry grew by 10 per cent a year in Britain and by more than 30 per cent a year in Norway. The output decline (registered for other countries and prior to 1970) reflects the contraction of the coal-mining industry (Britain in the 1950s and 1960s, Germany, France and Belgium in the 1960s and 1970s); the output growth in Britain, Norway and the Netherlands witnesses the exploitation of the Western European resources of petroleum and natural gas. Whether output declined or expanded, the growth of the real value added per person employed was in general substantial; thus employment contracted. In coal mining, which represented a substantial share of the total value added and employment of the industry in Britain, Germany, France and Belgium, the economic productivity growth resulted partly from the selectivity of the contraction process: the pits which escaped closure, or which were the latest to be closed, were generally the best endowed by natural conditions and/or the most suitable for modernization. In petroleum and gas extraction, which represented a new element of the industry in Britain and Norway in the 1970s (and in the Netherlands in the 1960s), the rapidly growing output per person employed reflects the apparent mismatch between numbers employed and actual production in the early phases of the industry: labour is used to put installations into use, not only for current production operations.

The growing commodity production in this period—and the associated changes in the scale and localization of production facilities—entailed expanding distributive work. The expansion of such work was recorded as output growth in wholesale and retail trade as well as in transport, storage and communication. As the increase in the real value added of these industries was not accompanied by an equally rapid growth of output per person employed, both industries reported increased employment, Substantial productivity gains were made in both industries. In retail trade, some firms had already introduced self-service in order to lower labour costs in the early 1950s. This raised the value added per hour of paid work, as part of the distributive work was taken over by the customers.[4] As for commodity transport, productivity growth resulted from the use of more efficient and adaptable means of transport, short-cuts in carrying operations and various measures to reduce the handling of goods in transit (e.g. 'containerization').

The scanty output and employment data available for banking, insurance, real estate and business services suggest that the real value growth of these intermediary industries was in general much stronger than the growth of the output per person employed. This is compatible with the strong employment growth of the industries. But it cannot be ruled out that employment growth also resulted from temporarily declining value added per person employed (such as for Sweden in the 1960s and Denmark in the 1970s). The reduction of average working time exceeded the gains in efficiency arrived at through rationalization.

What characterized commodity provision was thus a rise in real value added (or output) per person employed. To some extent this counteracted the effect on employment of rising output. In the agricultural sector it even caused a declining employment. The increased output per person employed was generally a token of increased economic productivity, a rise in the real value added per hour of work. The productivity gains resulted from rationalization of production processes, the disappearance of the least efficient and adaptive firms, changes in the product structure of the output, and also to some extent a transfer of some work to the customers, or (as in the case of agriculture) to other industries where it could be carried out more efficiently. Transfers of work to the customers characterized not only retail trade, but also was a typical reaction to rising labour costs in the hotel and restaurant industry.

In agriculture, where a large and growing share of all workers were their own employers (or assisting family members), the productivity increase essentially reflected a motivation of farmers to attain a standard of living (for themselves and their families) which was on a par with that of other social groups, probably not only industrial workers but also the urban middle classes. In the pursuit of this end they also relied on political means, exploiting their central position in the traditional left–right spectrum of voters. As potential supporters of the ruling or aspiring Social Democratic or Christian liberal parties, they could count on agricultural policies which reserved the national market for themselves as domestic producers, or, with the development of the agricultural policy of the EEC, the Western European market for the producers of the Community. Considering the highly competitive structure of the industry, it can be maintained that the productivity growth of agriculture followed from the structural positions of the individual producers. They were compelled to rationalize their production, simply because other farmers did so, even if they did not expect any improvment in their profitability as a result of their rationalization efforts. By means of labour-saving (and other) practices, many agricultural producers could at best safeguard their relative position as income earners and consumers *vis-à-vis* other groups. As the rationalization of farm work mainly affected the number of agricultural employees, it made the family farm an even more pronounced feature of Western European agriculture.

In other areas of commodity provision, where the productive and distributive activities were dominated by large firms, increased productivity reflected the quest for corporate consolidation and growth. Technical modernization of operations, substitution of low-wage labour for high-wage labour, self-servicing by customers, and product diversification towards more sophisticated goods or services which could command a higher price per unit of labour costs, were all standard means used by firms in order to secure a corporate levy which permitted some growth (or, at least, survival). Practices introduced by the large and growth-oriented firms were adopted by the members of the competitive sub-sector, producers who were engaged in ancillary or complementary activities, or who catered for some fringe of the markets of the big firms. As in the large firms, productivity-enhancing practices were essentially reactions to rising nominal employee compensation, attempts at evading the negative effects on profits of growing labour compensation.

The productivity gains in the commodity sector allowed political decision-makers to appropriate a growing share of household incomes (and the sales turnover of firms) for the purpose of public service provision, notably higher education and welfare services. The expanded activities of the public sector promoted further productivity growth in the private sector; they implied, for instance, provision of physical infrastructure and other facilities which could not be financed by individual firms, educational and vocational programmes which raised the technical and professional competence of the labour force, research activities which added to the available knowledge capital of the countries, and not least, a redistribution of private consumption opportunities of the inhabitants in such ways that the sales potential of commodity producers was enhanced and firms could operate closer to their full production capacity. As long as the expanded public services enhanced the economic productivity of the private sector, they thus created some of the necessary conditions for further employment growth of the public sector. The virtuous circle seemed to work for a large part of the period studied, and it was generally not until the late 1970s that governments experienced difficulties in providing the financial means for the accomplishment of the objectives of the state.

The employment growth in the industries of public administration and defence, education and research and medical and welfare services was compatible with the values, goals and priorities of the political parties which were brought to ascendancy in the post-war period. But a major force behind the growth of these industries was also, as already emphasized, the producers' interests in the growth of their services. The growth derived some of its momentum from the attempts of the public technostructures to expand their own institutions and spheres of activity. The leaders of the various branches of the public sector pointed out social needs which could not be satisfied unless their own branch of the public sector were allowed to expand; conditions were highlighted which called for the type of services that they were the most suitable to provide. By promoting the growth of their own institutions, it was possible for the leaders of the public technostructure to enhance their own positions and the careers of their subordinates; at the same time they contributed to the creation of a more responsible and a more equitable society.

The moderate growth of public administration and defence was conditioned by, on one hand, a curtailment of armed forces (which resulted from both modernization of warfare and collapsing imperial aspirations), and on the other hand, the expansion of the regulatory functions of the state (e.g. the development of regional and local planning activities which, in many cases, required public employment of professionals for functions which were formerly carried out by administrative laymen as part of some civic duties). The more conspicuous growth of education and research reflects the rapid development of the system of higher and professional education which added to the employment of the public sector, particularly in the 1960s. Between 1960 and 1970 the number of university students more than doubled in Britain; in the Netherlands and Belgium it increased by about 150 per cent; in France by 200 per cent and in Sweden by 250 per cent.[5] As for medical and welfare services, rapid employment growth showed the enhanced public responsibility for some functions which had traditionally been carried out by the households as unregistered and unpaid work (in some cases supplemented by the work of domestic servants). The growth of the industry provided access to the labour market for women in particular; it also implied the kind of institutional transfers of socially necessary work that was discussed in connection with economic growth in Chapter 2.

Other industries which derived their employment growth from the widened responsibilities of the state were recreational and cultural services, as well as sanitary and other personal and household services. In the former industry, one branch of employment growth was radio and television broadcasting; in the latter industry, employment opportunities were created through increased responsibility for public sanitation.

The growth of professional, trade and labour associations reflects the increased participation of organized interest groups in the political decision-making and administration of the state, the tendency of governments to involve major organizations in the settlement of political issues.

The development of restaurants and hotels was probably affected by various labour-saving devices, such as the introduction of self-service and the use of industrially processed inputs in restaurant cooking. The growing number engaged in the industry, as reported for some countries and intercensal periods, can be related to such factors as the growth of mass tourism, or the observed tendency of people to start a small service business of their own when general employment prospects are bleak. The restaurant and hotel trade offered opportunities for small business and self-employment although increasingly this became an area for growth of large corporations.

The contraction, or in some countries almost the vanishing, of domestic services witnesses the changing lifestyle of the middle class, processes of change urged by economic necessity: work which was typically carried out by a domestic (and female) servant was taken over by the food industry or the public sector (if it was not done by the former employers as unpaid and increasingly mechanized household duties). The sharp decline of domestic service employment also reflects the reduced labour force demands of agriculture. Many economically active persons who had been classified as domestic servants carried out diverse indoor tasks in rural households, which were, in fact, part of the daily farm work. As paid household work was probably one of those areas where clandestine work became more frequent in the period studied, reservations should be made as to the truth of the reported decline. It is possible, if not likely, that it also resulted from a growing tendency of employers not to report their reliance on paid household work. Untaxed work could have been a preferable alternative for both employer and employee.

Redistribution of Productivity Gains

The crucial factor behind the differential growth and decline of industries in the 1950s, 1960s and 1970s was the increased economic productivity of the commodity sector. The substantial rise of real value added per man-hour neutralized, partly or entirely, the employment growth effect of output expansion which was implied in the growth of the GDP. In the agricultural sector, the productivity growth even brought declining employment. The number of persons engaged in the sector in some countries reduced by more than two-thirds in the three decades.

The recorded growth and decline of the industries also implied transfers of these productivity gains both within the private sector (and its various industries and firms), and between the commodity sector and the sector of public service provision. As represented in Figure 3:12, some productivity gains were used for investments in new, expanded and more efficient physical capital, or in the employment of workers embodying human capital (engineers, scientists, etc.) The investments in physical and human capital affected the output capacity and efficiency of almost all industries engaged in commodity provision, including the intermediary industries of banking, insurance, real estate and business services (which were among the most rapidly growing industries in the period). Parts of the productivity gains in the private sector accrued to those employed in the sector, either as falling real prices or as higher real wages. Some part of the real wage increase was used for private consumption purposes; it was thus channelled back to private sector producers in the form of sales revenues which could be used by firms for further expansion or modernization. Another (and, during this period, increasing) part of commodity producer wage increases was appropriated by the state and used for the provision of public administration and defence, education and research, medical and welfare services or some

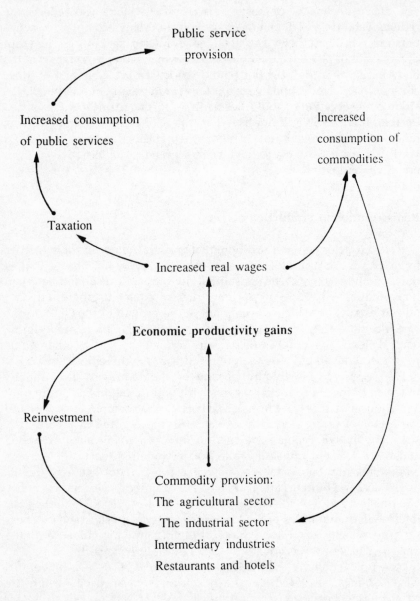

Figure 3.12   Industrial redistribution of economic productivity gains; commodity provision and provision of public services

other surplus-financed activities (such as recreational and cultural services). The expanded services of the state probably contributed, as a rule, to the private sector productivity growth and expansion potential; to some extent they thus created the economic requirements for their own growth.

The 1970s brought disturbances in the smooth working of this system of transfers which affected, above all, the public sector. Stagnating private sector output growth and a curtailment of private sector employment (in terms of man-hours) reduced, as was elaborated in Chapter 2, the potential for further employment growth in public services (and other activities dependent on surplus appropriation by the state). It should be observed, though, that the mounting financial difficulties of the state had a very limited effect on the number of persons engaged in public services (as registered in the population censuses of 1980). The major exception appears to be education and research, which seemed to approach an equilibrium in the late 1970s and early 1980s (probably not only for financial reasons, as the number of applicants for higher studies tended to stagnate). The financial crisis of the state mainly affected public investment. It contributed therefore, first and foremost, to a reduction in the number employed in the industrial sector.

Notes

1. The tripartite classification of industries was established by A.C.B. Fisher, *The Clash of Progress and Security* (London: Macmillan, 1935), C. Clark, *The Conditions of Economic Progress* (London: Macmillan, 1940) and S. Kuznets, *Modern Economic Growth: Rate, Structure and Spread* (New Haven & London: Yale University Press, 1966). For the notion of tertiary services, see also M. Lengellé, *La Révolution Tertiaire* (Paris: Editions Génin, 1966) and *The Growing Importance of the Service Sector in the Member Countries* (Paris: OECD, 1966).
2. The decline of the Norwegian international sea transport industry, as reported by the population censuses, is partly due to a growing share in total employment of workers residing abroad. As these workers are not considered members of the Norwegian population, they are not covered by the censuses.
3. For the performance of the manufacturing industry, see also Chapter 2, Table 2:17, Table 2:19 and Table 2:21.
4. In Sweden, one of the few countries reporting hours of work in wholesale and retail trade, the real value added per hour increased by more than 80% between 1950 and 1963, and by almost 25% between 1963 and 1971 (estimates from data in various editions of *Statistiska Meddelanden, Series N*). For a comprehensive account of post-war changes in retail and wholesale trade, see, for example, J.A. Dawson, *Commercial Distribution in Europe* (London & Canberra: Croom Helm, 1982).
5. P. Flora et al., *State, Economy and Society in Western Europe 1815–1975* (Frankfurt: Campus, 1983).

4 Occupations, 1950–80

Grouping of Occupations

When considering the development of the working population from the point of view of the kind of work, or functions that people perform, six broad categories, comprising in all 13 occupation groups, have been distinguished:

1. *Administrative, clerical and communication work.* This category encompasses *administrators, managers, jurists and accountants* and *clerical and communication workers*, i.e. those who are either involved in the administrative control of the state, a business firm or some other organization, or who carry out office work ancillary to such functions of control (typing, recording, data processing and transfer of information). Both kinds of worker are typically found in various bodies of public administration and the judiciary, or in non-operative departments of larger firms (head offices and other administrative units). But both are also numerous in offices providing banking, insurance and business services.

2. *Technical and scientific work*, i.e. functions implying either technical control (such as product research and development, design and construction, or supervision of operative work), professional counselling or development of basic or applied knowledge (not associated directly with teaching). This category includes the occupational groups of *architects, engineers and technicians* and *scientists and other professional workers*.

3. *Operative work.* This category comprises *agricultural and non-agricultural production-process workers, sales workers*, and *transport equipment operators*. Operative work is the typical work of farms, mines, factories, warehouses and shops of retailers, craftsmen and repairers, i.e. establishments where physical commodities are given their definite or intermediary form, where they are packed, reloaded or kept for further shipment or where they are made available to the customers. But operative work can also be implied in non-material commodity provision (e.g. personal transport services).

4. *Medical and social care, teaching and entertainment.* This category includes the four occupation groups of *medical and related workers, social workers and workers in religion, teachers* and *journalists and artists.* The functions are person-oriented and (with the exception of the last-named group) typically provided by the public sector.

5. *Personal service workers.* This group includes domestic servants, hairdressers, cleaners, undertakers and service personnel of restaurants and hotels. While Category 4 represents the expanding service functions of the state, Group 5 contains the traditional service work supplied by small firms and paid household workers.

6. *Protective service workers and armed forces.* This category represents the preventive and law-enforcing functions of the public sector, activities which are intended to secure the defence, integrity and cohesion of the nation-state, the authority of its leaders, the custody of law and order, etc. Protective service workers includes policemen, customs inspectors, fire brigade personnel, prison custodians and privately employed watchmen and guards.

Growth and Decline of Occupations

The growth and decline of the various types of occupations in the thirty-year period is demonstrated in Figures 4:1–4:7. The number of adminis-trative, clerical and communication workers increased in all the countries studied (see Figure 4:1). The increase was most rapid in Germany, France, Switzerland, Finland and Ireland, which are countries reporting considerable industrial growth in terms of both real value added and employment. (Many members of the occupation category work in the industrial sector.) In France and Switzerland the category grew by about 150 per cent, in Germany and Ireland by more than 200 per cent. Rapid growth was also recorded in technical and scientific work (Figure 4:2). Between 1950 and 1980, the number doubled in most countries.

The number of persons carrying out operative work declined. This decline was mainly due to dwindling employment opportunities for farm workers. The development of production process work outside agriculture is shown in Figure 4:3. Decreasing numbers were reported for all countries but Ireland (where production process workers increased in the 1960s and 1970s) and Switzerland and Finland (where the group increased prior to 1970). In the thirty-year period Britain lost about a fifth of its production process workers outside agriculture, in absolute numbers more than 2 million persons. In Germany, the group (which includes miners) declined by almost one million. The number of sales workers (such as shop assistants and supermarket cashiers) increased in most countries, as did the number of transport equipment operators. The growth of these groups was most rapid in the 1950s and 1960s.

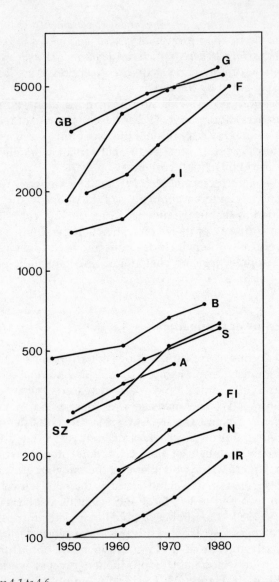

Figure 4.1   Administrative, clerical and communication work (000s workers)

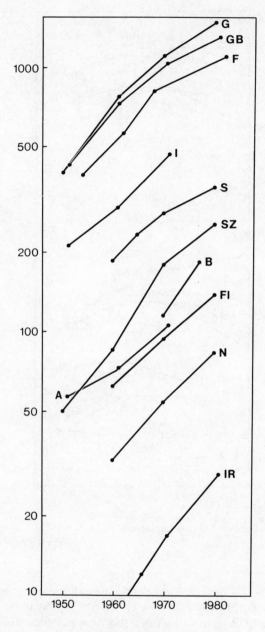

Figure 4.2   Technical and scientific work (000s workers)

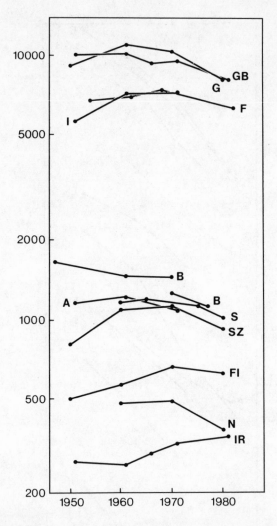

Figure 4.3   Non-agricultural production process workers (000s)

Medical and social care, teaching and entertainment engaged growing numbers in all countries (Figure 4:4); the growth was extraordinarily swift in Sweden, Denmark, Switzerland and Finland. For only a few countries the curves reveal a slower rate of growth in the 1970s than in the 1960s (Belgium, Finland and Norway). For personal service workers (Figure 4:5), some countries reported increasing numbers, others decreasing. Among the former was Finland, among the latter were Ireland and Norway. As shown in Figure 4:6, the number of protective service workers and armed forces declined in Britain between 1951 and

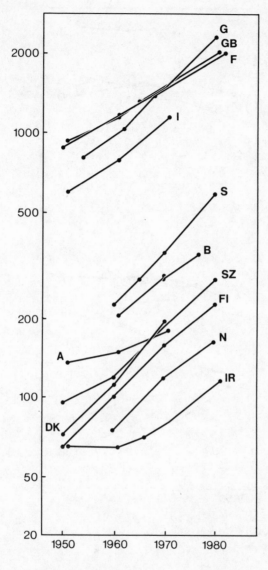

Figure 4.4 Medical and social care, teaching, and entertainment (000s workers)

1961, and in France and Belgium in the 1960s. All countries reported growing numbers for the 1970s.

The series of figures confirms the standard image of the occupational transformation of the working population: while fewer persons took direct part in physical production processes, more were engaged in administrative, clerical and communication work, technical and scientific work or medical and social care, teaching and entertainment. What were

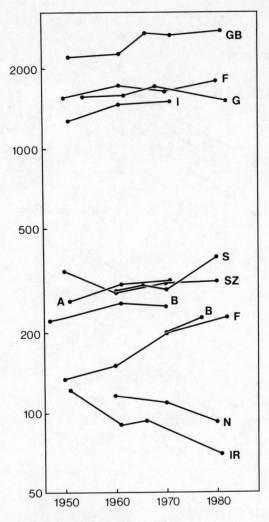

Figure 4.5   Personal service workers (000s)

the underlying processes and social forces of this transformation? Some answers to this question will be given in the following causal analysis.

Causal Analysis

This analysis will first focus on processes which worked in the sphere of commodity provision, i.e. practices adopted by small and large firms which, by enhancing profits, seemed to secure their potential for growth or survival. These practices were geared towards either the rationalization

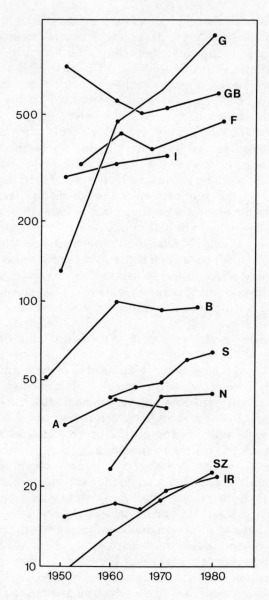

Figure 4.6 Protective service workers and armed forces (000s)

of operative work or the expansion of the firm's sales volume. In connection with commodity provision, the effects of transfers of work from the commodity sector to the households (such as work associated with the spreading ownership and use of private cars) will also be considered. Subsequently, the development of some occupations will be related to the expanded provision of public services. The major forces of change are assumed to be the postulated interests and goals of, on one hand, the *corporate technostructures* and, on the other, the *public techno-structures* and their financial supporters within the political decision-making communities. The crucial factor behind the occupational restructuring of the working population is considered to be the increased efficiency and economic productivity of the commodity sector, which followed from the attempts of firms to rationalize their operations and/or increase their sales volume in real terms. The growth and decline of occupational groups will be related to a recurrent redistribution of productivity gains which took place either *within* firms, *between* firms, or from the *commodity* sector to the sphere of *public service provision*. The character and direction of this redistribution will be considered in a comprehensive presentation of the processes and forces of change (see p. 103).

In the commodity sector, rationalization reduced the demand for production process workers, agricultural as well as non-agricultural. Mechanization, automation and labour-saving reorganization of the firm's whole system of work (or some establishments), were the standard measures adopted by employers to neutralize the cost effects of the rising nominal and real wages which characterized much of the post-war period. By economizing on the use of hired labour, it was possible for managers of firms to further their personal and organizational goals. In the corporate sub-sector, rationalization of operative work seemed to be the standard reaction of managers preoccupied with the problem of realizing an amount of gross profit which gave the firm the required financial strength and potential for adaptation to future changes in the demand for its products, technology of the industry or wage demands of employees. In other parts of the commodity sector, rationalization was often the main way in which the firms could cope with more intense competition, or the means by which self-employed owners of firms could secure an income which matched the achievements of other social groups. In agriculture, rationalization brought a sharp decline in the number of production process workers; production work outside agriculture contracted in most countries only in the 1970s, when declining physical capital formation produced a break in the post-war trend of economic and industrial sector growth. For most of the period studied, the growth of the sheer volume of work was swift enough to outweigh the effect which the increased efficiency of physical operations had on the number of production process workers.

A concomitant effect of the efforts of firms to curb the rise of labour costs through rationalization was a growth in the numbers of technical and scientific workers, an expansion of the workforce taking only indirect part in the production process. Centralized co-ordination and technical control (which includes the development of new production methods and modes of organizing production work) were key factors in the increased efficiency and economic productivity in both the agricultural and industrial sector of commodity production. The functions of co-ordination and control, which engaged increasing numbers of engineers and other technicians, could take place at great geographical distances from the production process, or in other industries. This is most evident in the case of agriculture, where the crucial changes in methods of production were based on research and development in large manufacturing firms which supplied vital parts of the required machinery, chemical inputs and, not the least, adopted agricultural technology. The stagnating, or declining, number of persons doing production process work, and the accompanying rise in the number of technical and scientific workers, epitomize the division and physical separation of conception and execution, brain and hand, to use the words of Braverman.[1] Behind a given number of production process workers there was an increasing number of production planners and co-ordinators, operation analysts, programmers, industrial sociologists and psychologists, time-study workers, constructors of machines and automatic production equipment, agricultural scientists and consultants. As these non-production workers produced a great amount of information to be handled and processed by assisting clerical workers, changes in the ways of producing goods and organizing production work were also a factor in the growing number engaged in administration, clerical and communication work.[2]

The technical and scientific employees created, by their diverse activities, the basic requirements for the growth of real value added per hour of operative work. And they thus also produced some of the necessary economic conditions for their further growth (considered as an occupational category), i.e. an economic surplus which could be used by the firms (or the public sector) to strengthen the available instrumental knowledge concerning production processes. In the corporate sub-sector of production, the derived economic productivity gains were to a large extent redistributed within the firms and used for internally determined consumption of more technical co-ordination and control (an expansion of the technical and scientific staff of the firm, or purchases of more consultancy services). In small firms, such as those operating in agriculture, efficiency gains were paid for by the firms through the purchase of capital equipment and inputs (and the technology embedded in equipment and inputs). Some of the efficiency gains were therefore channelled back to the producers of the capital equipment and inputs via the market.

The expanded commodity provision which characterized the period entailed growing sales and transport work. Both kinds of work were targets for rationalization. In retailing, where most sales workers are employed, the standard measure taken to reduce labour costs was the introduction of self-service, a transfer of some work formerly carried out by shop assistants to customers. Another factor which curbed the growth in the number of sales workers was the more frequent 'pre-packing' of distributed goods, which implied, in fact, a transfer of work from shops and wholesale storehouses to operative units in the manufacturing industry (where the work could be carried out more efficiently and often in direct connection with the physical transformation work). The increased part-time employment in retailing, and the varying national practices of coping with part-time employment in the censuses, make it difficult, however, to interpret the reported data on the number of sales workers. Substitution of part-time sales workers for full-time workers (adopted by employers as a device for labour-cost reductions) deflates the size of the occupational group if the required minimum number of hours worked (to be included in the working population) is high; figures are inflated if the requirement is low.

The growing commodity provision also affected the number of administrative, clerical and communication workers, as a substantial part of these workers are employed in banking and insurance firms. The growing demand for the functions of these workers was accompanied by rationalization (such as the introduction of electronic data processing), but apparently not to such an extent that the employment growth effect of the enhanced demand for those functions was outweighed. As has been shown in Chapter 3, the number of people engaged in banking and insurance increased substantially in the three decades.

The increased number of administrative, clerical and communication workers was also an effect of the growing organizational scale of commodity provision. The expanding sales, output and operative employment of firms, which resulted from frequent mergers and acquisitions, induced growing managerial and clerical employment, i.e. a rising number of non-operative employees responsible for the co-ordination and administrative control of the corporations. Of some importance for an understanding of the mechanism of this office-work growth is perhaps the fact that the work cannot be related directly to the output and sales revenue of the firms (as is often the case when firms consider their need for operative workers). The costs of additional workers in terms of salaries and social insurance payments can be ascertained, but not the contribution of the workers to the total sales receipts. Junior managers and clerical assistants are engaged, it has been maintained, as long as there is a general conviction among the members of the higher echelons of the organizations that they can free their highly paid working time from less demanding duties.[3] It is nevertheless plausible that the profit squeeze of the 1970s also aroused a general interest in rationalizing some kinds of work which had hitherto been exempted from efficiency considerations. (An example is the practice of substituting personal secretaries with secretarial pools.)

The growing organizational scale of commodity sector activities also explains, to some extent, the increased number of technical and scientific workers. When firms grow, their directors often find it worthwhile for pure cost reasons to engage specialized technicians or other professional workers for functions which were earlier carried out as parts of the more general responsibilities of some employees, or which were not carried out at all. If the firms did not find it justified to supplement their staff with the desired technical or professional expertise, it could probably be supplied on the market basis by independent consultancy firms. (For the rapid growth of the business service industry, see Chapter 3.)

The growing number of technical and scientific workers has been related to changes in the production process, and to the instrumental goal of management to keep down operative costs. But the growth can also be related to the attempts of firms to increase their sales revenues by means of 'market penetration' and 'market development', 'product development' and 'diversification', to use idioms of corporate strategy literature.[4] Corporations tried to increase their sales by means of advertising and other forms of sales promotion, by approaching new categories of customers, by means of changes in the form and function of their products, or by adding commodities to their product lines which seemed to have good market prospects. Such growth strategies necessitated the enrolment of product research and development workers, market researchers and promoters of sales, i.e. professional employees who could apply the knowledge of human behavioural and social sciences in the systematic search for growth opportunities. In the pursuit of such strategies, some corporations relied on, and even promoted, the technical modernization of the agricultural industry. By offering farmers the kinds of goods and services which seemed to be a remedy for their recurrent problems of profitability, some large firms could sustain the rationalization processes which were, in fact, a condition for their own viability. As farmers were actually compelled to rationalize their production by means of machinery, input and technology which were developed and supplied by large and oligopolistic firms in the manufacturing industry, it can be maintained that the declining number of agricultural production process workers reflects the aspirations and practices of the technostructures of these large firms. The eagerness and imposed necessity of agriculturalists to rationalize their production was, in other words, an important factor in the growth performance of some corporations, and one of the causes of growth in the number of non-production workers in the manufacturing industry. The same kind of reasoning can be applied to any kind of supplier–

customer relationship where buyers are forced to acquire the equipment or services which are supplied by some producer. Putting customers into such situations of actual dependency is part of the art of corporate strategy.

In connection with the strategic dispositions of large (and growth-oriented) firms it is proper to emphasize the role of the increased ownership and use of cars for personal transport. The post-war auto-mobilization of the Western European countries (which was touched upon in Chapter 2) can be considered the highly positive response of customers to a deliberate strategy of the major European car manufacturers: to combine mass production of small and medium-sized vehicles with emphasis on product differentiation (in a situation where intra-Western European trade was exempted from customs and other restrictions, while the competitiveness of non-European producers was for some time hampered by tariffs).[5] The developing automobile society provided an avenue of growth for many firms, not only European motor-car producers but also enterprises engaged in the ancillary part of the development block of the automobile (sale of cars, petrol and spare parts, car repairs, construction of roads and other infrastructure, not to mention activities which expanded as a result of the accompanying suburbanization and changing residential patterns, the altered ways of spending non-working time, etc.). As this development paralleled the evolution of the European corporte economy, it shall be mentioned among the factors which account for the growth of the occupational categories of administrative, clerical and communication work and technical and scientific work, the size of which can be related to the organizational scale of the firms. But it has also been maintained that the increased reliance of people on private cars implied a transfer of personal transport work from the private and public sectors of production to households.[6] As private cars were increasingly used to bridge the geographical distances between place of residence and place of work (or other destinations), paid work was replaced by unpaid work. Although it is not quite correct to regard the emerging automobile society as resulting wholly from such institutional transfers (see Chapter 2), it should be observed that the increased use of private cars affected the number of persons carrying out paid transport work. It contributed, no doubt, to the declining number of transport equipment operators.

The growth of the occupational category of medical and social care, teaching and entertainment shows the achievements of the welfare state, or the achievements of public technostructures (the members of which were interested in the expansion of the types of professional expertise they could provide). It implied, to restate a basis thesis, that some of the gains that followed from the increased economic productivity of the commodity sector were appropriated by the state, as health, social welfare and educational personnel could not expand unless the political decision-making communities of the countries could dispose of a growing private sector surplus. Some functions of medical and social care were, in the beginning of the period under consideration, to a large extent carried out as household duties. The growth of public care meant that much unpaid domestic and female-dominated work became modestly paid female-dominated work in hospitals, retirement homes and nursery schools.[7] The financial problems of the public sector in the late 1970s (see Chapter 2) do not seem to have had any substantial effect on the growth of the occupational category. As the tightened financial situation of the governments curbed the physical capital formation expenditure of the public sector (and thus also acted as a brake to the physical capital formation expenditure of the commodity sector), it can be assumed that it had a negative effect mainly on the number of production process workers outside agriculture. The productivity gains of the commodity sector also provided the financial means for a strengthening of the regulatory bodies of the state. They allowed for growing numbers of civil servants engaged in administrative, clerical and communication work or scientific work. Public regulation and surveillance increasingly required professional expertise, whether justified by changes in people's employment opportunities, or conditions of work or patterns of residence. Examples of public activities which required professionals are regional policy and physical planning. In the 1970s some disposable economic surplus was apparently also used to increase the personnel in the preventive and law enforcing functions of the state.

From the points of view of the various types of work, the causes of the occupational restructuring of the working population can be summarized as follows:

1. The growing number of administrative, clerical and communication workers was partly an effect of the growth of the corporate sub-sector, which implied a demand for managers who could be entrusted with the administrative control of the firms, as well as workers who could assist these decision-makers. The services of such workers were also requested by the increasing numbers of technicians and other professional employees caring for the technical control of the physical operations, or who carried out the marketing and sales functions of the firms. Other reasons for the growth of the occupational category were increased demand for banking and insurance services and increased public regulation. Efforts to save office labour were made by both private and public employers, but rationalization was not sufficient to neutralize the growth effect of the expanded volume of work.

2. The main factor in the growing number of technical and scientific workers was the increased demand for professional expertise in connection with rationalization of agricultural and non-agricultural production process work, or product development and research in large

firms; another factor was extended public regulation.

3. Operative work was subject to various forms of labour-saving rationalization. The moderate increase in agricultural output could not offset the effect of enhanced efficiency, and the number of production process workers in agriculture declined substantially. In other areas of commodity production, production process work was sustained during most of the period by expanded output. It was in general not until the mid-1970s, when industrial output contracted, that labour-saving practices brought an actual contraction. The number of sales workers was affected by the spread of self-service (and reliance on part-time employment) in retailing; the number of transport workers was affected by the increasing use of private cars for personal transport.

4. The growth of the occupational category of medical and social care, teaching and entertainment, which does not seem to have been interrupted in the 1970s, reflects the expanded provision of public services. The growing public care implied an institutional relocation of socially necessary (and female-dominated) work from households to public institutions.

5. Personal service work was rationalized through the introduction of self-service by the customers (a labour-saving device which changes the character and quality of the marketed services); or it became unpaid do-it-yourself activities of households when rising prices curbed the demand for private sector service work.[8] Rising wages also brought a contraction of paid domestic service work. Middle-class families, which had relied on domestic servants, were forced to look after themselves with the help of household machinery and/or to rely on clandestine labour.[9]

6. The declining number of protective service workers and armed forces registered in some countries in the 1950s and 1960s resulted from the decreasing labour-power requirements of military defence (the rationalization of warfare and national security functions through nuclear deterrence). The slight growth of the occupational category recorded for several countries in the 1970s presumably reflects a political demand for law and order (more police).

The crucial processes at work in the commodity sector reflected the growth and efficiency considerations of directors of firms. The increased provision of public services reflected political priorities and interests in public service growth among the leading public service providers.

The redistribution of economic productivity gains which enabled the growth of some occupations has already been emphasized. Some of these gains, which stemmed from the rationalization of operative work, were appropriated by the state and used to finance the expanding activities of the public sector. Increased provision of public services produced employment opportunities for increasing numbers of medical and social workers, teachers, administrators, clerical and communication

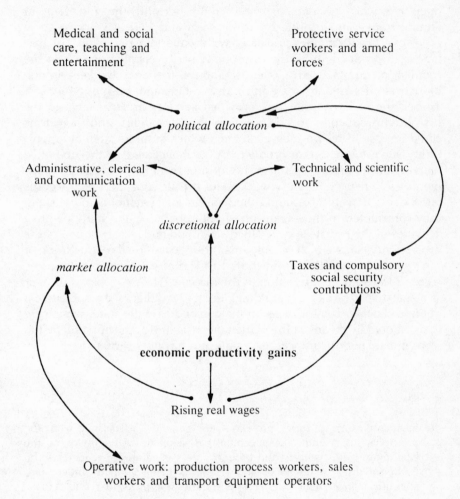

PUBLIC SERVICE PROVISION

Medical and social
care, teaching and
entertainment

Protective service
workers and armed
forces

political allocation

Administrative, clerical
and communication
work

Technical and scientific
work

discretional allocation

market allocation

Taxes and compulsory
social security
contributions

economic productivity gains

Rising real wages

Operative work: production process workers, sales
workers and transport equipment operators

COMMODITY PROVISION

Figure 4.7 Redistribution of economic productivity gains: occupational
categories

workers, as well as (civil) protective service workers. To the extent that it was a responsibility of the state to provide financially for cultural and recreational services, work was also created for the occupational group of journalists and artists. Some of the productivity gains were retained in the private sector and disposed of in the employment of more non-operative workers, persons who could perform the functions of administrative and technical control, sales and clerical work or some other 'overhead' activities associated with commodity provision. Further, increased productivity in the commodity sector enabled growth in the number of administrative, clerical and professional workers in the industries of banking, insurance, real estate and business services. These intermediary industries provided services indispensable to the expanded production and distribution of commodities, and their firms could impose levies on their customers which secured them an opportunity for growth. Some productivity gains accrued to the operative workers of the private sector in the form of rising real wages. As wage increases were used by these workers for private consumption purposes (after deductions of taxes and other compulsory payments to the state) they contributed to the expansion of both operative and non-operative activities in the private sector. The distribution and redistribution of the productivity gains which accompanied the occupational restructuring of the working population is illustrated in Figure 4:7. Some of the gains were allocated at the discretion of the directors of firms (as part of their strategic dispositions and spending decisions). Others were subject to a political allocation by the decision-making bodies of the state; some were redistributed by means of the market (such as those appropriated by the firms in banking, insurance, real estate and business services).

Notes

1. In manufacturing, these processes are generally associated with the principles of 'scientific management', developed by F. Taylor in the beginning of this century and brought into general and extended use by European firms in the 1950s and 1960s. As pointed out by Braverman, scientific management offered opportunities for firms to reduce labour costs: by splitting shopfloor work into detailed parts requiring various degrees of skill, firms did not need to use skilled and highly remunerated labour for the most simple tasks: these could be carried out by unskilled and low-paid workers (H.S. Braverman, *Labor and Monopoly Capital: The Degradation of Work in the Twentieth Century*, New York and London: Monthly Review Press, 1974, p. 112 ff.).
2. The concept of control embedded in scientific management requires, as emphasized by Braverman, that everything happening in physical production is replicated in paper form. Each step must be devised, pre-calculated, tested and laid out, assigned and ordered, checked and inspected,

and recorded on completion. The paper replica of the physical production processes calls into existence a variety of new occupations, the hallmark of which is that they are found in the flow of paper. The two aspects of labour are separated, but both remain necessary to production and in this the labour process retains its unity (Braverman, op. cit., p. 125 ff). It should be observed, however, that technical control of the physical production processes no longer necessarily implies paperwork. In the studied period, non-paper media were probably used increasingly in the direction and supervision of operations.

3. An example of such ancillary office work is the private secretary. From a functional point of view, the secretary came into existence as a device to extend the range of action and observation of the entrepreneur and proprietor. Later on, the secretary came to express the same kind of reasoning as that embodied in the principles of scientific management: it was wasteful to have managers spending their time typing letters, opening mail, sending parcels, making travel arrangements, answering the telephone, etc., when these duties could be performed by labour hired at one-third or less of the remuneration of the manager. The operation of this kind of thinking was further stimulated by the fact that managers organize their own labour and often tend to place an exaggerated value upon their time as compared to the time of others (Braverman, op. cit., p. 343).

4. I.H. Ansoff, *Corporate Strategy: An Analytical Approach to Business Policy for Growth and Expansion* (Harmondsworth: Penguin, 1971). When the business climate changed in the late 1970s, corporate strategists became more preoccupied with the appropriate dispositions for status quo or survival. A major concern became how to cope with increased competition. See M.E. Porter, *Competitive Strategy: Techniques for Analyzing Industries and Competitors* (New York & London: Free Press-Collier, 1980) and *Competitive Advantage: Creating and Sustaining Superior Performance* (New York & London: Free Press-Collier, 1985).

5. *The Future of the Automobile: The Report of MIT's International Automobile Program*, (London & Sydney: Allen & Unwin, 1984), p. 18 ff.

6. J.S. Gershuny, *Social Innovation and the Division of Labour* (Oxford: Oxford University Press, 1983)

7. R. Liljenström, *Kultur och Arbete* (Stockholm: Liber-Sekretariatet för Framtidsstudier, 1979), p. 116.

8. This is an argument presented by, notably, Baumol & Oates and Gershuny.

9. As pointed out by Gershuny, economic progress does not mean that most people are able to adopt the lifestyle of the wealthy: 'it may be true that at a particular historical juncture the rich had more servants, travelled more often by train, went more frequently to the theatre, than did the poor. But nevertheless, as the poor got richer over time, they did not employ more servants and buy more train and theatre tickets—instead they bought domestic machinery, cars and television sets' (op. cit., pp. 14–15.).

5 Self-employment, 1950–80

The Disappearing Petty Bourgeoisie

As for the *employment status* of the working population, this chapter focuses on the development of self-employment: to what extent do economically active persons provide paid work for themselves as small-scale employers or own-account workers? How has self-employment fared in the period 1950–80? The concern of this chapter is thus the changing numerical weight of 'the petty bourgeoisie', or the 'old middle class': people who run a small business of their own with a few employees or with no hired labour at all (independent farmers, self-employed craftsmen and repairers, shop owners, etc.)

The standard concept of an evolving industrial and capitalist society conveys the idea of a steady decline, and the eventual disappearance, of self-employment.[1] But, as pointed out by Giddens in a study summarizing its quantitative development up until the early 1970s, the actual gradient of the decline has not matched expectations: '[the] decay has taken the form of a slowly declining curve, rather than the progressive approach to zero'.[2] In more recent years, it has become even more difficult to vindicate the thesis of the disappearance of the self-employed. As will be demonstrated, there was actually, in some industries and countries, a tendency for self-employment to grow in the 1970s. The gradual, but far from regular, decline of self-employment in the 1950s and 1960s, and its subsequent (and partial) revival will be described here by means of population census statistics. Attempts will later be made to explain the recorded changes in absolute and relative frequency of self-employment.

Percentage and Absolute Numbers of Self-employed in the Working Population

A summary measure of the development of self-employment in the three decades is given in Table 5:1 (a and b). This table seems to confirm

Table 5.1(a) Self-employment (000s of persons)

	1950–1	*1960–1*	*1970–1*	*1980–1*
Great Britain	1,649	1,645	1,843	1,912
Ireland	326	286	259	232
Germany	3,412	3,238	2,571	2,311
France	4,110(a)	3,718(b)	3,334(c)	2,870(d)
Italy	4,605	4,134	4,066	4,012
Belgium	700(e)	663	531	483
Austria	588	533	428	398
Switzerland	409	366	313	299
Sweden	605	450	303	259
Norway	343	273	199	144
Denmark	414	404	322	383
Finland	401	395	302	214

(a) 1954   (b) 1962   (c) 1968   (d) 1982   (e) 1947
Sources: Population census reports.

Table 5.1(b) Self-employed as percentage of the working population

	1950–1	*1960–1*	*1970–1*	*1980–1*
Great Britain	7.4	7.0	7.8	8.4
Ireland	26.8	27.2	24.5	20.4
Germany	14.5	12.2	9.7	9.2
France	21.8(a)	19.5(b)	16.7(c)	13.4(d)
Italy	23.5	21.1	21.6	20.1
Belgium	22.7(e)	19.6	15.1	13.7
Austria	17.6	15.8	13.8	11.7
Switzerland	19.0	14.5	10.4	9.7
Sweden	19.4	13.9	8.9	–
Norway	24.8	–	13.6	10.5
Denmark	21.5	20.1	14.0	14.6
Finland	20.2	19.4	14.3	9.6

(a) 1954   (b) 1962   (c) 1968   (d) 1982   (e) 1947
Sources: Population census reports.

the idea of a long-term, and inevitable, decline of the class of petty employers and own-account workers. In France the relative share of this group in the entire working population drops from about 22 per cent in 1954 to less than 14 per cent in 1982. In Switzerland and Finland the overall rate of self-employment declined from about 20 per cent in 1950 to less than 10 per cent thirty years later. The decline is even more pronounced in Sweden, where less than 4 per cent of the economically active population was self-employed in 1975. Yet, for some countries, there appears to have been a break in the long-term trend of contraction: the decline is less rapid in the 1970s than in earlier decades, and a few countries actually report some growth as they approach the 1980s. In Britain the rate of self-employment rose in the inter-censal period 1966–81; in Denmark the rate increased between 1970 and 1980. In both countries self-employment grew in absolute numbers as well; in Britain more than 300,000 more were reported as self-employed in 1981 than in 1966.

Moving to particular industries, it is even more difficult to maintain the thesis of an inevitable decline in self-employment. In agriculture and forestry the *rate* of self-employment increased substantially in the three decades. According to population census reports, the percentage of self-employed persons in the rapidly contracting workforce of these industries was in some countries twice as high around 1980 as it was in the early 1950s. In Denmark, which belongs to this group of countries, almost 80 per cent of all workers in agriculture and forestry were reported as self-employed by the 1981 census. The rate rose substantially in the 1970s; in Ireland, for instance, from 48 per cent in 1951 to 74 per cent in 1981. The rising relative weight of self-employment in agriculture and forestry reflects the diminishing reliance of farmers on hired labour. It was this part of the agricultural labour force which declined most rapidly in the post-war period.

In the industrial sector, the rate of self-employment declined in almost all countries prior to 1970. But in the 1970s, it increased in Denmark, France, Ireland, Britain and France. With the exception of France, these countries could also report growing *absolute* numbers of self-employed workers in the industrial sector. In Britain, where aggregate industrial employment contracted substantially, self-employment rose from 268,000 persons in 1961 to 570,000 in 1981. The increased importance of self-employment within the industrial sector was due particularly to its absolute and/or relative growth in construction. In Britain the absolute number of self-employed persons in this industry increased from 133,000 in 1951 to 360,000 in 1981; in Italy the number increased fourfold in the same period. But great differences could be observed among the countries in the importance of self-employment in the construction industry (see Table 5:2 (a and b). Whereas the rate approached, or exceeded, 20 per cent in Britain, Ireland, France, Italy and Denmark by the end of the period, it was less than 10 per cent in Germany, Austria, Switzerland and Finland.

In wholesale and retail trade, which have traditionally housed many small and owner-run firms, self-employment declined, although apparently at a slower pace in the 1970s than in earlier decades. For land transport (excluding railways), the pattern is less evident: while the rate

Table 5.2(a) Self-employed persons in construction (000s)

	1950–1	1960–1	1970–1	1980–1
Great Britain	133	162	322	359
Ireland	7	6	11	17
Germany	215*	180	166	159
France	251(a)	260(b)	261(c)	330(d)
Italy	87	117	255	356
Belgium	48(e)	45	43	40
Austria	14	22	14	15
Switzerland	25	24	26	19
Sweden	28	32	32	–
Norway	23	21	23	19
Denmark	25	26	29	34
Finland	10	10	9	10

(a) 1954   (b) 1962   (c) 1968   (d) 1982   (e) 1947

* Excluding Saarland.

Sources: Population census reports.

Table 5.2(b) Percentage of self-employed in construction

	1950–1	1960–1	1970–1	1980–1
Great Britain	9.6	11.9	19.3	22.4
Ireland	7.5	8.8	11.4	16.7
Germany	11.5*	7.8	8.2	8.4
France	18.5(a)	15.4(b)	12.6(c)	18.7(d)
Italy	5.9	5.0	12.4	19.3
Belgium	24.3(e)	18.1	14.9	16.1
Austria	6.0	6.7	5.2	5.0
Switzerland	14.3	10.0	9.1	8.6
Sweden	11.4	11.0	9.8	–
Norway	18.0	16.0	18.0	15.2
Denmark	19.2	17.6	13.7	17.2
Finland	8.1	6.0	5.0	6.6

(a) 1954   (b) 1962   (c) 1968   (d) 1982   (e) 1947

* Excluding Saarland.

Sources: Population census reports.

of self-employment declined in Denmark in the latter part of the period studied, it rose in Britain and Ireland. Other industries with growing self-employment (in absolute or relative terms) were restaurants and hotels and business services. In the former industry, absolute numbers increased during the 1970s in Britain, Ireland, Germany, Austria and Denmark. In business services, which was one of the most rapidly growing industries in the thirty-year period, the rate of self-employment increased during the 1970s in Germany, France and Britain.

While the number of self-employed persons in non-agricultural commodity provision declined in almost all countries in the 1950s and 1960s, it tended to grow in some countries in the 1970s (see Table 5:3). In agriculture and forestry, where the rate of self-employment increased throughout the thirty-year period, the absolute number of independent workers declined substantially (Table 5:4).

Causal Analysis

The declining importance of self-employment in non-agricultural commodity provision, which characterized most of the post-war period, illustrates, first of all, the encroachment of large and medium-sized firms into the traditional realms of small-scale traders and independent service providers. Repairing, retail trade and various personal services, where self-employment once seemed to be the rule, offered growth avenues for large firms. Work done by independent mechanics and garage proprietors was taken over by the service departments of large automobile dealers and petroleum companies. Retailing chains and supermarkets penetrated the markets of small retailers of food and other daily goods. Large firms entered the restaurant trade by establishing chains of branded and highly advertised eating-places which could deliver quick and standardized food in stylized environments. Repair and service work also tended to be organized on a larger scale; it became standardized, mechanized, marketed and subject to the control of large and growth-oriented firms, in some industries even transnational corporations.

Many factors mitigated this development. One was the temptation of large firms to rely on subcontracting; to buy goods and services which would otherwise be provided within the firm. (Subcontracting provides work for many self-employed persons, although it is not limited to small owner-run firms.) Another obstacle, which barred the complete takeover by large firms in retailing was 'franchising', i.e. the practice of large wholesalers helping small retailers to establish themselves in a particular trade (so as to make them future buyers of their goods and services and, in fact, highly dependent). In some industries and countries there were also political factors impeding the total disappearance of small-scale

Table 5.3　Self-employed persons in non-agricultural commodity provision (000s)

	1950–1	1960–1	1970–1	1980–1
Great Britain	1,619	1,310	1,581	1,689
Ireland	90	74	76	91
Germany	2,144	2,097	1,909	1,848
France	2,194(a)	2,041(b)	1,941(c)	1,903(d)
Italy	2,063	2,200	2,637	3,673
Belgium	540(e)	493	416	400
Austria	276	255	223	216
Switzerland	238	225	209	219
Norway	187	137	116	91
Denmark	219	214	171	235
Finland	113	116	93	90

(a) 1954　(b) 1962　(c) 1968　(d) 1982　(e) 1947
Sources: Population census reports.

Table 5.4　Self-employed persons in agriculture and forestry (000s)

	1950–1	1960–1	1970–1	1980–1
Great Britain	344	335	262	223
Ireland	237	212	183	141
Germany	1,269	1,140	662	463
France	1,916(a)	1,676(b)	1,394(c)	767(d)
Italy	2,543	1,935	1,430	938
Belgium	230(e)	170	116	83
Austria	312	278	205	183
Switzerland	171	140	104	80
Norway	156	136	83	53
Denmark	194	190	127	148
Finland	288	279	208	124

(a) 1954　(b) 1962　(c) 1968　(d) 1982　(e) 1947
Sources: Population census reports.

traders and independent service providers; an ability of the self-employed to gain the support of certain factions of the political decision-making community (usually some centre/right-wing parties relying on petty bourgeois voters).[3] Such relationships of support help explain the relatively strong position of self-employment in agriculture, although the rising rate of independent workers in this industry mainly resulted from growing labour productivity. Technical and organizational innovations in agriculture benefited family farming, as they made it possible for farm-owners to run quite large production units without hired labour.[4]

The apparent revival of self-employment in the 1970s should be considered in the light of mounting unemployment. Establishing oneself as an own-account worker, or even as an employer, was probably far from an unusual response to actual or expected redundancy, although it may be a mistake to think that the dole made it possible for many unemployed workers to establish themselves as *de facto* self-employed workers in the 'black' sector of the economy (as has been suggested).[5] That actual, or threatening, perspective of unemployment worked as an impetus for persons to establish themselves as self-employed seems most probable in the construction industry, where barriers to such moves were low. Tools and other implements could be secured at reasonable costs or shared within a co-operative of workers; cars made independent workers more mobile and ready to take jobs far away from their homes. It is possible that growing income taxation promoted such moves. Declining profitability may have also made firms more inclined to subcontract self-employed workers in the 1970s than in earlier decades. A growing propensity among large firms to 'externalize' work is a probable cause of the rising number of independent workers in land transport (excluding railways). Large haulage firms are known to help their drivers establish themselves as self-employed by lending them the money to acquire a lorry. The independent drivers service their former employers on a piece-meal basis and are thus made responsible for the efficiency and cost-effectiveness of the operations. A growing fear among employers of getting bogged down in costly liabilities to their employees is also a possible explanation of the growth of self-employment in business services. Firms can cut labour costs by helping their senior and professional employees establish themselves in the consulting trade, buying their expertise for some time but without any commitment to do so for a longer period.

The rising number of the self-employed may also reflect increased opportunities, and a growing desire, for self-employment. New demands for goods and services, new technologies, the relative cheapening of tools and implements, the availablility of private pension schemes etc., has made it possible for more people to work for themselves.[6] People may have become influenced by the idea that self-employment provides more freedom, self-realization and even a higher income. Even the attitudes of governments to self-employment have changed considerably, as it seems to offer an alternative to unemployment. New policies *vis-à-vis* independent workers may have made it easier for people to establish and run a small business of their own.[7]

As to the *relative* frequency of self-employment in the entire working population, or a large part of it (such as the industrial sector), one should also keep in mind that variations in the rates of self-employed persons also reflect the accompanying changes in the industrial composition of the studied aggregate of activities. The declining rate of self-employment in the entire working population is partly due to the rapid growth of industries where self-employment is unusual or impossible (such as banking and public and public–private services); the less sharp decline in self-employment in the industrial sector in the 1970s is partly caused by the much reduced relative weight of industries where self-employed persons are almost non-existent (such as mining), and partly by the growing relative weight of repairing, where the rate of self-employment is comparatively high.

Notes

1. The self-employed belong to those 'third persons' who, according to Marx, were fated to be absorbed by either the capitalist or the working class. See A.L. Harris, 'Pure Capitalism and the Disappearance of the Middle Class', *Journal of Political Economy*, Vol. 47 (June 1939). More recent students of the social structure of the industrially advanced world have generally accepted the idea of the eventual disappearance of the petty bourgeoisie, although not necessarily as part of a two-class polarization (D. Bell, *The Coming of the Post-Industrial Society: A Venture in Social Forecasting*, London: Heineman, 1974). A numerical contraction of the self-employed class has also been considered as a corollary of modern economic growth. See, for instance, S. Kuznets, *Economic Growth of Nations: Total Output and Production Structure* (Cambridge, Mass.: Harvard University Press, 1971).
2. A. Giddens, *The Class Structure of the Advanced Society* (London: Hutchinson, 1973) p. 179.
3. Such political factors were, according to Silos Labini, the main reason why self-employment outside agriculture rose in Italy. Favouring the class of small manufacturers, shop-owners and service providers was seen by the Christian-Democratic and coalition governments as a means to forestall social and political instability. P. Silos Labini, *Saggio sulle Classe Sociali* (Bari: Laterza, 1976) p. 12.
4. The Common Agricultural Policy of the European Communities imposed, as pointed out by Silos Labini, restrictions on governments which would have been inclined to maintain a 'middle-class policy' *vis-à-vis* the farmers. Silos Labini, op.cit., p. 12.
5. R.E. Pahl, *Divisions of Labour* (Oxford: Basil Blackwell, 1984) p. 93.
6. It has been maintained that the need for service and repair work grows as larger amounts of household income are spent on dwellings, cars and other durables—items which always require some maintenance work. Mass consumption of industrial goods thus creates a market for service work which is often provided by self-employed workers. See Silos Labini, op.cit., p. 13. Consideration of the effects of heavy taxation may very well relegate a substantial part of this service work to the non-registered sector of the economy.

7. As pointed out by Scase & Goffee, self-employment is seen nowadays by some governments as offering not only a solution to the economic problems confronting Western society, but also as a potential cure for some of its alleged institutional, attitudinal and cultural ills. The popularity of such ideas is reflected in the economic and social policies of the British Conservative Government. Its strategy to rejuvenate the economy is based on a widely propagated belief that individuals should be responsible for their own lives. An economic climate must be created which prepares people to take risks; people must be allowed to stand on their own two feet. As the entrepreneurs must be satisfactorily rewarded for their economic risks, there must be a reduction in the level of direct taxation; in addition to increasing the incentive for entrepreneurship, lower taxes create resources for investment (R. Scase & R. Goffee, *The Real World of the Small Business Owner*, London: Croom Helm, 1980, p. 11 ff.).

6 Processes and Forces of Economic Change, 1950–80

In the foregoing chapters attempts have been made to explain the development of the gross domestic product and the working population by relating this development to certain and repeated practices of the main agents of the economy, i.e. to economic and political processes which make the statistically described change a matter of course. Processes of change were regarded as agent reactions to changing conditions which seemed compatible with their alleged organizational goals and group interests. In dealing with change in economies where large corporations gained weight and influence, it was considered proper to focus on processes which expressed the interests of the senior managers and technicians of such firms, that is their technostructures. But attention was also paid to supposed goals and interests of the technostructures of the public sector of production (who are professional employees implementing state policies), to political priorities of governments and other decision-making bodies (which provide the financial means for public sector activities), and to the claims for higher wages made by organized labour (which recurrently compel commodity providers to reconsider their use of the hired labour force). A short chapter also dealt with self-employment, the members of the economically active population who gain their living by running a small business of their own.

This chapter offers a summary of the causal analysis in Chapters 2–5. Major processes which transformed the national economies in the period 1950–80 are highlighted and their effects spelled out in terms of the various categories of both the gross domestic product and the working population (i.e. types of expenditure, industries and occupations).

The economic growth of the three decades studied essentially reflects, as was maintained in Chapter 2, the achievements of large and growth-oriented firms, i.e. the ability of corporations to expand sales (in real terms), to reduce (or abate the rise of) costs, to use a substantial share of their gross profits (or corporate levy) for investments in expanded, more appropriate and efficient production facilities. To the extent that corporate technostructures were able to follow these imperatives for growth of the firm, they secured most of the requirements for a large and rising gross domestic product. The economy of the Western European countries hence derived its main momentum from the growth of a comparatively small number of oligopolists. These large firms dominated the commodity sector, and they conditioned, through their strong influence on aggregate commodity provision and private sector employment, the development of the public sector.

A main area for sales expansion not only of the large corporations, but also of many smaller and partly dominated commodity providers, was the sector of unpaid household work. Functions which were traditionally carried out by households (according to principles of reciprocity) were taken over by the commodity sector and organized in such ways that they allowed for economies of scale and specialization. The functions, which more often assumed the form of 'goods' than 'services', replaced household work and allowed people to spend more time on activities which required the daily use of industrially produced commodities. The households acquired consumer durables which made it possible for them to 'internalize' services which were formerly bought on the market. The strategic dispositions of the firms in order to expand sales combined with various measures to reduce production costs; market and product development brought new products, and new variants of products within the reach of new categories of customers. Mass consumption and mass production of industrial goods serving domestic needs conditioned the capital accumulation of the firms. Although the increased availability of machinery for household work (and recreation) paved the way for transfers of work from the service-providing industries to the sector of unpaid household work, it can be taken for granted that the relocation of household work had a positive net effect on the aggregate output of the commodity sector, at least as long as the development blocks which these transfers induced were still expanding through investments in an enlarged production capacity.

Other areas which offered avenues for sales expansion of both large and small firms were agriculture and the public sector. Agriculture was an important outlet for machinery and industrially produced inputs. The demand for such goods was part and parcel of the rationalization of farm work, and derived its strength from the attempts of the agricultural producers to secure a fair share in the rising national income. Agricultural policies helped them realize these aims, but guaranteed, above all, the ability of the farmers to buy sophisticated machinery and appropriate inputs. Agricultural policies thus also helped the producers of such commodities to accomplish their growth objectives. The public sector was an expanding market for a variety of industrial products which seemed indispensable to a welfare state which also cared for the military defence of its citizens and the efficiency and competitiveness of its industries. The growth of the commodity sector allowed for substantial capital formation in the public sector and it was not until the deteriorated terms of trade *vis-à-vis* the oil-exporting countries (and less rapidly growing exports to the United States) brought balance of payments problems that governments were forced to restrict their spending.

The efforts of firms to reduce costs implied rationalization of all kinds of operative work: mechanization, automation and changes in the organization and overall scope of the concerned work activities; in the service industries the quest for lower costs also induced the introduction of self-service, in fact transfer of work to the customers. Whatever its actual form, rationalization brought increased labour productivity, that is, a larger real value per hour of paid work. Rationalization was induced by the demands of labour for higher wages. It is thus possible to relate the increased productivity to the achievements of organized labour, its successful attempts to capture a larger share of the real value of the private sector output.

The propensity of firms to use a large share of their gross profits for techni-cal modernization, expansion and other adjustments of their production facilities was manifested in the substantial physical capital formation of the private sector, in fact the most decisive single factor behind the high rates of economic growth in the pre-1973 period. It entailed a large volume of paid work in terms of man-hours and accounted for the almost 'full employment' which characterized most of the sub-period. The large, and probably growing, volume of work in the private sector created, as it combined with increased labour productivity and net transfers of work from households, the economic requirements for public sector growth, i.e. the creation of remunerated work and incomes guaranteed by the state.

The growth of the public sector reflected political priorities, but also the group interests of service providers themselves; it evidenced their ability to argue convincingly for larger public commitment in areas where their organization had a stake and they personally felt professional responsibility. The increased productivity—and sheer expansion—of the commodity sector provided the economic requirements for the expanding service provision and it was not until the late 1970s that governments were forced to curtail spending for public investment purposes. Public employment and public consumption expenditure increased throughout the whole thirty-year period (although apparently less rapidly in the 1970s than in the two previous decades).

Public sector growth implied, as did the growth of the commodity sector, transfer of work from households. Unpaid work and reciprocal social liabilities became public responsibilities and the paid work of public employees. The formalization of household work created jobs for people who would have otherwise presumably been redundant because

of declining labour needs in the private sector; and it also added therefore to aggregate commodity demand. The public sector contributed in
various ways to the increased productivity of the private sector and
created to some extent the economic requirements for its own growth, at
least as long as the growth of the commodity sector was not barred by
factors which could not be controlled by the individual nation-states.

In Chapter 2, economic growth was regarded as an effect of increased
labour productivity, full employment and transfer of work from households. These three factors, which were said to account for the expanding
gross domestic product, resulted from three types of process and three
types of social force (i.e. agent motives). The social forces of economic
growth, were:

— the growth motives of corporate technostructures;
— the income aspirations of farmers and other small-scale commodity
    providers;
— the interests in public sector growth attributed to public techno-
    structures and their political allies.

The three kinds of process which 'produced' the changes in the size of
the gross domestic product (through increased labour productivity,
expanding employment and transfers of work) were rationalization,
measures used by firms to expand their real sales, and various practices
of the leading public service providers to enhance the development of
particular public services (i.e. 'public sector growth processes'). The
effects of these forces and processes in terms of various types of
expenditure were also spelled out in Chapter 2: growing private consumption (in particular, expenditure on consumer durables), physical
capital formation in the private sector (induced by growing private
consumption), growing public consumption, and (as a further induced
type of expenditure) public sector capital formation. The same agent
motives, and kinds of processes, appear in Chapters 3–5, which
attempt to explain the changes in the size of the various working
population sub-sets.

The 'retroduction', or 'backward analysis', of the preceding chapters
also makes it possible to 'move forward', to trace the composite effects of
the basic motives and processes. Rationalization, which was motivated
by the income aspirations of small-scale producers and the growth
objectives of corporate technostructures as these agents were confronted
with claims for higher real wages, implied substantial physical capital
formation. The resulting rise in the ratio of physical capital to labour
(and output) was compatible with growing labour productivity: a rise in
the real value added per hour of paid work. Rationalization reduced the
need for operative labour in agriculture, the industrial sector and the
intermediary industries (to be more specific, in wholesale and retail
trade and transport). The contractive effect on employment by the

reduced need for operatives was mitigated by the concomitant increase in the need for technical and scientific workers in the commodity sector, and probably also the need for administrative and clerical personnel to handle the control routines of the mechanized, automated and redesigned work processes. Rationalization, and the ensuing productivity increase, was also a major cause of the rising rate of self-employment in agriculture. Farmers became less dependent on employees, i.e. hired farm workers.

The (on the whole successful) attempts of large firms to expand real sales entailed growing output and employment not only of corporations, but also of the competitive commodity sub-sector, part of which was dominated by large firms. The increased sales of the commodity sector as a whole implied growing private consumption expenditure, mitigating to some extent the contractive effect of rationalization on employment, partly because of the sheer increase in the volume of provided consumption goods, partly because of the ensuing investments of firms in expanded production capacity. The growing private consumption of households implied transfers of work to the commodity sector.

The output expansion of the commodity sector added to the demand for labour in the industrial sector and the intermediate industries, particularly banking, insurance, real estate and business services, where labour-saving devices seemed less feasible or urgent. In manufacturing and other parts of the industrial sector there was a tendency over time for the negative effect of rationalization to outweigh the positive effect of increased output on employment. Employment growth, which characterized the industrial sector at the beginning of the period, was succeeded by employment stagnation and decline. The gradually decreasing and countervailing effect of rationalization and increased productivity can also be registered in the development of operative labour outside agriculture. The number of production process workers declined, as did also (in most countries) the number of sales and transport workers.

The increased availability of durables helped households serve themselves instead of relying on the market for personal services; it thus affected both the demand for private services and private service employment. The growing expenditure on consumer durables supported the manufacturing industries and the intermediary industries; by enhancing the commodity demand as a whole, they presumably had a net positive effect on private sector employment. The most important household appliance was the private car, which opened up new activity patterns and changed use of time. Household use of private cars affected the demand for paid personal transport services but at the same time enhanced a host of private and public sector activities.

The growth processes and growth aspirations of the public sector, which could be realized through growing output and employment in the commodity sector, were manifested in national account statistics as growing public consumption expenditure. Public sector growth also entailed substantial physical capital formation, and added therefore to the demand for industrial commodities and labour force in the private sector. Expanding public consumption, which to some extent meant transfers of work from households, carried with it growing employment in public industries and an increasing number of persons engaged in medical and social care, teaching and entertainment. It also brought growing numbers of administrative and clerical workers, although the growth of these occupational groups mainly reflected the larger organizational scale of the commodity sector operations. Larger organizations mainly resulted from company mergers and acquisitions.

The economic growth and accompanying restructuring of the working population implied the redistribution and changing use of spending power, i.e. the capacity to command economic resources by means of the market. In connection with the rationalization of the firms and the commodity sector's increased productivity, earlier chapters touched upon the transfer of spending capacity from firms to their employees, the rising real wages of the labour force. The rising hourly compensation of the labour force brought declining profitability, although not necessarily declining gross profits as the growing real wages of the labour force were used for private consumption purposes (or for public consumption which carried increased demand for private sector goods and services). The rising hourly compensation of the employees were 'recycled' by the firms by means of their sales promotion measures and thus secured the capital accumulation of the firms. This was an important facet of the redistributional regime of the period studied, an order which affected the access to consumer goods of large segments of the population as well as the growth opportunities of firms.

Spending power was at the same time transferred from the commodity sector to the public sector, or rather from the employees of the private sector to the state. Governments could appropriate a growing share of household incomes and, due to the growing commodity provision, finance a growing public sector which enhanced both private sector output and employment. In the late 1970s many governments experienced difficulties in financing further public sector growth. The most critical factor was the balance of payments problem most countries encountered because of their deteriorating terms of trade with oil-exporting countries (and less rapidly growing exports to the United States). It was no longer possible to expand aggregate demand by means of traditional policy measures. The external constraints to such remedies gave way to a reconsideration of the responsibility of the state, for example, the 'privatization' of public health and welfare services.

The causal analysis has also emphasized the tendency of firms increasingly to invest in human knowledge capital, to engage scientific and technical workers who can co-ordinate, control and even execute operative work (if it is automated). This tendency witnessed the recurrent adaptation of the production system to the rising wages of operative labour. It was compatible with increased productivity in both physical and economic terms as well as the declining physical capital formation in the commodity sector. The 'material' content of the rationalization process was lessened, the knowledge content was increased. The firms could raise their productivity with smaller investment in physical production facilities, and larger spending on a professionally trained labour force. The changing use of the investment power of firms also had redistributional implications for the labour force. It promoted the growth of technical and scientific workers, and lessened the need for operative workers.

The redistribution of income, and the changes in the redistributional regimes of the economies witnessed the political and labour market achievements of the working class and the improved conditions of the class of essentially operative workers. Among the main factors in the economic change in Western Europe in the three decades of the post-war period, one should probably emphasize *the political mobilization of the working class*, as it was that factor which, in the specific geopolitical situation of the Western European countries, brought mass consumption, rationalization, increased welfare state spending, and substantial physical capital formation.

Economic growth in the pre-1973 period was furthered by the United States through aid, demand for European exports, and direct investment. In the post-1973 period exports to the United States lost some momentum due to the depreciation of the dollar. On the other hand, exports of capital goods to Third World countries contributed to the sustainment of growth processes in this sub-period.

7 Tendencies in the 1980s

Introduction

The previous chapters have accounted for economic change in the thirty-year period 1950–80. This final chapter deals with more recent tendencies in Western European economies. It concentrates on factors which conditioned capital accumulation and private sector growth in the 1980s. The economic performance of Western European countries is related to developments in other parts of the world. Views of some other writers concerning recent economic change in industrial countries are presented. The chapter first considers the evolution of consumer demand. Has mass consumption, which was the backbone of economic growth during most of the post-war period, been curbed in the 1980s? The question will bring a short discussion of the thesis of social (and timely) limits to economic growth and the possibility of deficient consumer demand as a restraint to economic growth and capital accumulation. The latter issue is considered in connection with the alleged 'crisis of Fordism', the thesis presented by members of the French 'regulation school'. A closely related theme is the global shift in the location of industries supplying consumer durables, notably the rise of Japan as the creator and exploiter of popular style in the 1980s. It is assumed that Western European economies have suffered from a leakage of effective demand for consumer goods, caused by inroads made by Japanese (and other East Asian) producers into the home and traditional export markets of European firms. Some comments will then be made on what has been termed 'the second industrial divide'; i.e. customization and flexible specialization allowing for highly efficient small-scale production of sophisticated industrial goods. Does this paradigm offer Western Europe a solution to the problem of increased competition from non-European producers? The rise of Japan as the world's leading supplier of sophisticated durables illustrates how capital accumulation in Western Europe is conditioned by political, economic and social developments in other parts of the world. Another case in point is offered by the debt crisis of Third World countries, which impinges upon the ability of developing countries to import machinery and other investment goods from Western Europe. A further illustration of external conditioning is provided by the changing economic inter-course of Western Europe with the United States, in fact the dependency of the Western European economies on the policies of the United States. These external influences are highlighted.

A further set of questions relates to productivity growth and the capacity of firms to invest: how have manufacturing productivity, labour costs and gross profits in the manufacturing industry evolved in the 1980s? After a short account of the recent performance of the public sector, and the ideological shifts of governments concerning public service commitments, the situation of Western European economies is summarized with reference to physical capital formation, the kind of aggregate expenditure which was of paramount importance for variations in economic growth rates in the period 1950–80 (and which still is the crucial factor of growth).

The third part of the chapter addresses the question of a possible return to substantial and enduring physical capital formation expenditure and strong economic growth. Are there any conditions in the imaginable future which could induce large investments in physical production facilities, strong growth and reduced unemployment? The question is raised with reference to the idea of 'long waves' in the development of industrial capitalism. After a presentation of views of some leading long-wave theorists, this section concentrates on the apparent propensity of large commodity providers in the 1980s to postpone physical investment and instead engage in financial investment. A scenario where substantial physical capital formation and higher rates of economic growth could be instigated is presented: reduced real interest rates within the framework of an enlarged, widened and deepened European Community. Finally, the chapter sketches the post-1980s development of the working population: for which groups of industries and occupations can employment growth be reckoned? Which groups have declined? The chapter ends with some remarks concerning future productivity growth, which will be a crucial factor in any restructuring of the working population.

A Curb on Mass Consumption?

The post-war period brought, as has been emphasized in earlier chapters, mass consumption and mass production of standardized household goods, items for everyday use provided for in the long run predominantly by large firms. New and modified consumption goods were available to substantial segments of the population as part of the private sector productivity gains were captured by the households in the form of lower relative prices and higher wages. Sophisticated sales promotion and large-scale marketing schemes secured economies of scale not only in the production of the commodities but also in their distribution. Mass consumption allowed firms to rationalize their diverse activities at the same time as they were able to regain a substantial share of the rising labour costs through increased sales. In other words, the employees of the firms providing consumer goods were to a large extent buyers of consumer goods. Through their willingness to spend their earnings on commodities in the production of which they had taken some part, they created the effective demand which was a requirement for capital accumulation of both large and small producers in the private sector.

In the vein of thought of Fred Hirsch, one could possibly argue that there are inherent *social* constraints to further growth of mass consumption: The 'satisfaction' that individuals derive from certain types of goods, such as a car or a country cottage, depends (under the regime of mass consumption) on not only their own use of the good, but on the use of similar goods by other people as well; growing and extending consumption incurs disutility on all users as the conditions of use deteriorate because of the increased number of these goods in use.[1] To the extent that this disutility curbs consumer demand, it also imposes obstacles to the growth of firms providing consumer goods.

It could also be maintained that built-in constraints to growing mass consumption are implied in the observation of Linder: as people engage in the use of various consumer goods they also allocate, in effect, their disposable time;[2] as the consumption of some types of goods restricts the scope for consumption of other goods, there are limits—because time is finite—to increased satisfaction. If marginal satisfaction declines, people become less motivated to consume.

The reasoning of Hirsch and Linder concerning the welfare effects of increased consumption seems reasonable, but do these limits to the increased satisfaction of individual consumers impose constraints on the effective demand for consumer goods? And have such limits been experienced, as yet, in the actual development of private consumption expenditure?

Although there certainly are limits to the satisfaction, or welfare, that individuals get from increased consumption, doubts can be raised as to such limits constraining the aggregate consumption expenditure and the mass of commodities to be provided. One reason is that people are often forced to bear the burden of other people's consumption. Mass consumption may very well create disutilities, and even mass frustration, but most people would be even worse off if they refrained from using the goods. (This necessity to consume is implied in what Hirsch called 'tip-toeing'.) Another reason is substitution for 'obsolescence' in the wide sense of the word: people acquire better and more up-to-date makes of consumer goods when such are offered by the producers and their own incomes grow. A third reason is that disutilities arising in the consumption of some types of commodity do not impede consumption of other types of commodity which satisfy other wants and needs. Producers often help people discover new wants and needs as incomes grow. One should also reckon with an ability of firms to develop commodities which do not suffer from the shortcomings described by Hirsch, consumer goods to be used almost in privacy (such as the Walkman recorder, the personal home computer and video equipment). The limits to welfare growth described by Hirsch and Linder do not necessarily mean limits to mass consumption and large-scale provision of consumer goods (though such limits may force producers to develop new types of commodity).

National accounts statistics compiled by the OECD show that household spending for private consumption purposes lost momentum in the 1970s; but the growth rates of consumption expenditure rose in the first half of the 1980s (according to OECD, *National Accounts 1974–1986*). This resurgence makes it difficult to argue convincingly that diminishing marginal satisfaction, or even the constraints of time, have as yet acted as a brake on mass consumption in Western Europe. To the extent that private consumption expenditure stagnates or declines, one has to look for other reasons for the fall in demand.

The thesis of social limits to growth implies that people refrain from buying consumer goods because such commodities provide less marginal satisfaction. In the light of the high unemployment rates which characterized the post-1973 period and the first half of the 1980s, an equally plausible impediment to growth would be insufficient spending power: effective consumer demand stagnates because fewer people command the economic means to fulfil the rising social norms of private consumption. According to Aglietta and other members of the French 'regulation school', such a constraint amounts to a *crisis of Fordism*, the mode of accumulation which has shaped the development of the advanced capitalist countries in the post-war period.[3]

In the writings of Aglietta, Fordism denotes 'a series of transformations in the labour process closely linked to those changes in the conditions of the wage-earning class that give rise to the formation of a social consumption norm' and that tend to 'institutionalize class struggle in the form of collective bargaining'.[4] Historically, it marked 'a new stage in the regulation of capitalism, the regime of intensive accumulation': the capitalist class seeks overall management of the production of wage labour by connecting the relations of production to the commodity relations in which the wage-earners purchase their means of consumption.[5] The Fordist regime is thus the principle of linking the process of production to a mode of consumption.[6] By creating a norm of working-class consumption governed by individual ownership of commodities, in particular the *standardized owner-occupied housing* as the privileged site of individual consumption, and the *automobile* as the means of transport compatible with the separation of home and workplace, commodity providers were able to secure the continuity of the consumption process.[7] For a couple of decades after the Second World War, Fordism appeared to have definitely resolved the contradictions of capitalism and abolished its crisis. The 'consumer society' brought a relatively regular rise in real wages, made possible by a continuing fall in real social wage costs, a fall which also meant a rise in the rate of surplus value.

The crisis of Fordism is first of all the crisis of a mode of labour organization: the semi-automatic assembly line. But, according to Aglietta, it extends to the sum total of production and exchange relations and upsets the entire regime of intensive accumulation. The development of the department producing means of production is barred when further mechanization does not generate sufficient savings in direct labour time to compensate for the increase in the organic composition of capital, i.e. the curtailment of the mass of wages which follows when machinery is substituted for labour and the increased productive capacity is not matched by increased capacity to consume. Profits decline and further capital accumulation is hampered. As producers try to get out of this impasse by means of automation, they save direct living labour, but only at the cost of extending and pushing to its limits the form of work organization and the working-class consumption norm. The result is on one hand growing job insecurity, conflict and confrontation challenging work disciplines and, on the other hand, a contraction of the demand for the kinds of commodities which are the very foundation of the mass consumption society: a falling proportion of people in younger age groups are able to buy their own homes; new automobile sales stagnate or even decline. The disproportion between investment goods industries and consumption goods industries could only be temporarily offset through higher wages paid by large corporations relying on economies of scale in mass production.

Also contributing to the crisis of the Fordist regime is its inherent and growing demand for 'collective consumption'. The dramatic rise in the costs of such consumption counteracts the general tendency towards a rise in the rate of surplus value to the extent that it eventually cancels its long-term growth trend. Whether the rising social costs of growth are levied on the incomes of the wage-earners, or on profits, they become an obstacle to capital accumulation, and hence also to the further growth of mass consumption.

It is not possible to find empirical evidence for deficient aggregate spending power as a constraint to mass consumption, but OECD statistics show that it cannot be ruled out that consumer demand stagnated because of stagnating consumption capacity. The growth rates of the 'gross spending power' of all employees in real terms, operationally defined as the percentage of annual changes in total employee compensation adjusted for changes in the weighted average level of consumer goods prices, declined substantially between the beginning of the 1970s and the mid-1980s.[8] For some countries the rates were negative in the early 1980s; the aggregate spending power of employees also seemed to contract in absolute terms. The apparently crumbling spending power of the mass of employees suggests that the suppression of the growth rates of private final consumption expenditure reflects to some extent an inability of certain segments of the population to comply with the established and rapidly changing consumption norms. As evidenced by the OECD (in *Main Economic Indicators* Jan. 1982–Jan. 1987), unemployment rates continued to climb in the first half of the 1980s. In Belgium, France, Italy, the Netherlands and Britain, a tenth of the labour force was registered as unemployed in 1985.

In other words, it can be supposed that high unemployment rates affected the sales potential of the firms. But why did the growth rates of spending power tend to climb in the 1980s, in spite of remaining high rates of unemployment? It is tempting to raise the idea of a more marked dualism in the income development of the population, the emergence of what has been called a 'two-thirds/one-third society'. People who are in full and regular employment, as most of the working population are, benefit from high and rising incomes. As the incomes of these persons rise over time they compensate for the loss of aggregate income caused by the steeply rising unemployment in the 1970s. But an equally plausible cause of the upturn in growth rates of both private consumption expenditure and the spending power of households in the 1980s may be the surge of Western European exports to the United States (which will be dealt with below). As growing exports boost aggregate household incomes, it is no mystery that the growth rate of people's spending power rose in the mid-1980s.

The hypothesis of insufficient spending power, caused by high rates of unemployment, echoes the old (Marxian as well as Keynesian) idea of an 'under-consumption crisis' of industrial capitalism: there is

a tendency for the growth of demand to lag behind the growth of surplus value unless new sources of aggregate demand can be created (e.g. through increases in government spending, increases in foreign markets, increases in consumer credit, and in the rate of accumulation itself). In the absence of such new sources of demand, part of the surplus value will remain unrealized.[9]

A circumstance supporting such interpretations is that some sources of aggregate demand which guaranteed a high rate of employment for most of the post-war period have contracted since the mid-1970s, as governments curtailed public spending for investment purposes and applied tight monetary policies. Underconsumption was caused by (imposed) policy priorities. This means that the stagnation of the effective demand for consumer goods should be related to the inner and outer constraints on governments rather than to some inevitable logic of capitalist capital accumulation.

Unlike what is implicit in 'the crisis of Fordism' thesis, this study does not contend that the actual development of private consumption can be used as a proof of the inner destructive logic of industrial capitalism. The future development of private consumption demand will be dependent on many factors, but mainly on the propensity of commodity providers to make investment in physical and knowledge capital as a response to the pull of demand (which is, indeed, a very traditional Keynesian interpretation). The constraints on further growth of mass consumption are mainly economic policy constraints imposed on governments for one of a combination of reasons (ideology, balance of payments consider-ations, etc.).

The 1970s brought declining savings as a proportion of total personal incomes. The decline continued in the 1980s. In Britain (as shown by data compiled by the OECD) savings as a percentage of total incomes of households and unincorporated enterprises were more than halved between 1980 and 1986. In Sweden, where the percentage was earlier very low, household savings turned negative in the middle of the decade. The tendency probably reflects not only high rates of unemploy-ment, but also the extravagant spending of households (not affected by unemployment). The thesis of a growing dualism in the development of household incomes and spending behaviour is vindicated by reports of increasing consumer credit sales in many Western European countries. The income limits of private consumption were stretched by means of borrowing.[10]

International Relocation of Mass Consumption Industries

Another factor conditioning capital accumulation of Western European producers in the 1980s is the evident relocation of industries providing commodities for mass consumption, particularly the emergence of Japan as a leading producer of sophisticated durables, not to mention machinery and other capital equipment. Chapter 2 has already touched upon this shift in the gravity of the global industrial system which over a couple of decades has made the countries of Western Europe large importers of Japanese passenger cars and motorcyles, musical instru-ments, radios, televisions and tape recorders, electronic data-processing equipment, cameras and watches, as well as industrial robots and advanced machinery for factory and office use.[11] In recent years Hong Kong, Taiwan, South Korea and Singapore have followed the Japanese lead into the European markets, making the Europeans net importers in product areas where they could earlier benefit from comparative advantages (e.g. cars and electronic household goods).[12]

The changing trade relationships between Western Europe and Japan are illustrated in Table 7:1. The value of total Japanese exports to Europe already exceeded European exports to Japan in the mid-1950s. As indicated by the export quotients of the table (showing European export value divided by the value of Japanese exports to Europe) the imbalance increased in the 1960s and 1970s. As for *manufactured goods excluding iron and steel and non-ferrous metals*, the value of Western European exports to Japan was, by 1980, a mere third of the value of exports in the opposite direction; as for *machinery and transport equipment* (where Japan was a net importer from Europe in the 1950s) Western European exports to Japan were equivalent to no more than a fifth of Japan's exports to Europe. In the first half of the 1980s the asymmetry prevailed, although Western European exports seem to have kept pace with imports.

The infiltration of Japanese producers into the home markets of European firms (and their traditional markets abroad) no doubt represents a leakage of effective demand which afflicts the economic growth potential of many Western European countries. As European production for domestic or foreign markets is supplanted by non-European production, the countries experience an inverse import-replacement process.

Table 7.1   Exports from Western Europe to Japan (A)
Exports from Japan to Western Europe (B)

($m, f.o.b.)

| | Total merchandise export | | | |
	1955	1970	1980	1985
A	160	1,680	8,220	9,830
B	200	2,910	21,460	24,930
A:B	0.82	0.58	0.38	0.39

Manufactured goods excluding iron and steel, non-ferrous metals and machinery and transport equipment – SITC (6+8)-(67+68)

	1955	1970	1980	1985
A	20	420	2,330	2,700
B	60	730	6,800	7,600
A:B	0.39	0.57	0.34	0.36

| | Machinery and transport equipment | | | |
	1955	1970	1980	1985
A	40	600	2,300	3,070
B	20	1,310	11,890	15,340
A:B	1.61	0.45	0.19	0.20

Sources: UNCTAD, *Handbook of International Trade and Development Statistics 1983, 1985* and *1987*.

What makes a structural adjustment of European manufacturing industries particularly cumbersome is maybe not the allegedly superior efficiency of many Japanese firms compared to their European competitors, but the current Japanese 'monopoly of the exploration of popular style, the icons of the technological age', to quote a report on Japan published by the *Guardian Weekly* (27 December 1987). A reversal of 'the inverse import-replacement process' requires that European producers develop and launch products which help consumers in high-income countries discover new wants and needs (or new ways of satisfying wants and needs), as the Japanese have done in the field of household electronic goods; that they catch up with the high-quality standards of Japanese goods, and that they apply methods of production and marketing developed by leading Japanese firms. The ability of Western European producers to attain (or regain) leading positions in (at least some segments of) the popular and rapidly changing consumer goods markets will no doubt be dependent on proper industrial policies— daring and sagacious government initiatives which, if not formally discriminating against foreign producers, offer Western European firms comparative advantages in production and ancillary functions (such as research and development). Such policies cannot be restricted to particular countries; they need to be developed for Western Europe as a whole.

Flexible Specialization and Customization

It has been maintained that the industrially advanced countries should abandon their attachment to mass production and instead create the necessary conditions for *flexible specialization* and (which has been regarded as its corollary) *customization*. This refers to the use of new, highly adaptive technology for cheap and small-scale provision of sophisticated products satisfying particular buyer needs, the adjustment of products to specifications made by the customers. They should thus leave the market for mass-produced goods to the industrializing countries of the Third World.[13]

Flexible specialization *and* customization, which according to Piore and Sabel represent a *New Industrial Divide* comparable to the nineteenth-century watershed between machinery-aided craft production and skill-substituting 'machinofacture', are presented as offering more than simply a remedy to the manufacturing decline that many industrial countries have experienced in recent decades. In particular, these new options provide opportunities for small firms to capture worldwide markets for special-purpose goods. By exploiting the new possibilities for rationally organized, automated and customized production, small-scale firms are able to increase their relative weight in the commodity sector. Flexible specialization and customization make small firms less dependent on large corporations (as the new technology enables them to enter the markets for consumer goods and not just markets for subcontracted manufacturing services).[14]

It seems reasonable to assume that new devices for the control of production work have paved the way for flexible specialization, and that many European firms have responded positively to the new cybernetic technology, adopting it in both new and traditional product lines as a means of lowering costs and adjusting quickly to changing market requirements. But one should not expect that producers in other parts of the world are excluded from the use of the same technology. According to the study of Piore and Sabel, Japanese firms are among the most flexible producers of the world and there is no reason to think that some of the new industrial countries of the Third World are unable to adopt the new techniques and modes of organizing industrial work, although the incentives to do so are supposedly weaker because of low wages (unless the First World countries rely increasingly on protectionism). Flexible specialization does not offer a patent solution to European manufacturers experiencing market losses to firms in other parts of the world.

Nor is it evident that the new technology represents a threat to large corporations, which appears to be a tenet of Piore and Sabel. The new production facilities can be acquired in small lumps and at low costs, and are hence within the reach of many small firms. But large firms may also make use of the new technology in order to supply a more varied range of products and models. If there really is a tendency for flexible specialization to appear more often in small and medium-sized firms, then the new technology opens up a new scope for subcontracting. Corporations may delegate some or most of their manufacturing operations to smaller firms and concentrate on research and development, marketing, sales and physical distribution where economies of scale will still be existent.

Customization, which means that products are made *after* the specification of the buyer's needs, seems to require proximity to the customer. European producers should thus benefit from locational advantages when satisfying the specified needs of European buyers. Yet, even if customization could benefit European producers one should not take for granted that it will displace provision of pre-formed products. Many consumer durables and other kinds of manufactured goods are nowadays diversified rather than standardized, albeit provided in large runs. Large-scale production of a wide range of products and models has been allowed for by market extension (i.e. lower transport costs, trade liberalization policies and worldwide market scanning by producers). In other words, the notion of mass production needs some qualification. It connotes standardization of commodities produced.

However, it does not specify whether the standardized commodities are malleable *materials* (such as plastics and steel) entering a wide range of industrial products (which are more or less standardized or diversified or even customized); or if they are pre-made *components* entering standardized or non-standardized products; or *end products* for consumption or production purposes. Piore and Sabel seem to have standardized end products in mind when distinguishing mass production from customized production. It should be observed that many kinds of end products for producer or consumer use are nowadays highly diversified, but generally they contain standardized materials and components produced in large chunks. The production of diversified end products entails mass production and standardization in earlier stages of the production process. Diversification of a wide range of pre-formed end products (offered by competing producers and countries) substitutes for customization (which has never been a viable alternative outside the capital goods industries). A high degree of diversification characterizes, in effect, Japanese industries catering for world markets. A requirement for diversification has been access to standardized inputs.

The Debt Crisis of the Developing Countries of the Third World

A constraint to capital accumulation in the 1980s which stemmed from conditions outside Western Europe was the debt crisis of the industrializing countries of the Third World, as it impinged on the ability of European producers to export investment goods and other manufactures.

The post-1973 period saw a big increase in capital flow to the developing countries. The outstanding aggregate debt of these countries expanded more than tenfold between 1970 and 1985 (despite a decline in flows since 1981).[15] The most conspicuous feature of this growth was greatly expanded commercial bank lending. The surge of commercial bank lending to developing countries has been described as a consequence of the 1973 rise in oil prices and declining real interest rates (due to inflation).

Higher oil prices transferred income from moderate and low savers [industrial and developing countries] to [at that time] high-saving oil exporters. The resulting excess supply of world savings put downward pressures on world output and interest rates. In real terms, interest rates turned negative for several years.[16]

The OPEC surpluses were in subsequent years recycled to developing countries via commercial banks, largely as a result of the OPEC countries' reliance on the Eurocurrency market for deployment of their trade-balance surpluses.[17]

The oil exporters and the commercial banks of the First World thus financed the investment programmes of the developing countries and allowed these countries to maintain, or even raise, their GDP growth rates and imports from the industrial countries. Without this industrial and economic growth of Third World countries, concludes the World Bank, the recession in the industrial world would have been much deeper in the 1970s. But with their expanded debt, and with a much higher proportion of it carrying floating interest rates, the borrowing countries became more exposed to the policies of the industrial countries.

This was made clear in the early 1980s when the industrial countries went into a deep recession coupled with stark inflation. As large budget deficits ruled out the option of escaping the recession by means of fiscal stimulus, many governments saw no alternative to a tight monetary policy. This implied high interest rates (to match the high rates of inflation). The soaring interest rates had major implications for developing countries with a large share of their debt at floating rates, or who were in need of refinancing. The rise in prices in 1979–80 failed to stop the increase in real interest rates. OPEC surpluses were short-lived, and the monetary restraint in the major industrial countries was much higher. 'Developing countries were thus having to pay higher interest rates on their external debt at the same time as demand was falling in their main export markets'.[18] Reasons why the history of the 1970s did not repeat itself in the 1980s were, according to Tew, first and foremost that commercial banks, in contrast to 1974, 'were not starting with a clean sheet but were already heavily lent, if not overlent, to the developing countries'.[19]

The debt service ability of the developing countries has deteriorated markedly since the beginning of the 1970s. The ratio of their foreign debt to the gross national product has more than doubled, from 14 per cent in 1970 to 36 per cent in 1985. The debt service ratio to exports rose from less than 15 per cent in 1970 to more than 21 per cent in 1985 (and 22 per cent in 1986).[20] Interest rate payments on debt increased in relation to the GNP and added heavily to the balance of payments deficits in developing countries. Debt servicing difficulties have necessitated many reschedulings.

In the mid-1980s, economic recovery in the industrial world helped ease some of the liquidity pressures. Real interest rates softened somewhat but remained at high levels as the industrial countries continued to run large budget deficits. A circumstance of vital importance to the indebted countries was mounting protectionism in developed countries, which made it difficult for them to service their debts by exporting more goods and services than they import. 'The debt crisis,' summarizes the UNIDO *Global Report* of 1986, 'illustrates not so much the excess flow of capital to developing countries as the stringent terms attached to the debt'.[21] It distorted the economy of the debtor countries and forced them to cut back on imports, reduce expenditure on poverty relief and delay improvements to the social infrastructure. An exportable surplus was squeezed from their income by means of fiscal measures which had their greatest impact on the poor. The debt crisis required a reduction of subsidies and public services available at subsidized prices. International agencies often made rescheduling conditional on the introduction of austerity programmes, which depressed the rate of economic growth in debtor countries. In the end, they restricted the export opportunities of the industrial countries.

Although many developing countries have captured markets for their consumer goods industries in the industrially advanced countries since the beginning of the 1960s, it is unlikely that imports from the Third World countries *en bloc* represent a major threat to capital accumulation and economic growth in Western Europe—unless protectionist measures in the First World invoke retaliation on the part of the Third World industrializers (which is less likely, as the latter have little to gain from a trade war).

As shown in Table 7.2, while total exports of developing (OPEC and non-OPEC) countries to Western Europe tended to grow faster than European exports to such countries in the 1950s, 1960s and (particularly) the 1970s, an opposite tendency seems to characterize the 1980s. In 1985 (as in most years in the first half of the decade) the value of the total European merchandise exports exceeded the value of developing countries' exports to Europe. As the latter declined more than the former, the quotient of Western European merchandise trade with developing countries rose between 1980 and 1985. The rise in the quotient was supposedly mainly due to declining prices of oil (and other primary commodities), which reduced not only the relative weight of these commodities in the total export value but also the ability of Third World countries to import goods from industrial countries. Another possible explanation is increased protectionism in Western European countries. In the second half of the 1970s, many industrial countries stepped up their restrictions on imports from developing countries, sometimes by increasing tariffs, but more often through import quotas or 'voluntary' agreements to restrain exports. They also used restrictive 'quality' requirements and health regulations to achieve protectionist ends. Subsidies on capital goods exports benefited developing countries buying such goods, but harmed those who were competing with industrial countries in the capital goods market.[22]

Despite increased barriers to imports from developing countries in the 1980s, the quotient of Western European exports to these countries declined for some commodity groups, such as *manufactured goods excluding iron and steel and non-ferrous metals* and *machinery and transport equipment* (see Table 7:2). In the case of the former commodity group, exports from Western Europe declined more than exports to Europe;

Table 7.2 Exports from Western Europe to developing countries (A)
Exports from developing countries to Western Europe (B)
($m, f.o.b.)

Total merchandise trade

	1955	1970	1980	1985
A	9,000	18,740	140,790	117,290
B	9,540	21,610	188,230	110,900
A:B	0.94	0.87	0.75	1.06

Manufactured goods excluding iron and steel, non-ferrous metals and machinery and transport equipment — SITC (6+8)-(67+68)

	1955	1970	1980	1985
A	2,590	4,060	30,020	25,710
B	320	1,560	18,350	16,300
A:B	8.07	2.61	1.64	1.58

Machinery and transport equipment

	1955	1970	1980	1985
A	2,860	8,480	61,810	48,770
B	20	170	4,440	8,240
A:B	143.00	50.47	13.91	5.92

Sources: UNCTAD, *Handbook of International Trade and Development Statistics 1983, 1985* and *1987.*

in the case of machinery and transport equipment, the current value of exports from Western Europe declined, while there was an increase in the value of exports from developing countries to Western Europe.

Although many Third World countries are forced to run large export surpluses in order to service their debts, and must therefore be competitive in the markets of the First World, it can be supposed that their continued industrialization creates more sales opportunities for European firms than are supplanted by their consumer goods exports. As emphasized by many writers, the present protectionist measures of the First World create more difficulties than they help resolve. By adding to the debt burden of the industrializing countries, they deal blows to these countries as buyers of capital equipment and technology.[23] The issue of European protectionism will be addressed in a wider context below.

It should be observed that Third World countries, as a consequence of their industrialization, have become less dependent on industrialized countries for capital equipment. As demonstrated by Table 7:3, the share of the total export value of exports of machinery and other equipment to developing countries from other developing countries has increased substantially since the mid-1950s. Although the share had not amounted to more than 12 per cent in 1985, it means a deflection of the non-European demand for European products which, if it continues, will afflict core industries in Western Europe. The tendency of developing countries increasingly to import capital equipment from other Third World countries emphasizes the need to ease the burden of the most debt-ridden industrializers (or to find alternative solutions to the stagnated demand for investment goods supplied by Western European firms).

Table 7.3   Total exports of machinery and transport equipment to developing (OPEC and non-OPEC) countries (A)
Of which exports originating from developing countries (B)
($m, f.o.b.)

	1955	1970	1980	1985
A	5,390	19,280	147,730	135,400
B	90	630	12,470	15,900
B:A (%)	1.7	3.3	8.4	11.7

Sources: UNCTAD, *Handbook of International Trade and Development Statistics 1983, 1985* and *1987.*

The Altered Role of the United States

Economic history since the late 1940s has offered ample evidence of Western Europe's dependence on the United States, and the changing relationship between these regions merits particular consideration in any attempt to assess the current and future growth opportunities of the Western European countries. The economic performance and policies of the United States have conditioned, and will condition, the development of European economies (unless Western European countries are able to provide for self-sustained economic growth by means of deepened, widened and pan-European integration policies).

The United States emerged from the war as the dominant world economy. As its exports were in high demand, it could run a growing trade surplus with other countries; it assumed the role of the major creditor country, an exporter of capital to a host of countries in both the First and Third World. The dollar was easily established as the leading international currency.[24]

At that time, it was evident that the productive capacity of the war-stricken countries could only be rebuilt through a rapid inflow of US capital equipment. The problem was usually described as 'dollar shortage', diagnosed as an inability of the weakened countries to trade with the United States as equal partners. It coincided with the inception of the Cold War and American concern for the political stability of the Western world. Faced with a worldwide challenge to political and economic freedom, the government of the United States embarked on a vast programme of economic assistance combined with military aid. The programme, later known as the Marshall Plan, provided substantial aid which helped Western Europe to recover. The United States simultaneously expanded its defence spending in Western Europe (and other parts of the world). It encouraged an outflow of dollars. In addition to foreign aid and military expenditure, it allowed, and even encouraged, protectionism and discrimination against the dollar in its client countries; the leverage of the Marshall Plan was used to encourage devaluation of many foreign currencies.[25] Such measures combined to create a deficit in the US balance of payments (in spite of a trading surplus), which increased the liquidity of the international economy.

The ending of Marshall aid did not put an end to the flow of capital to Western Europe. From the mid-1950s, US venture capital poured into Western European countries attracted by profit opportunities offered by the abolition of tariffs and more far-reaching economic integration policies. The prospects of a huge, expanding and harmonized market for American goods and services worked as an incentive for US banks and corporations to establish subsidiaries in Western Europe. These direct investments (taking place within large firms) contributed to the striking deterioration of the US balance of payments with the rest of the world, although they alleviated the current account to the extent that the profits from these investments were repatriated to the United States.

It has been held that the capital outflow and the commitments to military spending resulted in a gradual deterioration in US international competitiveness.[26] Whether or not this argument is true, the capital outflow and large defence expenditure abroad produced a striking change in the situation of the United States *vis-à-vis* the other countries of the First World; while the dollar shortage had been a key characteristic of the early post-war period, the 1960s saw the emergence of a 'dollar over-hang', an excess of American liabilities over its domestic foreign exchange reserves.[27]

In the early 1960s it was made clear that while the dollar deficit had been of essential importance for the recovery and growth of the rest of the international economic system, it would in the long run undermine the economic strength of the United States. The value of the dollar relative to other currencies depended on the viability of US productive capacity and the policies of US governments. In 1971 the trade surplus had moved into a deficit and the American government was forced to announce that the United States would no longer convert dollars into gold on request; that it could not guarantee the value of the dollar relative to other currencies; and that it was forced to introduce restrictions on imports until the deficit was brought under control. The measures signalled, if not the end of an era of American economic hegemony, a significant change in the international monetary system. They soon gave rise to a series of devaluations of the dollar against the currencies of the major Western countries. When, in mid-1973, the dollar had been devalued against the stronger currencies by about 17.5 per cent, central banks had to accept that they could no longer guarantee stable exchange rates (which had been one of the main principles of the Bretton Woods agreements alongside dollar–gold convertibility). The 'adjustable peg' system gave way to 'managed floating', which gave more room for the authorities to deal with pressures on the economy of their country (albeit at the cost of increased instability of the international monetary system).

The late 1970s initiated an era of tight monetary policies, in which high interest rates were used to curb inflation, intensify competition and impose a restructuring of the production system. The US balance of payments moved back into surplus (as the high rates of interest attracted many foreign lenders) and the fall of the dollar was halted. The tight monetary policy was maintained in the 1980s, but the administration was forced to engage in large public borrowing to finance its increased military spending. The public sector deficit worked as a stimulus to the US economy. The unemployment rate began to fall and output to rise.[28] The combination of a large public sector deficit and high interest rates (to secure the necessary public borrowing) attracted large amounts of foreign money to the United States in the 1980s, at the same time as it pushed up interest rates elsewhere. The high interest rates in the United States (and the ensuing high demand for American securities) led to an appreciation of the dollar which reduced the competitiveness of US manufacturing industry. A trade deficit resulted, which was large even by American standards.

By keeping US interest rates high, it was possible for some time to create a demand for the dollar which appreciated its value compared to other currencies, at the same time as the inflow of foreign currencies was secured. Policies affecting the capital account were used as a remedy for the deficiencies of the current account. The value of the dollar compared to the currencies of other major industrial countries peaked at the beginning of 1985; later its value declined, partly as a result of an international agreement as to its overvaluation by the Group of the Five leading industrial countries.

The dollar depreciation in the 1970s, which followed a long period of almost stable (and partly undervalued) European currencies, curbed Western European exports to the United States. As it had a contracting effect on manufacturing output and employment, it added to the economic stagnation of Western Europe in the 1970s. In the 1980s the policies of the United States implied an appreciation of the dollar against several European currencies. As US imports from Europe became cheaper, many Western European firms experienced a surge of exports to the United States. The soaring exports were of great importance to the economic recovery of Western European countries in the first half of the 1980s. The United States resumed for some time its old role as the growth locomotive of Western Europe.

The changing trade relationships between Western Europe and the United States are illustrated in Table 7:4. While prior to 1970 the value of Western European merchandise exports to the United States expanded faster than US exports to Europe, the latter tended to outgrow Western European exports in the 1970s (when the dollar was depreciated in relation to not only the Deutschmark, but also to such currencies as the Dutch guilder and the Belgian franc). The 1980s saw a surge of European exports to the United States while the value of US exports to Europe actually declined. For *manufactured goods excluding iron and steel and non-ferrous metals* the quotient of Western European exports to the United States rose from 1.13 to 3.08 between 1980 and 1985; for *machinery and transport equipment* the quotient increased from 0.80 to 1.30.

The changing role of the United States *vis-à-vis* Western Europe is also mirrored in current and capital account transactions with Europe. As revealed by data published in *Survey of Current Business*, the US balance of merchandise trade with Western Europe deteriorated gradually in the 1960s and went, in effect, into the red in 1972. It improved subsequently as the US dollar was depreciated compared to most European currencies. The 1980s brought, however, a dramatic change, caused by the instigation of a tight monetary policy and by dollar appreciation. While the United States could report a $20 billion surplus in its trade with Western Europe in 1980, the figures for 1986 showed a deficit of almost $30 billion. Although the incomes of US direct investors in Western Europe exceeded the incomes of Western European direct investors in the United States, the merchandise trade deficit combined with increased defence expenditure to produce a large current account deficit in the mid-1980s.

Since the mid-1960s, the United States has not only been the main overseas market of the Western European countries; it has also received substantial amounts of European capital. Although highly volatile, the flow of capital from Western Europe to the United States has increased

Table 7.4   Exports from Western Europe to the United States (A)
Exports from the United States to Western Europe (B)

($m, f.o.b.)

Total merchandise trade

	1955	1970	1980	1985
A	2,380	10,990	44,350	74,300
B	5,080	13,960	63,100	51,760
A:B	0.47	0.79	0.70	1.44

Manufactured goods excluding iron and steel and non-ferrous metals and machinery and transport equipment — SITC (6+8)-(67+68)

	1955	1970	1980	1985
A	900	3,560	10,600	18,650
B	260	1,710	9,380	6,060
A:B	3.50	2.08	1.13	3.08

Machinery and transport equipment

	1955	1970	1980	1985
A	340	4,150	19,020	31,950
B	740	5,190	23,810	24,480
A:B	0.45	0.80	0.80	1.30

Sources: UNCTAD, *Handbook of International Trade and Development Statistics 1983, 1985* and *1987*.

substantially since 1960. A growing part of the capital flow is due to direct investment by Western European firms in the United States. The outflow of capital funds from the United States to Western Europe has also increased (as measured in current dollars). In the 1980s there was, however, as in the late 1960s and early 1970s, a net outflow of funds from Western Europe to the United States.

The inflow of capital from Western European countries has alleviated the problem of the deteriorating current account balances. Due to capital inflows from Western Europe, and in spite of the mounting current account deficits, there was a growing net flow of funds from Western Europe to the United States. The United States could continue to import a large volume of goods from Western Europe.

The growing Western European exports to the United States in the 1980s, allowed for by the sanguine expansionist US policy and the overvalued dollar, had a strong impact on most Western European economies. They were probably the major cause of the resurgent growth of private consumption expenditure and the spending power of households, and they caused a surge of physical capital formation expenditure (see below). But because at the same time the US policies offered Western European investors opportunities for profitable financial investments and takeovers in the United States, while there were few incentives to make productive investments in Europe, the export opportunities diverted investable capital from Europe, money capital which could, under different conditions, have created an enhanced potential for production, marketing, sales and research and development in Europe. Some of the Western European takeovers of US firms can probably be seen as part of offensive market strategies: buying into America in order to strengthen the hold on the US market or acquire valuable technology and know-how (to be used in a later expansion at home or abroad).

Productivity, Labour Costs and Gross Profits

The preceding chapters have emphasized private sector productivity growth, the increased value added in real terms per hour of work derived from rationalization. Increased productivity restrained the rise in labour costs, and guaranteed some financial potential for investment. It was thus a main factor in private sector growth (and, in effect, the growth of the gross domestic product as a whole, since it provided the economic base for expanding public services). It was at the same time a major factor in the redistribution of economically active persons between industries and occupations, from the agricultural and industrial sector to intermediate industries and public services, from operative work to various kinds of service work (predominantly medical and social care, teaching and entertainment).

The development of the productivity growth rate in manufacturing is shown for twelve industrial countries in Table 7:5. All countries experienced slow-downs in the 1973–9 period compared to the period 1960–73. Seven countries report higher productivity growth rates for the years 1979–85 than for 1973–9, but the United States and the United Kingdom are the only two countries which increased their productivity growth enough in the first half of the 1980s to surpass their pre-1973 rates.

Productivity growth rates are not pure tokens of rationalization and technical change. Short-term variations reflect ups and downs in sales which are not matched by changes in the amount of employed labour. As the decline in productivity rates in 1973–9 compared to 1960–73 may be due to contracting demand not met by reductions of the labour force,

Table 7.5 Annual rate of change in manufacturing productivity: output per hour

	1960–73	*1973–9*	*1979–85*
Belgium	6.3	6.0	6.0
France	6.5	4.8	3.3
Germany	5.8	4.3	2.9
Italy	7.5	3.3	5.4
Netherlands	7.4	5.5	4.4
Sweden	6.4	2.8	3.5
United Kingdom	3.1	2.2	4.7
Denmark	6.4	4.2	1.8
Norway	4.3	2.1	2.6
Canada	4.5	2.1	2.7
United States	3.2	1.4	3.4
Japan	10.3	5.5	5.8

Source: 'International Comparisons of Manufacturing Productivity and Labor Costs', US Department of Labor, Bureau of Labor Statistics, *News* (July 1988)

one reason why rates were lower in the first half of the 1980s than in the 1960s may be slowly growing sales. In other words, modest productivity growth in the 1980s does not necessarily indicate a reduced scope for labour-force savings. It may equally reflect a reluctance (or inability) of employers to make short-term adjustments in their labour force. In the 1980s many manufacturers (particularly large corporations) were engaged in product lines where a large proportion of their employees represented not variable, but fixed, costs. Highly qualified personnel are not laid off in situations of slackening sales, as they embody the skill and knowledge potential of the firms. From the competitive point of view of the firm, they represent investment in human capital paid off only in an undefinable long-term future.

In the first half of the 1980s, labour costs did not rise as fast (in nominal values) as in the 1970s. As shown in Table 7:6, the annual growth rates of hourly compensation in manufacturing were, in all twelve countries, lower in 1979–85 than in 1973–9. For seven countries, hourly compensation growth rates were in the first half of the 1980s even lower than in the years 1960–73. As the reduced growth of hourly compensation combined with increased productivity in the first half of the 1980s, the growth rates of unit labour costs in manufacturing slowed down compared to the 1973–9 period (as shown in Table 7:7). For Belgium, Germany, the Netherlands and Japan, the growth rates of unit labour costs (at current values) were lower than in 1960–73; for Japan the rate turned negative in the first half of the 1980s.

Table 7.6 Annual rate of change in hourly compensation of employees in manufacturing

	1960–73	1973–9	1979–85
Belgium	11.0	14.0	7.8
France	10.0	16.1	13.0
Germany	10.3	9.5	6.0
Italy	13.5	20.6	17.2
Netherlands	12.9	11.6	5.1
Sweden	10.5	14.2	10.0
United Kingdom	9.2	19.4	10.9
Denmark	12.2	14.0	8.1
Norway	10.0	13.4	9.9
Canada	6.2	12.0	8.6
United States	5.0	9.5	6.9
Japan	15.1	12.8	4.9

Source: 'International Comparisons of Manufacturing Productivity and Labor Costs', US Department of Labor, Bureau of Labor Statistics, *News* (July 1988)

Table 7.7 Annual rate of change in unit labour costs in manufacturing

	1960–73	1973–9	1979–85
Belgium	3.8	7.5	1.7
France	3.3	10.8	9.4
Germany	4.3	4.9	3.0
Italy	5.6	16.7	11.1
Netherlands	5.2	5.8	0.7
Sweden	3.9	11.2	6.3
United Kingdom	4.8	18.0	6.0
Denmark	5.5	9.4	6.2
Norway	5.4	11.1	7.1
Canada	1.6	9.8	5.8
United States	1.8	8.0	3.3
Japan	4.3	6.9	0.8

Source: 'International Comparisons of Manufacturing Productivity and Labor Costs', US Department of Labor, Bureau of Labor Statistics, *News* (July 1988)

The low rates of manufacturing productivity growth in the second half of the 1970s compared to the 1960s are compatible with the interpretation of the crisis of Fordism offered by Lipietz: capital accumulation presupposes profitability of investments but

capital can only remain profitable on two conditions: unless increased productivity of the producer goods sector offsets the rising technical composition of capital [i.e. increasing volume of fixed capital per worker], the proportion of immobilized assets will become dangerously high; and unless increased productivity in the consumer goods sector balances the rise in mass purchasing power, the share of wages in total value added will climb to the detriment of profit.[29]

As was demonstrated in Chapter 2, hourly compensation in manufacturing industry as a whole rose in the 1970s much faster than output per hour. The consequently sharply rising unit labour costs combined with stagnating demand, thereby depressing not only gross profitability but also the mass of gross profits.

In the late 1960s and 1970s productivity growth rates declined, according to Lipietz, because of difficulties in advancing the application of principles of scientific organization of labour (absenteeism, strikes and other forms of obstruction on the part of the workers). When the employers tried to counter by increasing the amount of fixed capital per worker, they caused a rise in the technical composition of capital (i.e. the value of fixed capital compared to wages) which depressed the rate of profit (as labour cost savings constrained the sales potential of the producers). A reason why this profitability crisis did not spiral into depression (but assumed the form of stagnation) was the high proportion of indirect labour in total employment; total demand did not contract substantially although the number of unemployed persons increased.[30]

Contrary to the position put forward by Lipietz, this study maintains that the cause of reduced productivity growth in the 1970s was largely declining output, rather than resistance towards labour-saving rationalization; the lower growth rates reflected, above all, a lower degree of capacity use in manufacturing industries providing investment goods. The reluctance (or inability) of employers to adjust their payrolls to declining sales was, of course, due to (as observed by Lipietz) 'the high proportion of indirect labour in total employment'; the employees represented, to a very high degree, indispensable human capital.

The more favourable labour-cost situation of the 1980s (mainly due to reduced growth of nominal compensation) allowed for increased corporate leverage. While, as shown in Table 7:8, the estimated mass of gross profits in the manufacturing industries of the seven countries contracted in the first years of the decade, many manufacturers seem to have experienced growing gross profits in 1983, 1984, 1985 and 1986. The readiness of the firms to use their growing profits for physical capital investment will be discussed below. Suffice it to say that growing, rather than declining, gross profits characterized the manufacturing industry of Western Europe in the mid-1980s. In contrast to the pre-1973 period, the growing mass of gross profits implied improved 'gross profitability': the growth of the aggregated compensation slowed down compared to the growth of the value added at current prices. Co-operativeness and willingness of organized labour to permit labour-saving measures may be a cause of the improved profitability, but the most crucial factor was probably the more modest demands for nominal wage increases. The restraint of labour may reflect less militancy in the face of high rates of unemployment, but also reduced rates of inflation (which make nominal wage increases less urgent).

Also contributing to the improved financial situation of manufacturing industry in the 1980s (as well as the reduced rates of inflation), were the falling prices of crude petroleum and other primary commodities, as they translated into cheaper inputs. The development of world export prices of various categories of primary commodities in the 1980s is shown in Table 7:9. The export prices of petroleum, which rose steeply in the late 1970s, and peaked in 1981–2, declined smoothly in the following three years, and plummeted in 1986. The export prices of non-ferrous base metals dropped by almost 30 per cent between 1980 and 1985; the prices of agricultural non-food commodities fell at the same time by 25 per cent.

One should keep in mind that the kind of human capital investment that firms pursue when they engage highly qualified professionals and workers reduces the gross profits of the industry (as the compensation of these employees add to current costs). Gross profits serve only as a crude measure of the firms' capacity to make physical capital formation expenditure.

The Public Sector

The financial situation of the public sector has not improved significantly in the 1980s. As shown in Table 7:10, five of the seven countries shown registered public spending deficits in the first half of the decade. As in the 1970s, governments were dependent on public borrowing, or forced to cut public expenses in real (if not nominal) terms.[31] The growth rates of government final consumption expenditure, which crumbled in the 1970s, hence remain low compared to the pre-1973 period, although (as evidenced by OECD statistics) government consumption regained momentum in some countries in the mid-1980s. Public investment expenditure continued on its route of decline: in Belgium the volume of government gross fixed capital formation contracted by almost 50 per cent between 1980 and 1986, in the Netherlands and Sweden by 15 per

Table 7.8 Indices of estimated aggregate gross profits of manufacturing industry* (1980 = 100)

	1980	1981	1982	1983	1984	1985	1986
Belgium	100	74	117	138	138	143	163
France	100	92	94	97	101	105	115
Germany	100	95	96	105	109	115	127
Italy	100	99	95	94	103	107	114
Netherlands	100	88	115	120	149	150	179
Sweden	100	86	104	136	153	150	157
UK	100	89	113	131	146	170	184

* Gross product at fixed prices (i.e. real value added or output) multiplied by (1 – compensations of employees in current values divided by gross product at current prices).

Based on data from US Department of Labor, Bureau of Labor Statistics.

Table 7.9 Indices of world export prices of primary commodities and non-ferrous metals (1980 = 100)

	1980	1981	1982	1983	1984	1985	1986
Food	100	89	78	77	74	66	74
Agricultural non-food	100	93	82	86	91	74	75
Minerals	100	112	110	97	95	93	57
Iron ore	100	92	96	92	85	84	82
Fuels	100	112	110	97	95	94	57
Petroleum	100	112	109	96	93	91	54
Non-ferrous base metals	100	88	77	78	76	71	70

Source: UN, *Monthly Bulletin of Statistics*, Vol. 42, No. 11 (Nov. 1988)

cent. As shown in Table 7:11, Britain was among the (very few) countries where public investment expenditure increased in the first half of the decade. The volume growth by almost 50 per cent between 1980 and 1986 should be considered, however, in the light of the sharp cut in public investment in the second half of the 1970s. As a matter of fact, public investment expenditure at fixed prices was not brought back to its early 1970s level. The feeble performance of the public sector confirms its dependence on the private sector. Modest growth of aggregate commodity value added in real terms, which

Table 7.10 General government: current income surplus/deficit as percentage of current incomes

	1980	1981	1982	1983	1984	1985	1986
Belgium	−10.7	−19.8	−16.1	−17.8	−14.0	−12.5	−15.3
France	8.1	3.8	2.0	0.7	1.2	1.1	1.1
Germany	4.1	1.0	0.9	1.6	2.3	4.4	4.1
Italy	−14.4	−21.4	−20.4	−18.8	−19.7	−18.5	−17.3
Netherlands	1.5	−0.9	−4.4	−3.6	−3.1	−1.0	−2.3
Sweden	−0.4	−2.2	−4.3	−2.3	−0.1	−2.1	2.5
UK	−4.0	−3.6	−3.1	−3.8	−4.9	−3.1	−3.0

Source: OECD, *National Accounts*, Vol. II, *Detailed Tables 1974–1986* (Paris: OECD, 1988)

Table 7.11 Gross fixed capital formation at fixed prices: Producers of government services

	1980	1981	1982	1983	1984	1985	1986
Belgium	100	90	82	73	65	56	52
Germany	100	91	82	76	75	75	80
Italy	100	94	84	76	82	95	96
Netherlands	100	95	87	84	91	84	76
Sweden	100	96	92	91	89	86	85
UK	100	85	114	119	128	135	148

Source: OECD, *National Accounts*, Vol. II, *Detailed tables 1974–1986* (Paris: OECD, 1988)

characterizes the 1980s, does not provide much scope for expanding public commitments.

But the development of the public sector is also conditioned by the ruling ideologies and priorities of the political decision-making communities. In a longer twentieth-century perspective, it can be contended that the post-war welfare state expansion in the advanced industrial countries was founded on the political mobilization of working-class people during the recession of the 1930s and the Second World War. As pointed out by Dunleavy, this mobilization affected virtually all liberal democracies:

Even in those countries without socialist parties, the construction of a reformatist electoral coalition based on a core of working class and organized labour-movement support was vital either in directly introducing welfare state measures after decisive electoral victories, or triggering preemptive concessions from parties and governments of the Right.[32]

The vigorous private sector growth in most of the post-war period allowed for compensation of people for their sacrifices in the 1930s, during the war, and in the first years after the war (when left-wing radicalism seemed to threaten the political stability of several Western European countries). People who had been in their early twenties at the beginning of the 1930s, and in their middle thirties at the end of the war, could be offered an increasing array of public benefits as they approached their fifties and sixties; the costs of these benefits, which people had to pay for in the form of direct and indirect taxes, seemed reasonable, and did not preclude access to a growing range of private consumption goods and services.

The political climate of the 1980s has been less conducive to public sector growth. Because the economic base for public services is only growing slowly, and because there is a tendency for the services to become more expensive over time as private sector productivity grows (and the pay of public servants is allowed to keep pace with the incomes of private sector workers), differences in group interests between private and public sector workers have become more visible. As pointed out by Dunleavy, sectoral cleavages have supplanted class-based cleavages in the political life of the industrially advanced countries.[33] Public sector growth has created a growing 'middle class' of public sector workers prone to support parties with programmes of increased public commitments. But as public sector workers increase in absolute and relative numbers, the general awareness of public sector growth (and its costs) also increases. The greater prominence of public sector unions, their use of militant industrial tactics covered by the mass media, and the increasing scale of overall tax deductions from average salaries, combine to make private–public sector differences more controversial.

Campaigns against 'bureaucracy', 'waste', and 'big government' have become increasingly potent mobilizing tools for parties and movements of the Right. In particular, they open up a plausible basis on which parties of the Right can appeal across social boundaries to private-sector and non-union working class voters.[34]

The partial realignment of political parties and conflicts around private–public sector issues cross-cut traditional social class divisions and undermined the class-based electoral coalitions which initially constituted the political driving force behind welfare state growth. But despite the more pronounced rhetoric of conservative and neo-liberal political leaders, Dunleavy concludes, 'the chief policy implications have been a stabilization or incremental reduction in welfare state spending and a marginal rollback in other forms of intervention'.[35] It has been noticed that public consumption expenditure stagnates, while public investment expenditure contracts.

The situation of the public sector in the 1980s may signal an end to the working-class dominance of political life in Western Europe, what Esping-Andersen has called the 'social democratization of capitalism'. According to this author, the welfare state is the collective political expression of 'demands that logically flow from the position in which wage earners find themselves'.[36] Social policy, which created the welfare state, is an arena for the accumulation of working-class power resources; its overriding principle is to substitute social redistribution for market exchange. Social democratization of capitalism means:

1. decommodification: that citzens' rights supplant market distribution;
2. restratification of society along solidarity principles: that individuals can uphold normal standards of living without the compulsion to work;
3. redistributive corrections of market-induced inequalities:
   that the evolution of the capitalist economy—backed by progressive taxation and social transfers—resolves most of the lingering problems of inequality; and, above all,
4. the institutionalization of sustained full employment.

Full employment is the basic financial underpinning for decommodification and solidarity, as well as enhancing the chances of radical income redistribution.[37]

The 1980s have provided greater scope for distributional regimes which are less integrative, comprehensive and societal than that offered by social democracy. The liberal model, which establishes narrow boundaries for government intervention but maximum scope for markets, has gained more acceptance. Liberalism emphasizes voluntary private contractual insurance schemes, comparatively meagre public benefits, and standards which encourage private insurance initiatives. In the 1980s its agenda has even included 'privatization': the transfer of public sector services to the commodity sector.

From a utilitarian point of view, the end of the social democratization of capitalism can be interpreted as diminishing marginal benefits of welfare state services: financing the services by means of taxation (which requires extraordinary power mobilization) means nowadays that the majority of the electorate cover the expenses for the public support of political minorities, a redistribution of resources not from a wealthy minority to a needy majority, but from people in general to people in particular.

Physical Capital Formation

As shown in Table 7:12, positive and rising growth rates of physical capital formation expenditure have been recorded in the 1980s. But, as

Table 7.12   Rates of growth of gross fixed capital formation

	1980	1981	1982	1983	1984	1985	1986
Belgium	−16.4	−1.7	−4.2	2.1	1.0	3.7	7.6
France	−1.9	−1.4	−3.6	−2.6	2.8	2.9	3.7
Germany	−4.8	−5.3	3.2	0.8	0.1	3.3	1.8
Italy	−2.3	−5.7	−0.1	5.3	2.6	1.4	5.2
Netherlands	−10.4	−4.1	2.1	5.4	6.8	8.2	1.6
Sweden	−5.3	−1.1	1.6	5.1	6.0	−0.6	6.2
UK	−9.6	5.4	5.0	8.6	3.8	0.9	5.5
US	−0.1	−8.7	8.8	15.9	6.9	0.9	3.1
Japan	3.1	0.8	−0.3	4.9	5.8	6.0	10.3

Source: OECD, *National Accounts*, Vol. I, *1960–1987* (Paris: OECD, 1989)

shown by the national accounts statistics of the OECD, the rates recorded for the first half of the decade fit into a jigsaw pattern of peaks and troughs at 3–5 year intervals which has characterized gross fixed capital formation since the early 1950s (OECD, *National Accounts*, various editions). In a post-war time perspective they may as much suggest a long-term depression of physical capital formation as a turnaround from stagnation to growth. Growth rates in the range of 2–4 per cent a year, such as were registered in Belgium, France, Germany, Italy and OECD Europe as a whole in the middle of the 1980s, do not indicate a return to the situation of the 1950s and 1960s. Although depressed unit labour costs may have combined with increased domestic and US demand to improve the profit situation of the commodity sector in the 1980s, the rates do not suggest that commodity providers have engaged in investment programmes which will instigate a new era of sustained and rapid economic growth.

As has already been observed, public investment expenditure tended to decline rather than grow in the first half of the decade. Gross fixed capital formation in the form of machinery and transport equipment (excluding passenger cars) recovered in some Western European countries in 1985 and 1986 afer a downturn in 1981–3. According to OECD data, expenditure on residential construction contracted in most countries.

The feeble investment performance of the Western European economies since the middle of the 1970s is reflected in moderate, very low and even negative rates of economic growth in the first half of the 1980s. But its significance lies, perhaps, first of all in the fact that it is only by means of physical capital formation that new technology materializes into new products and production methods. A probable implication is that Western European firms (on average) did not gain much competitive

strength compared to firms in countries where physical capital formation was more impressive (for example Japan and other East Asian
countries).

Long Waves

There has been no need so far to refer to 'long-wave theory', the thesis
of quasi-secular cycles of economic ups and downs in the history of
industrial capitalism. Students of long waves adopt a very long-range
view on economic change; they are all preoccupied with an alleged
pattern of *regularity* in the behaviour of the economy since the British
industrial revolution.[38] Although the shift from economic growth to
stagnation in the 1970s (or late 1960s) has been used as proof of the
existence of regular long-term swings (and spurred renewed interest in
long-wave theory), the topic of long waves, as such, is regarded as
beyond the scope of this study.

Approaching the issue of the requirements for a return to sustained
physical capital formation, high rates of economic growth and reduced
unemployment, it may be appropriate, however, to consider some
interpretations of recent economic change offered by leading long-wave
theorists. Do their explanations of the post-war boom and the subsequent stagnation help us understand the present situation of the
Western European economies? Do they indicate conditions for a new
round of rapid economic growth? The discussion will be restricted to the
contributions of a few well-known writers.

In the neo-Schumpeterian interpretation of the post-war boom
presented by Freeman, Clark and Soete, 'the upward swing of the pre-
1973 period' is regarded as the result of 'the simultaneous explosive
growth of several major technologies and industries, particularly
electronics, synthetic materials, drugs, oil and petro-chemicals and
(especially in Europe and Japan) consumer durables and vehicles'.[39]
Emphasis is placed on *new technology systems*, constellations of innovations which are not more or less random groupings of innovations
appearing in a certain period, but rather clusters of innovations which
have a clear relationship to each other. The macroeconomic effects of
any basic innovation are scarcely perceived in its first years, but most
often much later; what matters is the diffusion of the innovation, the
extended swarming process when other firms realize the profit potential
of the new product or process and start to invest heavily: 'Once
swarming does start it has strong multiplier effects in generating
additional demands on the economy for capital goods (of new and old
types), for materials, components, distribution facilities, and of course
labour'.[40] The diffusion process involves a string of innovations as an
increasing number of producers get involved, learn the new technology

and strive to gain an edge over their competitors. It is this diffusion process which has significant economy-wide effects on investment and employment. The bandwagon effect is thus extraordinarily important and the main explanation of the upswings in the long waves.[41] The boom phase of the post-war period resulted from the roughly simult-aneous rolling of several new technology bandwagons: the computer bandwagon, the television bandwagon, the transistor bandwagon, the drug bandwagon and the plastics bandwagon, as well as the band-wagons of various consumer durables:

In the major boom periods new industries and technological systems tend to generate a great deal of new employment, as the form that expansion takes is the installation of completely new capacity and the building up of associated capital goods industries. Since the technology is still in a relatively fluid state and standardized special plant and machinery is not yet available, the new factories and plants are often fairly labour-intensive.[42]

As a new industry or technology matures, several factors interact to reduce the amount of employment generated per unit of investment. Economies of scale become increasingly important, and work in combination with technical and organizational changes associated with increasing standardization. The profits gained through innovation are diminished both by competition and by rising costs. A process of concentration is likely to occur, and competition forces increasing attention on technologies, allowing for reduced costs. In the early period of a long boom the emphasis is thus on rapid expansion of new capacity in order to get a large market share, and this investment generates a lot of new employment. As the new industries and technologies mature, economies of scale are exploited and the emphasis shifts to cost-saving innovations in process technologies. Capital intensity increases and employment growth slows down or even stops altogether.[43] This tendency plays an important part in the cyclical movement from boom to recession (or stagflation).[44] As for labour costs, it seems that the pressure for labour-saving technical change will be at its most intense during periods of labour shortages and a steep relative rise in labour costs (i.e. at peak periods). Because of the time lags involved in any such change of emphasis and the independent application of such innovations, the actual shedding of labour may occur later (i.e. in a period of stagflation or even depression).

The long-wave interpretation of the post-war boom and the subse-quent stagnation presented by Freeman, Clark and Soete is consistent with the analysis presented in Chapter 1. It relates the macroeconomic development to basic product innovations and changes in production methods. The authors highlight types of commodities which have been cores of important development blocks, they describe the conditions and forms of labour-saving rationalization which made economic growth possible but eventually contributed to stagnation. However, as the analysis is confined to what constitutes, in a strict sense, the production system, it provides only a partial explantion of the change from strong economic growth to stagnation. It does not assess the importance of the public sector and economic policies of governments; nor does it relate innovations to social forces of change, or institutional conditions such as the role of large and small firms, organized interests and public sector growth.

Attempts to regard the crucial technological development of the so-called fourth Kondratieff cycle in such a broader social and organizational perspective have been made by Freeman and Perez. What we are actually measuring when we detect long-wave behaviour in economic variables, emphasize these authors, is the increasing degree of 'match' or 'mismatch' between the techno-economic sub-system and the socio-institutional framework. Depression is not just a halt in economic growth

but a 'shouting' need for full-scale re-accommodation of social behaviour and institutions in order to suit the requirements of a major shift which has already taken place, to a considerable extent, in the techno-economic sphere. An upswing can only be unleashed by appropriate social and institutuional transformations that will re-establish structural coherence.[45]

The type of fundamental shift which underlies these periods of match and mismatch are successive *techno-economic paradigms* which transform the 'how' and 'what' of profitable production and which move the 'best practice frontier'.

The technological paradigm, which provides the direction and shape of the movement of the entire capitalist system, is, in the words of Perez, 'a sort of "ideal type" of productive organisation . . . which develops as a response to what are perceived as the stable dynamics of the relative cost structure for a given period of capitalist development'.[46] The establishment of a new paradigm is grounded on a constellation of technical and managerial innovations which lead to a level of factor productivity which is clearly superior to what was 'normal' in the previous technological paradigm. The productivity jump is made possible by the appearance of a particular key input in the cost structure, which can be supplied at descending relative costs for all practical purposes, which is all-pervasive, and which reduces the costs of capital, labour and products at the same time as it changes them qualitatively.

The technological paradigm of the post-war upward swing was embodied in the extension of the continuous-flow concept of the chemical industry to the mass production of discrete identical units made with energy-intensive materials, complemented on the organizational level by a separation of functions of administration control from operative work in accordance with the Taylorian ideas of scientific management. The 'ideal type' of firm was the 'corporation', a productive organization which 'benefited from economies of agglomeration and required an ever expanding highway network, together with oil and energy distribution systems for energy-intensive production, transportation and lifestyles'.[47]

The dominating technological paradigm not only brings about a particular pattern of inter-branch relationships and distribution of production between types of firm, but also affects the occupational structure of the working population and the distribution of income.[48] In the upswing of the 1950s and 1960s, Taylorism, or scientific management, was the seed out of which continuous mass production evolved into the fully-fledged technological paradigm. As firms reduced the size of their workforces in relation to output, and transformed their composition, new trends became visible in the occupational structure. With the growth of a new layer of white-collar workers between managers and foremen, and the reduction of the number of manual workers, a new pattern of income distribution evolved which translated into changing product demand. A middle-range demand pattern emerged and tended to grow.

The upswing of the economy after the Second World War was thus a period with a good match between the requirements of a paradigm of mass production and the socio-institutional framework. Among the main institutional changes which promoted this match were the expansion of the state's role in economic life, the rapid expansion of secondary and higher education to meet the demand for white-collar, technical and clerical employees, together with the expansion of the public health system, innovations such as consumer credit, commercial advertising, the mass communications industry and various forms of planned obsolescence, which strengthened the means of orienting the use of disposable income into intensive consumption of the various goods proper for the mass production paradigm. The institutional acceptance of the labour unions as representatives of the workers fostered the growth of disposable income, at the same time as it stimulated incremental labour-saving innovations. At the large firm level, the in-house research and development laboratory emerged. On the international level, international agreements established a solid basis for the regulation of international trade and investment.

The described socio-institutional framework of the techno-economic sub-system parallels much of the analysis in Chapters 3–5. It succinctly describes the social environment and underpinnings of the product and process innovations which contributed to the sustained economic growth of the boom. But it probably underrates the role of the state as an agent of economic change: governments and public technocracies provide conditions for capital accumulation, but do not by themselves represent social forces propelling economic change in one direction or another. In the authors' conception of the economy, government policies are apparently reduced to the servicing of the interests of capital.

The paradigm of a future upswing, maintains Perez, could be flexible batch production networks based on cheap and widely available micro-electronics and low-cost information handling. Its most proper type of productive organization brings together management and production into one single integrated system for turning out information-intensive and rapidly changing products. This technological paradigm, which will emerge on the basis of cheap, pervasive, readily available and cost-reducing micro-electronics, has a strong transnational dimension made possible by unprecedented data management and world-embracing telecommunications networks. It will thus suit large, complex and flexible transnational conglomerates, optimizing factor use and maximizing long-term profits on a global scale. Consequently, national policy solutions seem ill-adapted to nurture the new paradigm.

As the new paradigm gains weight there will be a tendency for 'intangible' capital investment to become more important than physical capital investment. (For a long time, firms in the computer industry have devoted larger resources to research and development than to physical capital investment.) As the information system available to firms, governments and other institutions is becoming the most critical resource, the balance will be tilted even more towards intangible investment.[49]

The thesis of flexible batch production networks based on micro-electronics as the leading technical paradigm of a future enduring boom echoes the idea of flexible specialization. As already mentioned, flexible specialization seems to be part of the economic reality of the 1980s, and will probably also be so in years to come. But it cannot be taken for granted that this avenue offers competitive advantages to Western European firms in particular, nor that it gives rise to substantial physical capital formation, as intangible investment characterizes the paradigm. Although the software applications of the new information technology will generate incomes and employment, doubts may be raised as to whether the emerging (or rather extending) paradigm will be tantamount to high rates of economic growth in Western Europe or the industrial world in general. In other words, application of the new technology will scarcely cause a sustained economic boom resembling that of the pre-1973 period, but rather propel some national economies which have acquired competitive advantages in the production of the needed physical equipment and software.

In the Marxist approach expounded by Mandel, the notion of long waves boils down to a statement that industrial capitalism may be divided into historic periods of almost equal length, each containing a long boom followed by a phase of relative decline. Although these movements can be related to the general laws of motion of the capitalist mode of production, it is not possible to specify their exact nature and causes without reference to prevailing historic *conjunctures* (as the waves manifest the reactions of the capitalist class to the specific combination of circumstances and trends which characterize the period).[50] 'Although basic innovations are bunched in a "countercyclical manner" during the depressive phases of long waves', as Schumpeter maintains,

> they do not *cause* the transition to an expansionary boom phase. Explanation of the turning points must be sought elsewhere. . . . Whereas the upper turning points from the boom to the depressive phase are determined largely by endogenous factors, especially the growing capital intensity, this is not true of the lower turning points. Exogenous 'system shocks' of various kinds are needed to propel the system out of the depressive phase.[51]

By emphasizing factors outside the production system *strictu sensu*, Mandel acknowledges the importance of political events and grand policies of states (e.g. wars, *ententes* between superpowers, multinational economic co-operation schemes). It suggests, in this respect, the kind of geopolitical economic approach to the development of the Western European economies that will be hinted at below.

The main cause of the post-war turn from rapid economic growth to stagnation was, according to Mandel, the significantly changed prospects for profits. While the long boom resulted from an interaction of many, and particularly autonomous, variables which led to an upsurge of profits, its end was essentially due to declining profits. Profit is, after all, what makes the capitalist system tick, and profit will not make it tick until external conditions precipitate a new round of vigorous capital accumulation. As capital accumulation implies investment in new production or servicing capacity, capital formation expenditure is also a critical factor in the Mandelian approach to the slump of the 1970s.[52]

Although Mandel treats profits in the traditional Marxist way as the *rate* of surplus value compared to the sum of constant and variable capital, he also acknowledges the relevance of the total amount, or *mass*, of surplus value. This entity may be regarded as an *analogue* to what has been called in this study 'the aggregated gross profits': the total sales revenues of all commodity providers less their expenditure for material inputs and labour, which can be disposed of for investment. An increase in the mass of surplus value is, according to Mandel, among the factors which may dampen the effects of the tendency of the rate of profit to decline; the mass of surplus value may increase due to a flow of capital into countries and sectors where the capital intensity is significantly lower than in the basic industrial branches.[53]

Among writers expressing scepticism about long waves as a systematic phenomenon affecting output is Maddison. Although many fascinating hypotheses have been developed in looking for them, this author argues that the case for regular long-term rhythmic movements in economic activity has not been proven. Explanations of major changes in the growth momentum should be sought, rather, in specific disturbances of an *ad hoc* character: 'Major system shocks change the momentum of capitalist development at certain points. Sometimes they are more or less accidental in origin; sometimes they occur because some inherently unstable situation can no longer be lived with but has finally broken down . . .'.[54] According to Maddison 'the institutional policy mix' plays a more important role in capitalist development than many long-wave theorists admit:

A system shock will produce the need for new policy instruments, and these are not always selected on the most rational basis, or they may require a long period of experiment before they work properly. There may also be conflicts of interest within and between countries which prevent the emergence of efficient policies. Hence there may well be prolonged periods in which supply potential is not fully exploited.[55]

Yet as most contemporary long-wave theorists do, Maddison considers the development since 1973 as a new phase of capitalist development, not just a temporary interruption of the unprecedented secular boom which started in the late 1940s. The 1974–5 recession affected virtually all industrial countries; the recovery was slow, halting and incomplete;

Although the recession in output was the most dramatic herald of change, there have been deeper causes. . . . The grounds for treating the post-1973 period as a new phase include observation of price as well as output behaviour, changes in government policy concerning the level of demand, change in expectations in the labour market, and changes in the international power balance, some of which occurred before 1973.[56]

As for the causes of the breakdown of the golden age of the pre-1973 period, Maddison emphasizes two changes in the international environment of the industrial countries: the collapse of the Bretton Woods fixed exchange system, and the tenfold rise in oil prices in the 1970s. Both of these factors meant an erosion of earlier constraints on prices and wages. The processes of wage bargaining and price fixing were no longer dampened by money illusion. When demand weakened in 1974–5, a very strong pressure for price increases continued, dominated by inflationary expectations acting as a fan instead of a damper. The oil price increase affected the general level of prices, and contributed considerably to expectations of further price increases. But the oil shock had several other important repercussions. Its adverse effects on trade balances were a major reason for the stringency of restrictive policies in most industrial countries. The considerable shift in the terms of trade with the oil-exporting countries lowered real incomes at a time when output fell for the first time in the post-war period. The oil shock was a major reason for the depth of the 1974–5 recession. The great structural change in prices also had a deflationary impact on demand. Demand for automobiles was badly hit, and the investment outlook became very uncertain.[57] Because of the change in expectations, and the many payments problems created by the oil price increase, virtually all governments changed their policy aspirations and tactics. Most of them pursued budget policies to counteract the impact of the recession, but not enough to offset the recessionary forces at work. The cautious policy stance was adopted in the hope that slack in domestic labour and goods markets would help break the exceptional momentum that was pushing up wages and prices, and would permit exports to rise to meet payments deficits.[58] Maddison pinpoints the structural constraints of policy-makers, a factor which has been emphasized in earlier chapters dealing with public investment and public sector growth.

In the vein of Maddison, one could argue that a return to sustained high rates of economic growth in Western Europe would require fundamental changes in the institutional framework of the world economy, a removal of external economic policy constraints as well as the creation of new investment and export incentives. Some of these requirements seem to be at hand in the 1980s, others are still faltering. The decade brought falling prices of imported oil and other primary commodities, reduced inflation, and an awareness among the governments of the industrial world of the need to co-operate and co-ordinate their policies. But although Western European exports to the United States increased in the 1980s, the incentives to invest were not strong enough to spur a new wave of massive capital formation.

By underlining the importance of changes in the international position and political framework of individual economies, Maddison indicates a more fruitful approach to inter-periodal variations in economic growth performance than most expounders of long-wave theory do. Economic growth and stagnation (and any envisaged future change) in Western Europe (or any individual country or group of countries) must be considered in the light of changes in the transnational and multinational economy.

The interpretations of recent economic change that have been given in the studies referred to earlier parallel and supplement the account presented in earlier chapters. However, in contrast to both Maddison and writers who have attempted to explain the situation of the second half of the 1970s and early 1980s in the perspective of long waves, this study hesitates to adopt the view of a clear shift, or turning point, from economic growth to stagnation. Chapter 2 provided evidence for a long-term tendency of depressed growth rates in the thirty-year period 1950–80. Although the post-1973 period differed greatly from the 1950s and 1960s, stagnation should be considered the result of many more or less contingent factors which accumulated in the whole post-war period to depress rates of economic growth. This view is confirmed by the records of physical capital formation expenditure (provided by, for example, the OECD). The rates are highly volatile, and in some years negative. But in the thirty-five-year perspective, they describe a falling trend rather than culmination followed by a marked decline. The troughs of 1974–5 are extraordinarily deep, and contribute strongly to the impression of a long-term contraction. But they fit into the pattern of (not very regular) ups and downs since the early 1950s. The significance of the upturn in rates in the middle of the 1980s cannot be completely assessed, but can nevertheless be regarded, at least partly, as reactions to a high US demand for Western European exports (caused by an overvalued dollar) rather than the signal of a new unlocking of strong forces of capital accumulation. On the other hand, in view of the apparent suspension of physical investments over a long period of time, it is plausible that growing obsolescence has called for modernization, i.e. investment in up-to-date machinery and other productive equipment.

It is possible that the falling trend of physical capital expenditure indicates increased productivity in a deeper sense than that of increased efficiency, or increased value added per hour, in that it signals that wants and needs can be satisfied with less physical work (but more ingenuity and brain-power). This may also mean that the material content of capital formation is bound to decline, and that increased material welfare (and less physical effort of people in their daily pursuits) can be attained with much lower rates of economic growth and substantially reduced input of labour. However, to discuss such an option needs a study of its own.

Postponing Productive Investments

In a situation of economic stagnation, such as that experienced recently in most Western European countries, many firms may deliberately wait and see before they engage in large programmes of physical capital formation; the firms may spend a substantial part of their gross profits on research and product development and even recruit scientific personnel and other qualified employees. Such investment in knowledge, skill and adaptive capacity enable them to launch new and appropriate products in a future phase of buoyant demand, but entail only modest investment in physical production facilities. If rates of interest and other premiums of pure financial investment are high— compared to experienced and expected rates of inflation—firms may also prefer to keep their gross profits in a highly liquid form (such as stock, bonds, foreign currencies and high-yielding bank deposits) rather than to invest in production facilities. Financial investment complies with the need of firms to be able to adjust expediently to emerging new prospects for profitable production; such investment also offers extremely short pay-off periods—although the acquired assets carry great risks, as they can be realized almost at the investors' beck and call. Such practices can induce a building boom in the financial centres of the world, but do not otherwise create much industrial employment. Employment expansion will be reckoned mainly in banking, insurance, real estate and business services. On the other hand, financial investments by commodity providers may help governments finance public sector employment.

The propensity of producers to *postpone* investments (or simply wait) in certain situations is a key element in Pasinetti's elaboration of the Keynesian approach to recurrent recessions or slumps.[59] As Pasinetti points out, Keynes explained the possibility of a drop in effective demand by means of two separate behavioural theories, one for total consumption expenditure, the other for total investment expenditure. As he was concerned only with short-term fluctuations, the composition of total demand did not matter.

To cope with the problem of the changing composition of total demand in an economy with technical change, Pasinetti contrasts the development of consumer demand with the development of investment demand. While consumer demand evolves as consumers decide according to their likings and preferences how to use additional earnings (after some deductions for savings), and is determined—so to speak—in an autonomous way, investment demand is dependent on consumer demand. If the economy is subjected to steady technical change, and hence the composition of consumer and producer demand is constantly changing, investment decisions must be expected to be much more unstable over time than decisions concerning consumption. According to Pasinetti, this is not because investment decision-makers are unable to scrutinize the preferences of consumers, but simply because investment has to be made in anticipation of the expected future growth of consumer demand. At any given time, consumers themsevles may be uncertain about the direction in which their demand is going to develop.[60] When per capita incomes rise (due to increased productivity) consumers are pushed in new directions, and into previously unexperienced fields of consumption (if they do not prefer to add to their savings). For investors, it may from time to time be very difficult to detect clearly the directions in which consumer demand is going to expand. In such situations, the propensity of producers to postpone the actual undertaking of investment will cause investment volume to decline.[61]

When some new lines of expansion have once been established, because consumers have found out their preferences and are able to decide how to spend their incremental income, the rates of growth of consumer demand are soon likely to become rather high. The growth rate of investment cannot be as high, as it takes time to build new plants and investors must adopt a long-term view of the expansion pattern. There will therefore be a (boom) period in which demand remains partly unsatisfied. Over time, demand saturates and the rate of demand expansion flattens by necessity. Yet sooner or later, the investors will realize that they are investing too much, with respect to the rate of expansion of demand. This is a crucial point, and an inevitable one, because of the very nature of consumer preferences:

When it comes, investors will be compelled to stop or slow down investment, unless they are able to find new outlets—for example by selling abroad, or by devoting the existing productive capacity to making new models or new products for which they can promote demand.[62]

This means that there is no inevitability about the slowing down of investment and the appearance of unemployment (as new outlets may be discovered after all). But there is, according to Pasinetti, an inevitability about the *periodic* emergence of the *necessity to find new outlets*. The growth of an economic system with technical progress is thus normally, but not inevitably, bound to take place by an alternating succession of expansion waves and 'pauses'. The latter are periods in which the growth rate of effective demand tends to fall short of the production potential growth. They are not necessarily depressions (i.e. sharp falls in demand and employment). Whether or not they will develop into large-scale depressions mainly depends on the type of existing institutional arrangements.[63] In line with the reasoning of Pasinetti, it can be inferred that such periods, when the growth of effective demand falls and does not keep up with the growth of the produciton potential, are periods when major product innovations are likely to appear; new (or substantially modified) products are launched to soak up unused productive capacity.

Although Pasinetti's analysis concerns 'an economy' and not (as does this study) a group of 'national economies', his elaboration of the Keynesian framework is highly applicable to the situation of Western European countries in the 1980s. If the consumers of a country, or group of countries, find that they want to spend their incremental incomes on commodities which are developed and produced with some competitive advantages in other countries, there will be a leakage of effective demand and also some relocation of the production that satisfies the demand of the consumers of the country (or countries) in question; in other words, the new demand will be satisfied by means of imports. What is alluded to is, of course, the theory that Japanese firms have been more successful than European firms in developing and marketing products on which consumers in Europe (and other parts of the world) are willing to spend their incremental incomes (for example various household electronics goods).

Pasinetti maintains that large multi-product firms represent a stabilizing factor in the economy. By continuously adapting the use of their disposable resources to new demand conditions, they are able to carry out efficiently and inside their own organization the process of structural change which secures a high rate of employment.[64] Large multi-product firms may also play a stabilizing role by keeping a stock of ideas to be used when needed.[65] One may add that such firms are presumably more apt to diversify into financial operations while they wait for consumer demand to find new directions. By postponing productive investment, but at the same time keeping their disposable gross profits in highly liquid form, commodity providers may secure (or even enhance) their future capacity to make productive investment. But the firms may also in this way add to the economic stalemate.

It is not possible to enumerate, and interrelate, all factors which influence the choice of a producer between using a disposable amount of gross profit for a productive investment and using it for a financial investment. Suffice it to say that such a choice involves some expectations as to the future prices of capital equipment, inputs and products supplied by the firm, as well as the future efficient return of the financial assets which are offered as alternative investment options for the firm. All other things being equal, it can be supposed that high rates of experienced and expected inflation make financial investment less attractive than productive investment, and that rising premiums of financial investment lessen the costs of refraining from, or postponing, productive investment. There is, of course, a trade-off between the various forms of financial asset (stocks, bonds, foreign currencies, etc.) and investors may take into account how, for instance, a rise in long-term interest rates affects the value and efficient yields of shares, before they make any dispositions. But if at any time financial investment seems to offer firms an unimpaired (or enhanced) potential for productive investment in the future, they should at least consider financial investment compared to productive investments.

The alleged propensity of corporations to postpone productive investment in periods characterized by both uncertainty as to the future development of demand and high effective returns of highly liquid assets may be a main cause of the economic stagnation of the 1970s and early 1980s.

In the second half of the 1970s, investors in most European countries experienced rising rates of interest and high but declining rates of inflation. High interest rates reflected tight monetary policies, but also the need for public borrowing. Declining profitability (due to rapidly rising nominal wages and input prices) combined with stagnating demand (for investment goods in particular) to curb the growth of the mass of gross profits; positive real rates of interest (which are rates exceeding inflation rates) made financial investment attractive to firms which commanded some gross profits, but felt uncertain that productive investment would pay off; physical capital formation expenditure

Table 7.13 Long-term interest rates (A)*
Rate of change of the deflator of gross fixed capital formation (B)

	1980	1981	1982	1983	1984	1985	1986
Belgium							
A*	13.0	14.0	12.7	11.9	11.6	9.6	7.7
B	5.4	6.3	4.3	3.6	3.7	1.3	6.7
France							
A	14.7	17.1	15.7	14.0	11.9	11.2	8.8
B	10.6	12.1	8.4	6.6	4.5	3.4	2.8
Germany							
A	8.9	9.7	7.9	8.2	7.0	6.5	5.9
B	4.9	2.9	2.0	2.3	1.7	1.3	1.3
Italy							
A	15.2	21.4	19.7	17.7	14.5	13.7	10.0
B	20.5	15.8	11.1	9.0	8.1	3.6	2.8
Netherlands							
A	10.5	11.3	8.4	8.5	7.4	7.0	6.4
B	6.6	3.6	1.3	1.5	1.1	−0.5	−0.3
Sweden							
A	12.6	12.8	13.0	12.0	12.6	12.2	10.5
B	9.5	8.8	10.1	5.5	5.7	4.5	5.2
UK							
A	12.1	13.9	10.2	9.9	10.0	9.9	10.1
B	9.9	2.9	3.3	4.2	5.5	4.9	5.1
US							
A	11.9	12.9	10.3	11.4	11.2	9.6	7.7
B	8.9	5.3	−1.2	0.1	0.3	2.3	1.1
Japan							
A	9.4	7.9	7.5	6.9	6.3	5.8	4.6
B	0.9	0.5	−0.7	0.1	−0.2	−1.9	−1.3

*Yield on long-term government bonds

Sources: OECD, *National Accounts*, Vol. I, *1960–1987* (Paris: OECD, 1989); OECD, *Main Economic Indicators 1964–1983* (Paris: OECD, 1984); *Main Economic Indicators*, Jan. 1988 (Paris: OECD, 1988).

contracted. In the first half of the 1980s interest rates declined, but as inflation simultaneously lost most of its momentum, interest rates exceeded inflation rates. As the gap between nominal interest rates and inflation rates tended to grow, there was actually a rise in real interest rates. Rising profitability of operations caused the mass of gross profits to grow, but there were small demand inducements to engage in heavy programmes of physical capital formation. If there were not widespread uncertainty among consumer goods producers as to the development of demand, firms were not certain that they could capture a sufficient

Table 7.14   Share price indices (1980 = 100)

	1980	1981	1982	1983	1984	1985	1986
Belgium	100	81	96	123	156	174	250
France	100	88	86	116	157	185	285
Germany	100	101	100	132	145	189	253
Italy	100	152	123	153	171	287	667
Netherlands	100	93	99	166	211	282	416
Sweden	100	113	131	165	196	242	300

Sources: OECD, *Main Economic Indicators, Historical Statistics 1964–1983* (Paris: OECD, 1984); *Main Economic Indicators,* Feb. 1987 (Paris: OECD, 1987)

market share of the evolving demand. Many Western European producers preferred to wait and see, investing their gross profits in highly liquid assets (such as securities offered by their own governments or shares and securities denominated in US dollars). When nominal interest rates were brought down, share prices surged; when the value of the dollar increased compared to Western European currencies in the first half of the decade, there was a stong inducement to prefer investment in dollar assets. (Attention has already been called to the resulting net flow of capital funds from Western Europe in the 1980s.)

The development of long-term interest rates and the deflator of the gross fixed capital expenditure (as a measure of both inflation and changes in the price of physical production facilities) is shown for some countries in Table 7:13. Table 7:14 documents the rocketing share prices in the 1980s.

Requirements of Substantial Physical Capital Formation

The situation in the second half of the 1970s and early 1980s has been described as a (temporary) stalemate of economic growth. The impasse was caused by circumstances which were beyond the control of the governments of individual nation-states. The forces of capital accumulation and commodity sector growth could not be mobilized unless certain conditions materialized which allowed gross profits to expand and lured firms to use a substantial share of their gross profits for investment. Until such conditions were at hand, physical capital formation and hence economic growth would be modest (as the public sector cannot be expanded to promote commodity sector growth as long as commodity providers shun large-scale investment). The 1980s apparently brought rising 'gross profitability' and growing gross profits but not sufficient physical capital formation to allow for a return to the standards of the pre-1973 period. It has been maintained that productive investment was postponed as firms hesitated to venture into some direction of the rapidly developing but unpredictable consumer demand (which to a large extent was captured by non-European producers).

Among probable conditions which could precipitate substantial physical capital formation are *lower real rates of interest*, or rather, changes in the fiscal and monetary policies of the United States which provide options for lower rates of interest in the global financial system as a whole.

Although nominal rates of interest dropped in the 1980s, real interest rates remained high in a post-war perspective. The main reason why nominal rates of interest exceeded rates of inflation by 3–5 percentage points was the reluctance of the US administration to cope with a mounting budget deficit through increased rates of taxation. Tax rates were cut sharply in 1981 with the monetarist claim that lower taxes would spur people's effort so much that public revenues would not fall but rise. What was produced was, in effect, a budget deficit with great impact on the world economy. The need of the United States to finance large and sophisticated defence programmes, as well as education, health and welfare by means of public borrowing, caused a widening gap in its external payments. (By 1987 the federal budget deficit and the current account deficit were both in the order of $150 billion.) As was developed earlier, interest rates were raised to attract foreign capital. Other industrial countries had to follow suit in order to avoid a flight from their currencies and/or inflation.

The dollar was first pushed up to a peak in 1985, then pushed down (under the control of foreign central banks, which did not want its value to dive so much that it would threaten the competitive strength of their countries in the US market). Other industrial countries

faced first the risk of inflation as their currencies fell against the dollar, and later the strain of industrial dislocation as they rose. The developing countries fared worse. Soaring dollar interest rates contributed strongly to the international debt crisis, leaving the debtor countries no choice but to cut deeply into their imports and their living standards . . . in buying less from abroad they made it all the harder for America—one of their principal suppliers—to keep its trade gap in check.[66]

By pushing up global interest rates, the peculiar US brand of monetary restraint and Keynesian expansionism exerted contrasting effects on the Western European economies: at the same time as it made it easier for European producers to export to the United States (i.e. as long as the dollar rate kept rising), it depressed the demand for investment goods by making financial investments more profitable compared to productive investments.

High real rates of interest meant high costs of borrowing for purposes of investment, as well as high opportunity costs of productive investment (i.e. high rewards offered by financial investment). When commodity providers found that productive investment did not cover the costs of borrowing, or that financial investment added (or added more) to their gross profits, they refrained from, or postponed, physical capital formation expenditure. High interest rates also meant high costs of residential construction, a very capital-requiring type of physical capital formation which had declined in most Western European countries since the middle of the 1970s. A further effect of high interest rates was the high cost of servicing public debt; as most governments had borrowed to cover public consumption expenditure there was little room for public investment. As most of the interest charges attached to the Third World debt are linked to the US prime lending rate, the high rates of interest also curbed the demand of the industrializing countries for Western European imports (at the same time as they forced these countries to become more aggressive exporters). The high real rates of interest thus affected capital formation expenditure in Western Europe, as well as Western European exports to the countries of the Third World. Although capital formation (and Third-World-directed exports) may very well entail considerable imports from other parts of the world, it seems most reasonable to assume that the policies of the United States constrained growth rates in Western Europe (and the world economy as a whole). As interest rate differentials (and expectations as to the development of the value of the dollar) attracted large amounts of capital from Western Europe, the policies of the United States caused a diversion of investable funds: European savings were not used to finance investment in Europe, but rather for public consumption in the United States. As industrial creativity materializes only by means of productive investment, it can also be maintained that the technological development of Western European firms was hampered by the policies of the United States.

High rates of interest have been used to curb inflation, but if self-occupancy of housing is frequent (as it is nowadays in many Western European countries) high interest rates may equally well promote inflation: wage-earners are urged to negotiate higher wages to compensate for the increased cost of servicing mortgages.

A fall in the real rate of interest (which requires changes in the policies of the United States) would make financial investment less attractive compared to productive investment at the same time as it would reduce the costs of financing productive investment by means of borrowing. It would also lower the production costs of residential construction, ease the terms of public borrowing, and provide more room for public investment. Lower real rates of interest would allow Third World countries to import more from Western Europe and other industrial countries. Yet lower real interest rates could spur physical capital formation only to the extent that they induce, or coincide with, growing internal and external demand for Western European commodities.

Among factors which could represent demand pulls *per se* (i.e. irrespective of a fall in real interest rates) are the completion of the internal market of the European Community and the very hypothetical (but not entirely unrealistic) option of a geographic enlargement of the Community.

In 1985 the Commission of the European Community launched its subsequently famous White Paper, *The Completion of the Internal Market*. The objective of the programme was the welding together of the twelve individual markets of the member states into a single market of 320 million people. The programme contained 300 items; it was to be realized by the end of 1992.[67]

The completion of the internal market means removal of

— differences in technical regulations between the member countries;
— delays and administrative work caused by frontier customs controls;
— restrictions on member-state competition for public procurements;
— limitations on the freedom of firms and individuals to engage in certain service transactions (such as finance and transport).

The completion programme supposed that remaining restrictions on free trade within the Community imply a considerable non-competitive market segmentation, and that their elimination will suppress a series of constraints that today prevent enterprises from being as efficient as they could be, and from employing their resources to the full. It assumed that a removal of these restrictions would both increase the efficiency of Community producers and create a competitive environment which would encourage firms to exploit new opportunities more fully.

According to an assessment of the potential gains of the programme made for the EC Commission, the creation of a true market may lead to a reduction of costs and prices in the order of 2.5 to 6.5 per cent of the aggregated GDPs of Community countries. In addition to these welfare effects, macroeconomic gains in the range of 4.5 to 7 per cent of the aggregated Community GDPs are expected. The gains (which are once for all) should materialize over a period of five or more years.[68]

The abolition of non-tariff barriers is considered to be synonymous with a reduction in production costs which, under the impact of greater competition, would largely be passed on in prices. Everything would then flow from that: improved purchasing power of incomes would stimulate economic activity, increased competitiveness would reinforce that upturn and at the same time improve the Community's balance on current account, the initial price reductions would prevent the upturn in activity from degenerating into inflationary pressure—there would even be disinflationary tendencies—and finally, public deficits could be alleviated through the twin effect of the opening up of public procurement and the upturn in activity. A virtuous circle could even be established which could prolong those beneficial effects into the medium term or even beyond: under the impact of increased competitiveness and the enlargement of markets to cover the whole of the Community area, firms would continue to cut their production costs (economies of scale, stimulus to innovation, and reduction in X-inefficiency).[69] The beneficial effects due to the productivity-induced reduction in production costs could thus be self-sustaining.

A reduction in employment in the initial stages of the process is feared, but after some years the completion of the internal market is expected to imply the creation of some 5 million jobs for the Community as a whole.

The 'completion of the internal market' has been officially presented as a sort of 'supply-side' programme to boost European economic growth. Of great importance are the expected strategic reactions of firms faced with a new competitive environment; it is maintained that the rate of technological innovation depends on the presence of competition and economies of scale, and that only an integrated market can offer the benefits of both scale and competition; that market segmentation damages the performance of high-technology industries; and that a full integration of the internal market will foster the emergence of truly European companies which are better suited to securing a strong place in world market competition.

But it has been argued that the programme of the internal market may also create a much more self-sufficient and self-centred Europe where member countries prefer to trade and invest more among themselves than with the rest of the world. As noted by *Far Eastern Economic Review* (5 May 1988), the price for outsider countries 'to gain access to the European "Club of 92" will be heavy by way of reciprocity'; the simple protectionism of national quotas could give way to 'Euro-protectionism enshrined in community-wide quotas'. These possible effects have not been examined in the various reports commissioned by the European Community, although it has been said that the integration of Europe should give European firms a better base for oligopolistic competition against US and Japanese rivals.

The perspective of 'Fortress Europe' emphasizes the component of protectionism inherent in economic integration policies such as those of the European Community: attempts are made to combine industrial protection with economies of scale and impetus to change, and non-discrimination of members with discrimination of non-members.[70] In other words, economic integration policies offer only second best to totally free trade, but also a lot of things which are not offered by free trade at all (such as the possibility of fostering new industries).

As a protectionist device, the internal market may create conditions for physical capital formation and economic growth by means of (what has been termed) trade diversion: the substitution of Community production for less costly imports (from the United States, Japan or the newly industrialized countries). The possible welfare losses of this substitution are the price to be paid for increased commodity production and employment. The demand pulls caused by both import replacement and increased mobilization of resources within the Community may provide necessary conditions for substantial physical capital formation if combined with lower real rates of interest.

Extended European Nationalism

A more self-sufficient and inward-looking Europe, capable of loosening the apron strings of the United States, has been advocated by Seers as a solution to the recent problems of stagnation and unemployment.[71] It is only within an enlarged, widened and deepened European Community that proper reflation policies can be conducted. In such a framework of Extended European Nationalism, technology and capital could be mobilized more easily. Behind its ramparts, there would be markets for sophisticated industrial products large enough for European producers to match the leading firms of the United States and Japan. The challenges to stagnating economies would be demanding but not overwhelming. Protective development would provide orders for European investment goods industries rather than for producers in the United States or Japan. Food and energy needs could be covered at stable prices, particularly if the Community entered long-term purchase and production agreements with non-member countries. Because of its bargaining power, it could protect its internal market without losing access to overseas markets or sources of supply. Community regulations of industrial output (such as those applied to steel) would probably spread to an increased number of industries, but Community initiatives could also be increased (in electronics for example), as well as European education programmes in technical and scientific subjects. The enhanced Community self-reliance would be the logical counterpart of the South-South co-operation promoted in other parts of the world. But it should not mean complete economic independence. Restricted imports of manufactures would release foreign exchange for the purchase of more primary products. Various measures could be used to reduce the import content of consumption and steer demand towards sectors which could produce more employment. Inflows of non-European capital could be monitored by the Community and, if threatening to strategic industries, prevented. The frantic and expensive competition for Japanese investment could be put to an end. Transnational companies with a base in

Europe could be dissuaded from creating industrial plants overseas that compete with European industries. European interest rates could be delinked from the interest rates of the United States (a kind of dependence that Seers also argued keeps activity in Europe depressed).

In such a Community framework, not only a large proportion of trade but also most service transactions would be internal. The European Currency Unit could be used as a currency of both account and settlement, which would greatly reduce the need for US dollars; it could, in fact, develop enough strength to be largely unaffected by fluctuations in the dollar. The European Monetary System could adopt some of the functions of a European Central Bank with its own reserves, capable of reinforcing Community economic policies. The envisaged Europe would be less 'liberal' than the Community Jean Monnet and its other progenitors had in mind, but it would also be more egalitarian than they thought necessary. Seers's scenario includes fiscal systems with a much larger budget to support the development of regions and industries with economic problems. The crucial role of Community leadership would probably be assumed by Germany, which has the most to gain but also more to sacrifice than other countries in a redistribution of income. This raises the historical spectre of German domination, but is modified by the fact that the political framework would also comprise other nations of great weight.

It should be a priority to integrate the less wealthy countries of southern Europe, but the most important task will be to overcome the East–West division of Europe. The Community should in due course also include the countries of Eastern Europe. Like southern Europe, these countries would be a natural outlet for agricultural surpluses of the Western countries. The demographic consequences would also be similar to the integration of southern Europe (as younger and more dynamic populations would be added). Closer economic co-operation with Eastern Europe needs to be complemented by non-aggression pacts which would make both NATO and the Warsaw Pact obsolete. An East–West framework could also allow for membership of Austria and Finland, as well as attracting Sweden and Norway. 'Is it, anyway, quite inconceivable,' asks Seers, 'that political developments within the Soviet Union, especially the growing independence of the Asian Republics, will ultimately lead to links between the Community and the European Soviet Republics?'[72] In sum, an expanding European Community, with growing internal homogeneity, self-sufficiency and bargaining power, provides, according to Seers, a coherent answer to the historic challenge of the Europeans. As Europe develops its resource base, the customary (and increasingly less feasible) interventions of its member governments in the political and economic affairs of overseas countries become less necessary.

Seers's scenario may seem unrealistic, but it is definitely less unrealistic in the final years of the 1980s than it was when his book appeared in 1983. Attempts by the countries of the European Free Trade Association to adjust their economies and align their legal system with that of the European Community have already been made. The EFTA countries seek nowadays, in effect, a customs union with the twelve countries of the EC, which would mean adopting the EC's common tariffs against outside goods. Their prime concern is 'not to lose out from the proposed abolition of all barriers to the movement of goods, capital, services and people within the community of 1992' (*Far Eastern Economic Review* 9 March 1989). Recent developments have also brought specula- tions about an association of the French Magreb countries of Algeria, Morocco and Tunisia, as well as Egypt, Syria and Jordan (not to mention Israel, too). We have already described the programme for the completion of the internal market, which could equally well be interpreted as attempts at protectionism on a continental scale, as a move towards global free trade and factor movements. New initiatives have been taken in the late 1980s to create a European Monetary Union with a common central bank.[73]

Economic integration policies also comprising Eastern Europe and the Soviet Union would entail, of course, the greatest difficulties, but functional integration of Eastern and Western Europe nevertheless appears to be a solution to economic problems facing policy-makers on both sides of the East–West border. It could ease the task of modernizing the Eastern economies by providing technology and direly needed capital equipment, raise private consumption standards, and help solve the severe environmental problems of the centrally planned Eastern countries. The West could help finance investment projects in the East, which would also generate substantial physical capital formation in the West. From the point of view of the Federal Republic of Germany, a broadly enlarged Economic Community is in line with the *Ostpolitik* already initiated in the late 1960s; it would provide a substitute for formal German reunification. But will a European Community stretching from the Atlantic to the Urals be accepted by the United States? And is it compatible with the geopolitical interests of Britain and France? Such questions open up a field of analysis which is beyond the scope of the present study. Suffice it to say that Western European commodity trade with the Soviet Union and other socialist countries of Eastern Europe has hitherto been modest, and that there is great potential for future growth.

As shown in Table 7:15, the combined Western European exports to these countries amounted to $36 billion in 1980. Exports from the East to the West in the same year totalled $44 billion. In the first half of the 1980s exports in both directions contracted. While Western European exports to the United States increased by almost 70 per cent in current values between 1980 and 1985, Western European exports to the socialist countries of Eastern Europe declined by 30 per cent. The combined

Table 7.15   Exports from Western Europe to socialist countries of
Eastern Europe (A)
Exports from socialist countries of Eastern Europe to Western
Europe (B)*

($m, F.o.b.)

	Total merchandise exports			
	1955	*1970*	*1980*	*1985*
A	1,100	5,840	35,820	24,880
B	1,420	6,230	44,120	39,840
A:B	0.77	0.94	0.81	0.62

	Manufactured goods excluding iron and steel and non-ferrous metals and machinery and transport equipment $-SITC\ (6+8)-(67+68)$			
	1955	*1970*	*1980*	*1985*
A	150	1,220	7,330	4,940
B	110	820	5,300	3,590
A:B	1.29	1.48	1.38	1.38

	Machinery and transport equipment			
	1955	*1970*	*1980*	*1985*
A	250	970	5,170	7,580
B	110	590	3,220	2,220
A:B	2.27	1.65	1.60	3.42

*Excluding trade between the Federal Republic of Germany and the German Democratic Republic.

Sources: UNCTAD, *Handbook of International Trade and Development Statistics 1983, 1985* and *1987*.

Eastern European exports to Western Europe have exceeded the combined Western European exports to Eastern Europe ever since the 1950s. As the former contracted less than the latter in the first half of the 1980s, the export quotient of Western Europe in relation to the Eastern countries declined. As for *manufactured goods excluding iron and steel and non-ferrous metals* and *machinery and transport equipment*, the value of exports from the West to the East has always exceeded the value of exports from the East to the West. As Western European exports of *machinery and transport equipment* increased, while Eastern European exports of such commodities contracted in the first half of the 1980s, the export quotient for the product group rose substantially. The figures indicate the distinction of the trade pattern between the two parts of Europe: while the East is mainly a supplier of energy and primary products, the West supplies machinery and other capital equipment. Total Western European exports to Eastern Europe in 1985 amounted to a third of Western European exports to the United States; Western European exports of *machinery and transport equipment* to the East was less than a quarter of Western European exports to the United States.

The Economically Active Population

How have industries and occupations evolved in the 1980s? The question can only be answered tentatively, as comprehensive census data will not be available until the mid-1990s.

With respect to industry groups, it is possible to make the following observations regarding the most recent developments by means of OECD employment statistics. The rate of employment decline in the agricultural sector was much lower in the ten-year period 1976–86 than in the 1960s (see Table 7:16). While the sector contracted by 4–5 per cent a year between 1960 and 1970, the rate was in the range of 2–3 per cent in more recent years. (An exception was Italy, where the rate of decline was much higher.) In 1986 agriculture, forestry and fishing comprised no more than 2–5 per cent of all employed civilians. In most countries the sector is probably not far from its minimum size and near equilibrium.

Industrial employment contracted by 1–3 per cent a year between 1976 and 1986 (see Table 7:17); in the latter year the industrial sector provided paid work for less than a third of total civilian employees. In

Table 7.16 Agriculture, forestry and fishing: number employed

| | Annual rate of change | | % of civilian |
	1960–70	1976–86	employment, 1986
Belgium	−4.9	−2.1	2.8
France	−3.7	−3.0	7.3
Germany	−4.0	−2.2	5.3
Italy	−5.6	−3.6	10.9
Netherlands	−3.4	−0.5	4.8
Sweden	–	−3.4	4.2
UK	−3.5	−1.3	2.5

Sources: OECD, *Labour Force Statistics 1959–70* and *1966–86* (Paris: OECD, 1972; 1988)

Germany the share was over 40 per cent. Manufacturing employment, which peaked around 1970, continued on its declining trend in the 1980s. In the middle of the decade it reversed in some countries— probably as a result of growing exports to the United States—and reassumed physical capital formation. Figure 7:1 relates the development of manufacturing employment in seven Western European countries to that of Japan and the United States; for the United States, variations in manufacturing employment reflect the development of the dollar rate since the late 1960s (growth in the second half of the 1970s when the dollar fell compared to major Western European currencies; a subsequent sharp decline when US policies caused the dollar to rise). For Japan, where manufacturing employment showed rapid growth in the 1950s and 1960s, a recovery from the 1974–5 recession was already recorded in 1980. The development of Japanese manufacturing employment for the 1980s thus differs from that of West Germany and Italy, the most successful exporters of manufactures in Europe. Although the number of employed increased in Germany in the mid-1980s, the pattern for the Western European countries conveys sustained contraction.

It is hardly surprising that the industries of banking, insurance and real estate, and business services, have expanded in recent years, as they did in the earlier decades of the post-war period (see Table 7:18). The sheer growth in the volume of business (due to more frequent use of cheques, consumer credit, household financing of owner-occupied homes, etc.) has required more staffing. In Britain, where the City of London has been a successful exporter of financial services to other countries, employment grew by more than 4 per cent a year between 1976 and 1986. The steady employment growth of banking and other financial services for many years means that these industries currently employ two, three or (in Britain) four times as many persons as the agricultural sector.

Table 7.17   The industrial sector: number employed

| | Annual rate of change | | % of civilian |
	1960–70	1976–86	employment, 1986
Belgium	0.4	−2.9	29.1
France	1.2	−1.9	31.3
Germany	0.6	−0.8	40.9
Italy	1.1	−1.0	31.1
Netherlands	0.9	–	26.8
Sweden	–	−1.2	30.1
UK	−0.3	−2.6	30.9

Sources: OECD, *Labour Force Statistics 1959–1970* and *1966–86* (Paris: OECD, 1972; 1988)

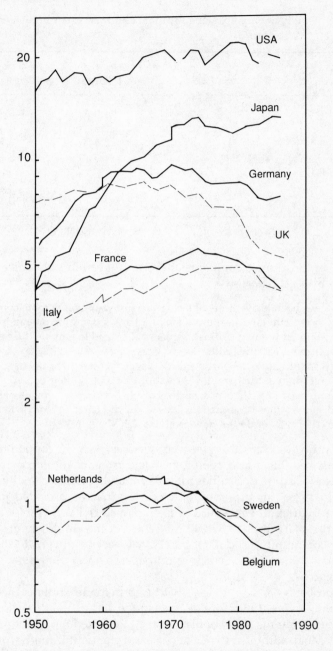

Figure 7.1 Manufacturing employees/employment (millions of persons)

Table 7.18 Employment in banking, insurance and real estate and business services

	Annual rate of change		% of civilian
	1960–70	*1976–86*	*employment, 1986*
Belgium	4.3	3.0	8.3
France	–	2.6	8.4
Germany	–	2.3	6.7
Italy	–	–	3.6
Netherlands	4.0	–	10.8
Sweden	–	3.1	7.7
UK	3.1	4.2	10.1

Sources: OECD, *Labour Force Statistics 1959–70* and *1966–86* (Paris: OECD 1972, 1988)

Banks and insurance companies have been keen to save office work. As noted by *The Economist*:

Big banks have been heavy users of technology for years. Mainframe computers have been processing and keeping track of a bank's domestic operations since the 1960s. Without them . . . British banks would need to employ the country's entire population to deal with the business they now do. . . . Even for technology smart banks, labour is still the biggest component in costs. British banks . . . reckon that their employees account for 65% of their operating costs. Most are employed in routine jobs, such as cashing cheques or opening letters of credit and getting those transactions logged on the bank's records. Relatively few sell to customers or design new products. (25 March 1989, p. 11)

Community, social and personal services, which contain mostly public services, have also been a growing category of employment in recent years (despite difficulties for governments in financing the public sector). In 1986, this grouping of service industries provided jobs for between a quarter and one-third of all employed civilians (Table 7:19). In Sweden the share approached 40 per cent. Yet the employment growth rates of community, social and personal services have declined in comparison to the 1960s, which in retrospect appear as the hey-day of public services.

It is probably a safe guess that 'information-handling' activities provide employment for more persons in the 1980s than they did in the 1970s, corroborating the popular image presented by Porat, among others.[74] Most administrative, clerical and communication work has been affected by office rationalization undertaken by private and public employers keen to save costs. Growth should be expected to characterize, in particular, technical and scientific work. The number of operative workers has certainly declined, at least in production, if not in sales and transport.

Table 7.19 Employment in community, social and personal services

	Annual rate of change		% of civilian
	1960–70	*1976–86*	*employment, 1986*
Belgium	2.6	2.2	32.2
France	–	2.3	29.8
Germany	–	1.8	25.9
Netherlands	2.4	–	34.2
Sweden	–	2.1	36.9
UK	1.7	1.2	29.9

Sources: OECD, *Labour Force Statistics 1959–70* and *1966–86* (Paris: OECD 1972, 1988)

Less impressive growth than in earlier decades probably holds for medical and social care, teaching and entertainment. The various types of work included in this group of occupations are financed to a large extent by public expenditure. Although some are carried out in areas destined for privatization, their growth momentum has probably been contained by the squeeze of public sector budgets.

Personal service work may have assumed greater weight in countries with high rates of unemployment and substantial immigration from less developed countries. The supply of such work tends to create its own demand (when people 'force themselves into the market' by establishing a small service firm of their own).

The occupation group of protective service workers and armed forces has probably neither expanded nor declined: the demand for internal (and privately organized) security work may have grown, but the manpower need of military defence has probably declined at the same time due to rationalization.

As for the future, it is possible to make the following remarks in a ten-year perspective.

The development of agricultural employment in the countries of a more or less enlarged European Community will be highly dependent on Community policy and, of course, the geographical scope of the integration scheme. Inclusion of some of the economies of Eastern Europe may create markets for the farming industry of the Western countries; if the Community evolves to include other Mediterranean countries, agricultural jobs in the current southern European member countries will be under threat. A crucial factor is future efficiency and productivity growth.

The development of manufacturing employment will also depend on the stance and scope of European integration policies. Factual (although not formally admitted) protectionism may very well allow for some employment growth, particularly if the Community evolves in the directions envisioned by Seers. The cost of creating manufacturing employment through protectionism may be higher prices of manufactures (or rather that the real prices of some types of consumer good will fall less rapidly than has been the case in recent years due to increased imports).

While the employment growth of banking and insurance will be brought to a halt in a ten-year perspective, it is possible that employment in business services will grow. Growth may reflect increased demand for 'producer services' but also an expanded supply of alleged professional expertise or sheer office work offered by small firms and self-employed workers.

The development of community, social and personal services will be dependent on the performance of the manufacturing industry in particular (as that industry will remain the economic base for real value growth, and thus the creator of conditions enabling employment growth in public service industries). Some private service industries may expand if rates of unemployment remain high and there is an influx of migrants from less developed southern (and eastern) countries. If migrants from such countries (and other persons pressing to enter the labour market) accept modest pecuniary compensation (and conditions of work shunned by most workers), traditional private service trades may even thrive. The same type of reasoning may apply to retailing, where the rate of self and family employment may be substantial even if distributive functions are overwhelmingly carried out by large firms.[75]

Of crucial importance to most industries and occupations is, of course, the future development of productivity. Will productivity, in the physical and/or economic sense of the word, increase at approximately the growth rates recorded in the time period studied?

From a technological point of view, which relates to both the efficiency of operations and the ability of firms to use their labour resources for the supply of more sophisticated (and highly priced) products, there seems to be a considerable potential for further productivity growth. One apparent source of efficiency gains is automation and flexible specialization, which may permeate the various industries and branches of the commodity sector (not only in manufacturing, but also in service trades). But (in the vein of traditional Marxist analysis) one can easily argue that automation will afflict aggregate demand and profits unless the rising efficiency is accompanied by a proportionate growth in aggregate incomes, and/or a substantial, and increasing share of the wages and salaries of those engaged in the automated industries are appropriated as taxes (or in some other form) and used to expand public services (or other industries). The same kind of reasoning holds for measures taken by firms to increase real value added per hour by means of diversification towards more sophisticated products. Such strategies may be successful for some producers, and even lead to the increased welfare for most people, but they will hurt average profits if spending power and a demand sufficient to soak up discharged labour is not generated simultaneously.

As a policy issue, the problem seems extremely tricky: on one hand, governments are forced to promote the efficiency and international competitiveness of their domestic industries, and on the other hand they cannot neglect the negative effects (on both profits and average household incomes) of continued rationalization. The very notion of employment and unemployment may be redefined and adjusted according to a situation where a declining portion of the labour force complies with earlier standards. Average hours can be reduced. But if such measures require higher taxes and/or rising hourly compensation (to evade the problem of crumbling or stagnating demand), they may be politically infeasible: higher taxes will be opposed by people in employment (and may have adverse effects on incentives to work), and increased hourly compensation will be opposed by employers and/or spur further labour-saving rationalization. If productivity growth afflicts aggregate demand and profits, it may lose some of its rationale in a wider social perspective. However, as long as profits remain the main motive of producers, the concerted dictates of product markets and organized labour will force firms to rely on rationalization to enhance real value added per hour. Productivity will grow, employment will be dislocated.

European agriculture offers an illustration of the 'dysfunctionality' of increased labour productivity. The social and political costs of the increased unemployment which is likely to be an effect of relaxed protection may serve, in effect, as an argument for the much criticized Common Agricultural Policy (CAP).[76] The opportunity costs, which are the 'true' economic costs of the protection of farmers (or any industry) seem to be small (as there are, for the time being, few other industries where redundant farmers can find regular and full-time employment). As the CAP creates sales opportunities and jobs in other parts of the Community sector (not to mention the Community bureaucracy and the public sector of member countries), it can be argued that a much larger portion of total employment is at stake (for example in manufacturing firms supplying European agriculture and using their sales in Western Europe as a base for exports to other parts of the world). The protection of farmers offers governments an opportunity to underpin European 'agri-business' as a whole, the *filière* of economic activities which is, in effect, dependent on modern agricultural production. The main argument against the CAP resides with the consumers (and countries where agri-business is small): these parties pay for the protection of farmers (and the support of linked industries) by spending more money on food than they would if non-Community producers had free access to Western European markets. But in a situation where unemployment rates exceed 10 per cent of the labour force, there is little reason (except for a country such as Britain) not to protect farmers. Of course, such reasoning has not taken into account that the present system of support does not solve the basic problems of increased efficiency; that it ties farmers to a productivity treadmill where they can safeguard their incomes only by means of increased sales (the main beneficiaries being producers of farm equipment and inputs); that the costs of the resulting overproduction (and high rate of capital intensity) are covered by the people in general; and that mechanization and 'scientification' of agriculture may have disastrous ecological effects.

There is little reason to expect a future common manufacturing policy to protect manufacturing in the way farming is protected by the CAP. But the creation of a 'true European market' may provide for a substitute that shields particular manufacturing industries from the competition of foreign producers. The completion of the internal market project will remove non-tariff barriers to intra-Community trade, but at the same time make discrimination against 'third countries' possible. Yet protection does not exclude productivity growth (as demonstrated by the much protected Western European agriculture). The firms of the partly shielded internal market will be forced to rationalize to cope with internal or external competition and demands for increased compensation on the part of their employees.

Notes

1. F. Hirsch, *Social Limits to Growth* (Cambridge, Mass.: Harvard University Press, 1978).
2. S.B. Linder, *The Harried Leisure Class* (New York: Columbia University Press, 1970).
3. The thesis of a crisis of Fordism has been developed with reference to the United States in M. Aglietta, *A Theory of Capitalist Regulation: The U.S. Experience* (London: New Left Books, 1979). According to Boyer & Mistral and Lipietz, the thesis is also applicable to the contemporary societies of Western Europe. See R. Boyer & J. Mistral, *Accumulation, Inflation, Crises* (Paris: PUF, 1978) and A. Lipietz, *Crise et Inflation: Pourquoi?* (Paris: Maspero, 1979).
4. Aglietta, op.cit., p. 116.
5. To speak of the regulation of a mode of production is to speak of the processes which reproduce the determinant structure of a society. Aglietta, op.cit., p. 12 ff.
6. Ibid,. p. 116.
7. Ibid., p. 158ff.
8. OECD, *National Accounts 1974–1986*. The data serve only as a crude measure of the spending power of households. They include contributions made by employers to social security schemes, private pension schemes and

family allowances, health, life and casualty insurance payments, etc. They are subject to taxation, and are supplemented by various payments made by government.

9. E. Olin Wright, *Class, Crisis and the State* (London: Verso, 1979) p. 140.

10. Household savings should be related to direct taxes and government transfers of incomes. OECD statistics disclose great differences among countries in both the relative weight of the net obligations of households towards government, and the direction of change of these obligations. Whereas aggregate direct taxes and social benefits tended to counter-balance each other in France and the Netherlands in the 1980s, taxes and social security payments net of social benefits were in the range of 10–15% of aggregate incomes in Sweden (where household savings became negative). While the share of net obligations declined in Britain, it grew in Belgium and Germany. One may expect small and declining net obligations to favour private consumption. Yet the causal link is far from simple. A high percentage share of direct taxes net of social benefits may very well promote mass consumption if it contributes to low rates of unemployment (as seems to be the case in Sweden).

11. A case in point is the Japanese automobile industry, where many of the major car producers of today started in the 1950s as assemblers of 'completely knocked down' kits under licence from European and US manufacturers. See, for instance, R. Jenkins, *Transnational Corporations and the Latin American Automobile Industry* (Basingstoke: Macmillan, 1987), Ch. 9. Another example is the consumer electronics industry, where Japanese firms account for more than half of the world market. The familiar products, such as television, videocassette recorders and audio equipment, are almost the very symbols of Japanese industrial success (K. Morgan & A. Sayer, *Micro-Circuits of Capital: 'Sunrise' Industry and Uneven Development*, Cambridge: Polity Press, 1988).

12. Since the late 1950s and early 1960s these countries have all expanded their gross domestic product by means of swiftly growing manufactured exports. Beginning with garments and textiles and progressing through a variety of miscellaneous products including electronic components, they have in the 1980s attained a steadily growing sophistication in their commodity exports. See N. Harris, *The End of the Third World: Newly Industrializing Countries and the Decline of an Ideology* (London: Penguin, 1986) p. 67. As for their exports of household electronics and automobiles, see Morgan & Sayer, op.cit. and *The Future of the Automobile: The Report of MIT's International Automobile Program* (London & Sydney: Allen & Unwin, 1984) p. 41 ff.

13. M.J. Piore & Ch. F. Sabel, *The Second Industrial Divide: Possibilities for Prosperity* (New York: Basic Books, 1984).

14. Great popularity has been achieved particularly by small firms in Italy (or rather 'the Third Italy') for being the visible expression of the new production regime. See A. Amin, 'Flexible Specialization and Small Firms in Italy: Myths and Reality', *Antipode* Vol. 21 (April 1989).

15. The World Bank, *World Development Report 1985* (New York: Oxford University Press, 1985) p. 2.

16. Ibid., p. 31.

17. Ibid., p. 89.

18. Ibid., p. 32.
19. B. Tew, *The Evolution of the International Monetary System 1945–1985* (London: Hutchinson, 1985) p. 225 ff.
20. *World Development Report 1985*, op.cit., and *1987* (New York: Oxford University Press, 1987).
21. UNIDO, *Industry and Development: Global Report 1986*, p. 134 (Vienna: Unido, 1986).
22. *World Development Report 1983*, p. 13 (New York: Oxford University Press, 1983).
23. UNIDO, op.cit., p. 134.
24. This and the following paragraphs on the changing economic intercourse between the United States and Western Europe draw heavily on E.A. Brett, *The World Economy Since the War* (London: Macmillan, 1985).
25. Ibid., p. 107, relying on J. Spero, *The Politics of International Economic Relations* (London: Allen & Unwin, 1982) p. 40 ff.
26. Brett, op.cit., p. 108. For the productivity growth of the US manufacturing industry compared to manufacturing in Western Europe, see p. 142.
27. Ibid., p. 110 ff.
28. Ibid., p. 130.
29. A. Lipietz, 'Towards Global Fordism', *New Left Review*, No. 132 (March–April 1982) 35. See also *Mirages and Miracles* (London: Verso, 1987).
30. A. Lipietz, 'Ackumulering och Kriser: Några Metodologiska Reflektioner angående Begreppet Regulering', *Nordisk Tidskrift för Politisk Ekonomi*, No. 17 (1984) 28 ff.
31. Repeated budget deficits implied growing public debt. Between 1975 and 1985 the ratio of net public debt to the GDP changed by 6.2% a year in Belgium, by 4.4% a year in Sweden, and by 3.7% a year in Italy. The corresponding figures for the Netherlands and Germany were 2.2 and 2.1%, for France 0.6 and for Britain –1.0%. See J.D. Sachs & N. Roubini, 'Political and Economic Determinants of Budget Deficits in the Industrial Democracies', *NBER Working Paper* no. 2682. Quoted from *The Economist* 7 January 1989.
32. P.J. Dunleavy, 'The Growth of Sectoral Cleavages and the Stabilization of State Expenditures', *Environment and Planning D: Society and Space*, Vol. 4 (1986), 135.
33. P. Dunleavy, 'The Political Implications of Sectoral Cleavages and the Growth of State Employment: Part 1, The Analysis of Production Cleavages', and 'Part 2. Cleavage Structures and Political Alignment', *Political Studies*, Vol. 28, Nos. 3 & 4 (1980).
34. Dunleavy, 'The Growth of Sectoral Cleavages', p. 141.
35. Ibid., 142.
36. G. Esping-Andersen, 'Power and Distributional Regimes', *Politics & Society*, Vol. 14, No. 2 (1985), 277.
37. Ibid., 227 ff.
38. For an overview of long-wave theory, see for example, M. Marshall, *Long Waves and Regional Development* (London & Basingstoke: Macmillan, 1987).
39. C. Freeman, J. Clark & L. Soete, *Unemployment and Technical Innovation: A Study of Long Waves and Economic Development* (London: Frances Pinter, 1982) p. 20.

40. Ibid., p. 65.
41. Ibid., p. 67.
42. Ibid., p. 65.
43. Ibid., p. 21.
44. Ibid., p. 75.
45. C. Freeman & C. Perez, 'Long Waves and New Technology', *Nordisk Tidskrift för Politisk Ekonomi*, (1984) No. 17, 8 ff.
46. C. Perez, 'Structural Change and Assimilation of New Technologies in the Economic and Social System', in *Design, Innovation and Long Cycles in Economic Development*, ed. C. Freeman (London: Frances Pinter/New York: St. Martin's Press, 1986) p. 32.
47. Freeman & Perez, op.cit., p. 10.
48. Perez, op.cit., p. 40.
49. Freeman & Perez, op.cit., p. 13.
50. E. Mandel, *Senkapitalismen*, Vol. 1 (Stockholm: Coeckelberghs, 1974), *The Second Slump: A Marxist Analysis of Recession in the Seventies* (London: New Left Books, 1978), *Long Waves of Capitalist Development: The Marxist Interpretation* (Cambridge & Paris: Cambridge University Press/Editions de la Maison des Sciences de l'Homme, 1980) and 'Explaining Long Waves of Capitalist Development', *Futures*, Vol. 13 (August 1981).
51. Ibid., p. 332.
52. Mandel, *The Second Slump*, op.cit., p. 166.
53. Mandel, *Long Waves*, op.cit., p. 14.
54. A. Maddison, *Phases of Capitalist Development* (Oxford & New York: Oxford University Press, 1982) p. 81.
55. Ibid., p. 83.
56. Ibid., p. 91.
57. Ibid., p. 143.
58. Ibid., p. 144 ff.
59. L.L. Pasinetti, *Structural Change and Economic Growth: A Theoretical Essay on the Dynamics of the Wealth of Nations* (Cambridge: Cambridge University Press, 1981) p. 232 ff.
60. Ibid., p. 68 (note on 'consumer learning').
61. Ibid., p. 234.
62. Ibid.
63. Ibid., p. 235.
64. Ibid., p. 228.
65. Ibid., p. 235.
66. *The Economist*, 24 September 1988.
67. J. Pelkmans & L.A. Winters, *Europe's Domestic Market* (London: Routledge, 1988), Chatham House Papers 43.
68. 'The Economics of 1992: An Assessment of the Potential Economic Effects of the Internal Market of the European Community', *European Economy*, No. 35 (March 1988).
69. Ibid., p. 163 ff. Reduced X-inefficiency means a better internal allocation of resources within the firms.
70. This interpretation of economic integration policies had already been offered by early students of customs unions. As Viner remarks: 'The literature on customs union in general, whether written by economists or

non-economists, by free-traders or protectionists, is almost universally favourable to them. . . . It is a strange phenomenon which unites free-traders and protectionists in the field of commercial policy, and its strangeness suggests that there is something peculiar in the apparent economics of customs unions.' If free-traders and protectionists agree, Viner continues, 'it must be because they see in customs unions different sets of facts, and not because an identical customs union can meet the requirements of both the free-trader and the protectionist'. While the latter sees tariff protection, the former sees benefits of increased division of labour within the group of countries forming a customs union. See J. Viner, *The Customs Union Issue* (New York & London: Carnegie Endowment for International Peace/Stevens & Sons, 1950) p. 41 and *passim*.

71. D. Seers, *The Political Economy of Nationalism* (Oxford: Oxford University Press, 1983).
72. Ibid., p. 180.
73. 'EMU in motion' and 'How to Hatch an EMU', *The Economist*, 22 April 1989.
74. M.U. Porat, *The Information Economy* (Washington, DC: US Department of Commerce, 1976). For an assessment of the evolving 'information economy' of Western Europe, see OECD, *Trends in the Information Economy* (Paris: OECD, 1986).
75. In the first half of the 1980s, the self-employed as a percentage of all workers in non-agricultural industries contracted in Italy and France. In Germany, the Netherlands, Belgium and Britain, self-employment outside the agricultural sector assumed an apparent equilibrium rate of 3–5% of all workers (OECD, *Labour Force Statistics 1966–1986*).
76. 'The EEC's common agricultural policy [CAP] . . . "protects" European farmers in three ways: it puts up barriers to imports, in particular "variable levies" which are equal to the differences between the EEC's target price for a commodity and the prevailing world price; it buys and stores surplus production within Europe; and it subsidises exports to non-European countries to get rid of what is left.' (*The Economist*, 15 April 1989).

References

Aglietta. M. *A Theory of Capitalist Regulation: The U.S. Experience*, London: New Left Books, 1979.

Ahnström, L. 'The Turn-Around Trend and the Economically Active Population of Seven Capital Regions in Western Europe', *Norsk Geografisk Tidskrift*, Vol. 40, No. 2 (1986).

Amin, A. 'Flexible Specialization and Small Firms in Italy: Myths and Reality', *Antipode*, Vol. 21 (April 1989).

Anell, L. *Recession, the Western Economies and the Changing World Order*, London & New York: Frances Pinter & St Martin's Press, 1981.

Ansoff, I.H. *Corporate Strategy: An Analytical Approach to Business Policy for Growth and Expansion*, Harmondsworth: Penguin, 1971.

Averitt, R. *The Dual Economy: The Dynamics of American Industry Structure*, New York: Norton, 1968.

Bacon, R.W. & Eltis, W. *Britain's Economic Problems: Too Few Producers*, London & New York: Macmillan, 1978.

Baumol, W.J. *Business Behavior, Value and Growth*, New York: Macmillan, 1949.

Baumol, W.J. 'On the Theory of the Expansion of the Firm', *American Economic Review*, Vol. 52 (December 1962).

Baumol, W.J. 'The Macroeconomics of Unbalanced Growth', *American Economic Review*, Vol. 57 (June 1967).

Baumol, W.J. & Oates, W.H. *The Theory of Environmental Policy*, Cambridge: Cambridge University Press, 1975.

Bell, D. *The Coming of the Post-Industrial Society: A Venture in Social Forecasting*, London: Heinemann, 1974.

Boyer, R. & Mistral, J. *Accumulation, Inflation, Crises*, Paris: Presses Universitaires de France, 1978.

Braudel, F. *Civilization and Capitalism 15th–18th Century*, Vol. III: *The Perspective of the World*, London: Collins, 1984.

Braverman, H.S. *Labor and Monopoly Capital: The Degradation of Work in the Twentieth Century*, New York & London: Monthly Review Press, 1974.

Brett, E.A. *The World Economy Since the War*, London: Macmillan, 1985.

Coase, R.H. 'The Nature of the Firm', *Economica*, Vol. 4 (1937).

Churchman, C.W. *The Systems Approach*, New York: Dell, 1968.

Clark, C. *The Conditions of Economic Progress*, London: Macmillan, 1940.

185

Dawson, J.A. *Commercial Distribution in Europe*, London & Canberra: Croom Helm, 1982.

Dunleavy, P.J. 'The Political Implications of Sectoral Cleavages and the Growth of State Employment: Part 1, The Analysis of Production Cleavages', and 'Part 2, Cleavage Structures and Political Alignment', *Political Studies*, Vol. 28, No. 3 (1980).

Dunleavy, P.J. 'The Growth of Sectoral Cleavages and the Stabilization of State Expenditures', *Environment and Planning D. Space and Society*, Vol. 4 (1986).

'The Economics of 1992: An Assessment of the Potential Economic Effects of the Internal Market', *European Economy*, No. 35 (March 1988).

Eichner, A.S. *The Megacorp and Oligopoly: Micro Foundations of Macro Dynamics*, Cambridge: Cambridge University Press, 1976.

Ellul, J. *The Technological Society*, New York: Vintage Books, 1964.

Ernst, E. (ed.) *The New Division of Labour, Technology and Underdevelopment: Consequences for the Third World*, Frankfurt: Campus, 1980.

Esping-Andersen, G. 'Power and Distributional Regimes', *Politics & Society*, Vol. 14, No. 2 (1985).

Eurostat *Employment and Unemployment 1984*, Luxembourg: Statistical Office of the European Communities, 1984.

Falk, T. *Changes in the Distribution of the Population — the 1960s in Focus*, Stockholm: EFI, 1976.

Fisher, A.B.G. *The Clash of Progress and Security*, London: Macmillan, 1935.

Flora, P. et. al. *State, Economy and Society in Western Europe 1815–1975*, Frankfurt: Campus, 1983.

Fourastié, J. *La Productivité*, Paris: Presses Universitaires de France, 1971.

Freeman, C., Clark, J. & Soete, L. *Unemployment and Technical Innovation: A Study of Long Waves and Economic Development*, London: Frances Pinter, 1982.

Freeman, C. & Perez, C. 'Long Waves and New Technology', *Nordisk Tidskrift för Politisk Ekonomi*, No. 17 (1984).

Frey, B.S. & Weck-Hannemann, H. 'The Hidden Economy as an "Unobserved" Variable', *European Economic Review*, Vol. 26 (1984).

The Future of the Automobile: The Report of MIT's International Automobile Program, London & Sydney: Allen & Unwin, 1984.

Galbraith, J.K. *The New Industrial State*, Boston: Houghton Mifflin, 1967.

Gallie, W.B. *Pierce and Pragmatism*, Harmondsworth: Penguin, 1952.

Gershuny, J. 'Post-Industrial Society: The Myth of the Service Economy', *Futures*, Vol. 9 (April 1977).

Gershuny, J. *After Industrial Society? The Emerging Self-Service Economy*, London & Basingstoke: Macmillan, 1978.

Gershuny, J. 'The Informal Economy: Its Role in Post-Industrial Society', *Futures*, Vol. 11 (February 1979).

Gershuny, J. *Social Innovation and the Division of Labour*, Oxford: Oxford University Press, 1983.

Gershuny, J. & Miles, I. *The New Service Economy: The Transformation of Employment in Industrial Societies*, London: Frances Pinter, 1983.

Giddens, A. *The Class Structure of the Advanced Society*, London: Hutchinson, 1973.

Giddens, A. *Violence and the Nation-State: Volume Two of Contemporary Critique of Historical Materialism*, Cambridge: Polity Press, 1985.

Gouldner, A. *The Dialectic of Ideology and Technology*, London & Basingstoke: Macmillan, 1976.

Harris, A.L. 'Pure Capitalism and the Disappearance of the Middle Class', *Journal of Political Economy* Vol. 47 (June 1939).

Harris, N. *The End of the Third World: Newly Industrializing Countries and the Decline of an Ideology*, Harmondsworth: Penguin, 1989.

Held, D. 'Theories of the State', in *The State in Capitalist Europe: A Casebook*, ed. S. Bornstein, London: Allen & Unwin, 1984.

Hirsch, F. *Social Limits to Growth*, Cambridge, Mass.: Harvard University Press, 1978.

Jacobs, J. *The Economy of Cities*, London: Jonathan Cape, 1970.

Jenkins, R. *Transnational Corporations and the Latin American Automobile Industry*, Basingstoke: Macmillan, 1987.

Kuznets, S. *Modern Economic Growth: Rate, Structure, and Spread*, New Haven & London: Yale University Press, 1966.

Lengellé, M. *La Revolution Tertiaire*, Paris: Editions Genin, 1966.

Lengellé, M. *The Growing Importance of the Service Sector in the Member Countries*, Paris: OECD, 1966.

Liljenström, R. *Kultur och Arbete*, Stockholm: Liber-Sekretariatet för framtids-studier, 1979.

Linder, S.B. *The Harried Leisure Class*, New York: Columbia University Press, 1970.

Lipietz, A. *Crise et Inflation: Pourquoi?*, Paris: Maspero, 1979.

Lipietz, A. 'Towards Global Fordism', *New Left Review* No. 132 (March–April 1982).

Lipietz, A. 'Ackumulering och Kriser: Några Metodologiska Reflektioner angående Begreppet Regulering', *Nordisk Tidskrift för Politisk Ekonomi*, No. 17 (1984).

Lipietz, A. *Mirages and Miracles*, London: Verso, 1987.

Maddison, A. *Economic Growth in the West*, New York: Twentieth Century Fund, 1964.

Maddison, A. *Phases of Capitalist Development*, Oxford & New York: Oxford University Press, 1982.

Mandel, E. *Senkapitalismen*, Vol. 2, Stockholm: Coeckelbergh, 1974.

Mandel, E. *The Second Slump: A Marxist Analysis of Recession in the Seventies*, London: New Left Books, 1978.

Mandel, E. *Long Waves of Capitalist Development: The Marxist Interpretation*, Cambridge & Paris: Cambridge University Press & Editions de la Maison des Sciences de l'Homme, 1989.

Mandel, E. 'Explaining Long Waves of Capitalist Development', *Futures*, Vol. 13 (August 1981).

Marris, R. *The Economic Theory of 'Managerial' Capitalism*, London: Macmillan, 1964.

Marshall, M. *Long Waves and Regional Development*, London & Basingstoke: Macmillan, 1987.

Mattera, Ph. *Off the Books: The Rise of the Underground Economy*, London & Sydney: Pluto Press, 1985.

Mingione, E. & Redclift N. (eds) *Beyond Employment*, Oxford: Basil Blackwell, 1985.

Morgan, K. & Sayer, A. *Micro-Circuits of Capital: 'Sunrise' Industry and Uneven Development*, Cambridge: Polity Press, 1988.

O'Connor, J. *The Fiscal Crisis of the State*, New York: St Martin's Press, 1980.

OECD *Trends in the Information Economy*, Paris: OECD, 1986.

Offe, C. *Contradictions of the Welfare State*, ed. J. Keane, London: Hutchinson, 1981.

Olin Wright, E. *Class, Crises and the State*, London: Verso, 1979.

Pahl, R.E. *Divisions of Labour*, Oxford: Basil Blackwell, 1984.

Pasinetti, L.L. *Structural Change and Economic Growth: A Theoretical Essay on the Dynamics of the Wealth of Nations*, Cambridge: Cambridge University Press, 1981.

Pelkmans, J. & Winters, L.A. *Europe's Domestic Market*, London: Routledge, 1988 (Chatham House Papers 43).

Penrose, E.T. *The Theory of the Growth of the Firm*, Oxford: Basil Blackwell, 1959.

Perez, C. 'Structural Change and Assimilation of New Technologies in the Economic and Social System', in *Design, Innovation and Long Cycles in Economic Development*, ed. C. Freeman, London & New York: Frances Pinter & St Martin's Press, 1986.

Perroux, F. *L'Economie du XX:e Siècle*, Paris: Presses Universitaires de France, 1961.

Perroux, F. 'La Firm Motrice dans une Region et la Region Motrice', *Cahiers de l'Institut de Science Economique Appliquée*, Suppl. no. 111 (March 1961).

Piore, M.J. & Berger, S. *Dualism and Discontinuity in Industrial Societies*, Cambridge: Cambridge University Press, 1980.

Piore, M.J. & Sabel, Ch.F. *The Second Industrial Divide: Possibilities for Prosperity*, New York: Basic Books, 1984.

Polanyi, K. *Trade and Market in the Early Empires: Economies in History and Theory*, ed. C.M. Arensberg & H.W. Pearson, New York & London: Collier-Macmillan, 1957.

Porat, M.U. *The Information Economy*, Washington, DC: US Department of Commerce, 1976.

Porter, M.E. *Competitive Strategy: Techniques for Analyzing Industries and Competitors*, New York & London: Free Press-Collier, 1980.

Porter, M.E. *Competitive Advantage: Creating and Sustaining Superior Performance*, New York & London: Free Press-Collier, 1985.

Prais, S.J. *The Evolution of Giant Firms in Britain*, Cambridge: Cambridge University Press, 1976.

Sabel, C.F. *Work and Politics: The Division of Labour in Industry*, Cambridge: Cambridge University Press, 1982.

Sachs, J.D. & Roubini, N. 'Political and Economic Determinants of Budget Deficits in the Industrial Democracies', NBER Working Paper no. 2682, 1989.

Salter, E.A.G. *Productivity and Technical Change*, Cambridge: Cambridge University Press, 1960.

Sayer, A. *Method in Social Science: A Realist Approach*, London: Hutchinson, 1984.

Scase, R. & Goffee, R. *The Real World of the Small Business Owner*, London: Croom Helm, 1980.

Seers, D. *The Political Economy of Nationalism*, Oxford: Oxford University Press, 1983.

Silos Labini, P. *Saggio sulle Classe Sociali*, Bari: Laterza, 1976.

Smith, A. *Wealth of Nations* (1776), Harmondsworth: Penguin, 1979.

Spiro, J. *The Politics of International Economic Relations*, London: Allen & Unwin, 1982.

Viner, J. *The Customs Union Issue*, New York & London: Carnegie Endowment for International Peace/Stevens & Sons, 1950.

William-Olsson, W. *Europe West of the Soviet Union*, forthcoming.

World Bank *World Development Report 1983*, New York: Oxford University Press, 1983.

Taylor, P. *Political Geography; World Economy, Nation-State and Locality*, London & New York: Longman, 1985.

Tew, B. *The Evolution of the International Monetary System 1945–1985*, London: Hutchinson, 1985.

Thomas, B. *Migration and Urban Development: A Reappraisal of British and American Long Cycles*, London: Methuen, 1972.

Toffler, A. *The Third Wave*, London: Pan Books, 1983.

UNIDO *Industry and Development: Global Report 1986*, Vienna: UNIDO, 1986.

Index

(Note: the letter 'n' indicates that the reference is in a note on the page indicated.)